# *No Bed of Roses*

Patti Walkuski was born in South Australia in 1940, and grew up from a working-class childhood to become a celebrated Madam. She has survived five marriages, countless beatings, a cluster of de factos, seven children, numerous abortions, two attempted murders, a mad psychiatrist, being born again, and arrest by the National Crime Authority.

David Harris is a writer, historian and adventurer. Among his eight books is *Black Horse Odyssey*, which describes his discovery of the lost city of Rome in the Gobi Desert. He lives in the Adelaide Hills.

# No Bed of Roses
## MEMOIRS OF A MADAM

### PATTI WALKUSKI
AS REVEALED TO DAVID HARRIS

WAKEFIELD PRESS

Wakefield Press
Box 2266
Kent Town
South Australia 5071

First published 1993

Many names have been changed to protect the innocent
and guilty.

Edited by Jane Arms
Designed by Ann Wojczuk
Typeset by Clinton Ellicott
Printed and Bound by Hyde Park Press, Adelaide

Cataloguing-in-publication data
Walkuski, Patti, 1940–   .
No bed of roses: memoirs of a madam.
ISBN 1 86254 310 0.
1. Walkuski, Patti, 1940–  . 2. Prostitutes – South Australia –
Biography. 3. Prostitution – South Australia. I. Harris, David,
1942–   . II. Title.
331.76130674092

Promotion of this title has been assisted by the South Australian Government
through the Department for the Arts and Cultural Heritage.

For all the girls who worked for me

# *Patti's note*

My thanks to Glennyse and Kate, my staunch friends, and to Ray and June Prettejohn, who were always there for me.

# Contents

## Madam

## Decline and Fall

*Childhood and Youth*

# St Patrick's Day

*'And what have we here today?'* Mr O'Reilly *leant on the handlebars of* his bike and looked down at me.

I held up the baby tooth and opened my mouth wide. I put my fingertip on the soft squashy hole in my bottom gum.

'Well, Patti, don't forget to put it under your pillow.'

I squinted into the morning sun. 'My Nan says there are no fairies.'

Mr O'Reilly took off his hat and wiped the back of his hand along his forehead. He looked furtively at our front bedroom window then leant down. 'Let me tell you something your Nan doesn't know. Every time anyone says there are no fairies, somewhere a fairy falls down dead,' he whispered. 'Mark my words, Patti.' Mr O'Reilly tapped me on the shoulder with his hat brim, straightened his back, balanced his kitbag between the handlebars of his bike and rode off.

I sat in the gutter, my back against a verandah rail, and scowled. How many fairies with wings like dragonflies had my Nan killed? I put my tooth close to my nose and sniffed its sweet rotten smell. I knew what I'd do to Nan. I'd believe so hard that no fairy would die. My wishes were much stronger than Nan's.

Anyway, Mr O'Reilly was right. Nan didn't know everything. She had never seen my secret sister who lived under the Singer sewing machine. I played with her there when I'd put a blanket over the sewing machine to make a cubby. I gave her rides up and down on the pedal. I sneaked her out to go into the lane beside our house where we looked for a four-leaf clover. But

3

my secret sister never went in our back shed where the rats ran along the rails and stared at me with red eyes. And she never went out near the toilet where the monster-man lived.

My sister was too clever for him. She hid when he reached out for me and only popped out to play in safe places. She enjoyed games and giggled when we hid together behind Nan's clothes that hung like black ghosts against the wall. My little sister had a dress covered in flowers. Mine had a big rip because I tore it on a nail when I climbed along the bottom rail of the back fence, my eyes shut, my feet on a mountain ledge, way up high.

Mr Moses was late. I stood up to feel in my pocket for the rent book and money. I grabbed the verandah post with one hand and swung round and round to make myself giddy. Then I tried to walk in a straight line to the next post. My eyes were on the post, but my legs kept taking me away from it.

It was good having a verandah on the footpath. I saw everything in the street and chatted to the people going by. Our place, Number 37 Pickering Street, had been a fruit and vegetable shop until Uncle Frosty had put up partitions to make it into a house.

I heard the clip-clop of horses. Around the corner came two giant draught-horses pulling a beer cart. I waited, watching their long manes and their feathery feet that danced as they trotted along. When they were level with me I ran beside them to the pub at the railway end of Pickering Street. I was only up to the horses' knees, but I flew along, breathing in their horsy smell. They nodded their heads at me, their harness jingling. The finishing line was the pothole by the saloon door. The man high up in the cart called out, 'Whoa-up.' The horses slowed down, and I just won, my arms stretched out in front of me.

I stood by the horses' heads while the man rolled barrels down a plank and rumbled them across the footpath to the cellar door. I wanted to touch the horses, but they were so big. The one nearest to me had a white patch on his forehead and long whiskers under his chin. Slowly, frightened in case he bit me, I lifted up one hand to stroke the powerful neck all hard with muscles. He turned to look at me, his big sad eyes rolling to show the browny-white under the eyelid. Hot air came out of his nostrils, and he champed at the metal bit, white froth coming out the corners of his mouth. The poor thing had to pull all those barrels. I touched his neck lightly and stroked his rough hair. I loved the horse, the heaving of his great chest, his hot sweet smell. While I patted him, a fly crawled on his leg, and his leg twitched. I shooed it away.

My eye caught a movement at the other end of Pickering Street. A man in black rode his bike towards Number 37. Oh, no, it was Mr Moses. If I wasn't there to pay the rent, Nan would belt my arse with her walking stick. I ran like mad. Before I knew it, Mr Moses was under our verandah, and leant his bike against the wall.

'Mr Moses,' I yelled. 'Wait.'

He looked towards me.

I ran all the way to him, and stood beside him puffing. He looked down at me and reached into his pocket for his purse. Mr Moses was a big black bear. He wore a black hat, black coat, a shirt with the collar facing the front, black trousers and black socks into which he tucked the cuffs to keep them off the oily bike chain. Our house was once his shop, but he never tried to come in. He reached out and scratched one fingernail at the flaking brown paint on the verandah post. 'How's life in the lion's den?' He gave a small smile, but I didn't know what the joke was.

I shoved my hand way down in the deep pocket of my torn dress and pulled out a handful of money and the rent book.

Mr Moses counted the money carefully, spreading the coins out in his palm. 'One pound, eighteen and six.' He opened his black purse and slipped the money in. 'He lives off the fat of the land,' Nan had said, 'while all we can afford is tripe, cabbage, bread and dripping, the rotten old bastard.'

Mr Moses licked the tip of a short pencil and wrote in rent book.

When I grew up, I thought, I was going to h money. People with money did whatever they li

Nan tapped angrily on the window with and waved her hand at me impatiently. I h the rent book and hurried inside. Nan sat on her bed, pillows behind her back, and puffed away on a cigarette. Her box of Bex powders was on the window sill. She glared at me with her piggy eyes. 'What day is it?' My heart sank. Nan was in one of her moods.

I made a wild guess. 'Wednesday?'

'No, you fool. What special day?'

Why was I always wrong? I shrugged and, ready to run, eyed the open door.

'Come on girl, *think*!'

'Sunday?' I was panicking.

Nan looked out the window and let out a long sigh. 'I don't know why I bother.' She leant forward and put her face close to the glass. Then she roared, 'Go on, get out of it, you little devil.' She waved her walking stick to show she meant it.

From outside came a child's voice. 'Fat and Skinny went to war. Fat got shot and Skinny swore. Fat, fat, fat. Old Ma Robbins is a tub of lard.'

Nan's face grew red and swelled. She pulled herself up and peered around to see who it was. There was a sound of running footsteps. 'Just wait till I get my hands on you,' she screamed. 'I'll thrash you to within an inch of your life.' Nan fell back against her pillows and closed her eyes. I could feel my heart beat. I didn't know whether to laugh or cry. When Nan opened her eyes, the eyelashes were all wet.

Nan tapped me on the head with her walking stick. 'That's enough of that now.' She moved her enormous bum on the blanket and took a last long puff on her cigarette, then ground the butt in the saucer beside her. 'That Visconsi brat and the dago girl. Time to fix their bacon.' Nan kept grinding the butt of the cigarette until it split open and bits of damp tobacco twisted out. 'You're to stop playing with those bloody dagos who come over here, take our jobs and jabber away so we can't understand them. If they want to live here, why don't they learn he King's English? Or go home?' Nan looked me in the eye. don't know what the world's coming to.'

held my breath. Mary Tarcento was my best friend. We did
es in Pickering Street while the boys stood around and

6

laughed and made farting noises. Now I would have to go to the end of Pickering Street to play with Mary.

Nan gave me the evil eye. 'Patti, you're too young to understand, but some places in Adelaide are no longer safe for decent people. They're taking over Hindley Street. Dagos with their flick knives and Mafia and foreign food. When you grow up, you stay away from Hindley Street. They'd stick a knife in you as quick as look at you.'

I thought of the Greek greengrocer shop around on Port Road. I loved running around there just to look at them. They shouted and waved their arms about, yelled words I couldn't understand. But their voices weren't angry, like at my place. The Greek mother yelled at the man, telling him where to put this box and that. She had a mole on her chin, which I stared at in wonder. Black hairs grew out of it and hung down like a little beard. The man yelled back at her and when he walked past gave her a little pinch on the arm, just above the elbow on the soft skin. She pretended to be cross and told him off. Even their little girl helped. She climbed up on a fruit box and polished the tomatoes with a rag. Their shop smelt lovely. I stood for ages and watched, thumb in my mouth. This was a family.

Not like my family. My mother ran away and left me when I was two. My father was a drunk. He stank and bashed me. If I waited long enough, if I was good enough, if I never stopped loving my mother, she would come back some day. She would walk down Pickering Street, knock on our door, and I'd run into her arms and she'd lift me up and kiss me and take me home to her house, where I'd snuggle up in bed next to her on cold mornings, and she would stroke my cheeks and play the game with my fingers, 'This little piggy went to market, this little piggy stayed home'.

Nan looked out the window. 'If wishes were fishes.' Then she brightened up and said, 'St Patrick's Day.'

I didn't move or say anything. I'd learnt the hard way not to show my feelings. Nan reached between her huge boobs and took out the purse with the brass clip. 'Here's two three-pences. One is for the milk and the other is to buy a flower from Mrs Barry.' I held up my hand and Nan pressed the tiny silver coins into my palm. Then she closed my fingers over the money. 'Mind you get it right, Patti. Who knows, maybe if you're good, you'll see the circus.'

I skipped down Pickering Street, going from one side to another. The billy can for the milk banged against my leg. St Patrick's Day. 'My Red Letter Day', Nan called it. St Patrick's Day was more important than Christmas, which we couldn't have anyway because my father got drunk and smashed things up. The best we did on Christmas was go to Aunty Jean's where I played the pianola, watching the holes in the paper go past as the song unrolled. I sang my made-up words, swaying with passion – 'Vilia, oh Vilia, my light of the moon' – and the song for my aunty – 'I dream of Jeannie with the light brown hair.' Tiritomba went so fast that all I could fit in was 'diddy dum dah, diddy dum day . . .'

St Patrick's Day was even more fun. Nan got out of bed and we went down to the pub for a drink. As I ran down to buy the milk I thought, Maybe today I'll see the circus. How many times at the table had Nan said, 'Stop pushing your food around. Just eat it up and you'll be able to see the circus.' I'd force down the cold cabbage and tripe in white sauce and I'd run out to sit on the footpath until it was dark, waiting for the circus.

As always when I went to get the milk, I stopped by the door of Barry's Bakery. The man in the white pinny stood by a large pot and stirred the pasty mix with the biggest wooden spoon in the world. Just as well Nan didn't have that spoon. The man grinned at me and jerked his head to me sideways. I sneaked in and hid behind the pot. He stopped stirring and passed me a bread roll that was still warm. 'Here you are, Smiley,' he said. I grabbed the roll, whispered, 'Thanks', and ran out into the street, where I sat on the edge of the footpath, picked a hole in the crust, tore out lumps of warm soft bread and gobbled them down.

I breathed in the warm morning air; a wonderful mixture of the bakery and the stables of the other baker around the corner. When I finished the roll, I went to Mrs Barry's house and knocked on the front door. Old Mrs Barry came up the passage and opened the door. 'Well, look who's here. If it isn't Patti Robbins. And what do you want, my dear?'

'Please, Mrs Barry, it's St Patrick's Day.' I held up the coin.

Mrs Barry was a plump lady who smelt like the flowers in her garden. That day she wore a little bunch of lavender pinned to the shoulder of her dress. The skin of her face was as clean as a newly washed baby. She smiled at me. 'St Patrick's Day. Well, I never.' She clicked her tongue. 'You'd better come in then, Patti.'

I followed Mrs Barry into her cool lounge room. Straightaway I ran over to the bowl of china fruit: pears, grapes, bananas, cherries, apples. The cherries glowed, so delicious I had to touch them. First I looked back at Mrs Barry, who smiled and nodded. I put my billy can on the polished wooden floor, stuffed the money in my pocket, pulled out the chair with the curved legs and climbed up on the seat, which was smooth and cool on my bare feet. I leaned over the table to caress the cold fruit and stared at the burning colours. My eyes searched in the hollows between the fruit that shone like jewels in Aladdin's Cave. It was a deep mystery to me. Why was there this cold fire in Mrs Barry's house, and a black coldness at Nan's?

'Come along, Patti. Time for your St Patrick's Day surprise.' I gave the cherries one last touch and climbed down. 'What will it be?' Mrs Barry said, her head tilted to one side and a finger tapping her chin. 'A pasty? No, not this time.' Maybe it would be a handful of the hard little purple and pink lollies that smelt so sweet. Mrs Barry's face lit up and she gave me a secret smile.

I followed her into her bedroom, which had a tall vase of red roses on the dressing table, so you could see the back of the flowers in the mirror. Her room smelt of roses. No, it wasn't just the flowers, nor the clean feeling, it was something lovely I felt but did not understand.

Mrs Barry opened a drawer of her dressing table and took out a white lace hanky. 'Here you are, my dear.' She lay it across my open palms. Almost too scared to touch it, I ran my finger-tip around the lace edges. The hanky was ironed and folded in a neat triangle. It was the most beautiful I'd ever seen. I didn't know what to do, so I reached out, grabbed Mrs Barry's dress and stood there tugging it, speechless, while I gazed down at the treasure in my hand. By magic, only for a moment, I felt like I was Mrs Barry's own grandchild.

Mrs Barry patted my hair once and then was gone. I heard her voice. 'I guess you've come for a flower.'

I suddenly remembered and took out the threepenny piece.

'No, no,' Mrs Barry said. 'I've got thousands of flowers.' Her back yard garden went way back to the cow paddocks.

'You've got to take it,' I said, 'or I'll be in the shit.' Nan said that not paying brought bad luck. You never got anything in life without paying.

Mrs Barry laughed and said, 'How can I refuse?' She took my money, and we went into the kitchen. 'Perhaps, because it is St Pat's, Mrs Robbins would like one of these.'

Lined up on the kitchen table were sprays of flowers, their stems wrapped in silver paper. Mrs Barry chose one and handed it to me. 'Tell Mrs Robbins they've only just been picked.'

I sniffed the purple flowers and the perfume of violets made me dizzy.

'Off you run now, or your Nan will wonder what you're up to.'

That afternoon, Nan and I went to the pub. We dressed to the nines. Nan was in her good black dress with white lace around the collar and the spray of violets pinned above her heart. Her long auburn hair was tied up in a knot. I wore the cardigan with red and green stripes that Aunty Jean had knitted for me. I had a green ribbon in my hair. I could hardly believe my eyes when Nan let me wear the pretty ribbon.

Nan hobbled along Pickering Street, her elephant legs clumping along, her feet squeezed into brown lace-ups. Nan's chest wheezed long before we got to the Brompton Park Arms on the corner. 'Get that later.' She pointed to a pile of poop a draught-horse had left on the road.

We held our noses as we passed the men's toilet. At last we reached the saloon door, its glass window the colour of a beer bottle. Nan put one arm against the wall, and waited a while until she stopped puffing.

Inside, the air was grey and musty with cigarette smoke. As soon as we went in I saw Aunt Maggie, from across the road. She sat with a fag in her mouth and a scarf around her hair. Aunt Maggie gave us a wave. 'Here's Mary and Patti.' She stood up and dragged up another chair to the round table. 'Come on you two, front up.' Aunt Maggie was part Aboriginal, but the hotel let her in. She lived just up the road in a house full of kids and spider webs. There were great brawls at Aunt Maggie's. Her husband was supposed to be having it off with her brother's first wife, or something like that, just like most of Pickering Street. It was a good excuse for a punch up. I liked Aunt Maggie. She was as tough as two goat's knees, and smelt like bleach from her job cleaning houses.

I climbed up beside Aunt Maggie and leant against her arm. 'Goodday, Patti,' she said. 'What'll it be. My shout.'

Nan answered. 'Now, don't you go giving that girl any ideas.'

'Who me?' said Aunt Maggie, her hand over her heart and her voice as sweet as pie. All the other women in the room cheered and yelled.

I nearly weed my leg with all the excitement of being with these gossipy old faggots – that's what Nan called the pub women. I banged my fist on the table and shouted the first words that came to my head. 'Brandy cruster, on the rocks!'

The women's laughter exploded in the room, and I looked around, wondering what I'd said. Then Nan cracked my ankle bone with the end of her walking stick, and I sucked my breath in with the pain of it.

'A chip off the old block,' somebody said. The room went quiet. Some people glanced at the front bar wall. My father – 'Bloke', as his mates called him – was on the other side. In the stillness I heard the men's shouts and the races on the front bar radio.

Aunt Maggie looked at Nan's face. It was red from the neck up. Nan's son might be a pisspot and a no-hoper, and she called him worse, but if anybody outside the family criticised him, her Irish went up.

Aunt Maggie stood up, put her hand on Nan's shoulder,

glared around the room and said, 'There'll be no unpleasantness today.'

Into the silence that followed, my Nan boiling away, Aunt Maggie said, 'I'll order for my friends, Mary and Patti. For Patti a lemonade and raspberry, in a pint glass.' People began to relax. I heard a whisper, 'A pint glass. She'll need a ladder to get to the bottom.' Aunt Maggie strode over to the little wooden shutter on the wall, and lifted it, put her face in the hole, and called to the barman, 'One pint lemonade and raspberry, and a stout for Mary Robbins' – Aunt Maggie turned out to those in the room – ' 'cos I reckon if anyone's a stout woman it's our Mary.'

I heard the breath drawn in, then Nan gave a chuckle. All the others shared in the laughter and turned back to gossip to their friends at their tables.

'Phew. I don't know,' said Aunt Maggie. 'Bloody den of iniquity in here.'

The barman handed the drinks through to Aunt Maggie. She lifted my glass down and I stared at the enormous drink with thousands of tiny bubbles wobbling up through the pink.

Aunt Maggie and I were mates. We were both cleaners. Once a week she came to our place to do the jobs that were too hard for me. I scrubbed the floors and climbed on a kitchen chair to wash the dishes. On Mondays I did the worst job: I had to go out all alone to the back shed that was full of rats. Out there I put kindling under the copper in the shed and boiled the water for the washing.

'I don't know what I'll do when she starts school,' Nan said once to Aunt Maggie. I was as proud as punch. I scrubbed the floors so clean you could eat a meal off them. I worked until my arms ached, so that Nan would be proud of me.

Every morning I took Nan her cup of tea and slice of toast. She sat on her single bed by the windows, and I perched on the edge of my big double bed.I watched her face carefully to see if the breakfast was just right. The tea must not be too milky, the toast still warm. If she took her first sip of tea and then closed her eyes and smiled, I let out a big sigh. If she frowned, I backed out the door quick smart. I tried to get it perfect. If I worked harder, I was sure she wouldn't hit me so much.

There was one job I refused to do, no matter how much Nan ranted and raved. I would not sweep out the back yard dunny. When Nan asked, I went stiff as a broomstick. She looked at me strangely. Nan didn't know about the man who waited there. The man who I had to call 'Uncle'. The sparrows knew. The creeper he hid in knew. At four years old I knew it hurt and was horrible, and I thought that's the way it was.

'A toast,' said Aunt Maggie. 'Come on, Mary. Up you get.'

Nan put down her glass of stout and struggled to her feet. She swept her eyes around the room. Everybody stopped talking. Nan held her glass up and said in a serious voice, 'To our patron saint, St Patrick, and to the shamrock.'

We all raised our glasses and clinked them to drive away the evil spirits. That day everybody was Irish.

'To St Patrick,' I said, feeling the importance of the occasion.

Then Nan started on the brandy and began to lay down the law about wowsers, Pig Iron Bob, Commies, the Yellow Peril, the Pope, you name it, my Nan had the answer. The more tiddly she got, the longer grew her words. She used big posh words I'd never heard. I listened in amazement. Nan sounded like someone on the radio. It must be true what I heard my father tell Aunt Maggie, that my Nan came from a good home and had been educated. That afternoon Nan took on all and sundry and talked them to a standstill. The saloon grew noisier and the air thicker. I was lifted onto the table and sang 'When Irish Eyes are Smiling' to loud applause. Then I sang 'the drunkies' song 'Goodnight Irene'. The women joined in, waving their glasses of plonk, fags hanging out of their faces.

St Patrick's Day at the Brompton Park Arms was a dream of an afternoon. I drank my lemonade and raspberry, but Aunt Maggie poured some of her drink in mine while Nan wasn't watching. Later I had a pasty with sauce, on a plate, a lime spider that frothed out of the glass, and another splash of Aunt Maggie's plonk.

My aunt Jean, who was cook over at the Hope Inn, called past for a quick beer with us all. She stood up and declared that Wirth's Circus was in town and she was going to take me there that night in a car. I just looked at Nan. I knew all about broken promises. Nan nodded. I leant my forehead on the edge of the table and cried and cried while they all laughed with happiness. It was such a wonderful afternoon that Nan and I sang all the way home, and then took it in turns to throw up in a bucket.

# *Spiritualism*

---

*I pushed open the butcher's glass door, the little silver bell jingling* above it.

'Hello, Dimples.'

'Hello, Mr Miller.' I breathed in the cool smell of damp saw-dust on the smooth wooden floor. Mr Miller stood behind the glass counter, which had trays of chops and sausages, silver beef that we could never afford, slippery brown lambs fry, and white tripe, which made me feel sick just to look at. There were skinny rabbits stacked together lying on their tummies, their sad little arms up in the air but without any hands. Beside them were thick coils of bung fritz – my favourite – horrible, veiny brains and fatty pigs' trotters with hairs sticking out of the tough skin.

I held up my note and Mr Miller leant over the counter to take it. His smile was kind. He thought the sun and moon shone out of me, Nan reckoned.

'Two lion chops.' Mr Miller pursed his lips and squinted through his glasses at my note.

'Yes, please.' I was proud of my writing. Soon I would be allowed to use a nib pen at school.

He smiled. 'Let me see. Lion. They must be pretty big chops. He turned to the row of sheep carcasses hanging on hooks from a high, metal bar. Each hollow sheep showed its ribs, and the kidneys dangled in fat.

'Maybe you'd better come around and help me choose.'

I ran round behind the counter and stood beside Mr Miller, who was so tall my eyes were only level with the bottom of the wooden holster where three large knives rattled about. He was my friendly giant. He let me into the secret world behind the counter, where I peeped at things that other people were not allowed to see – like the bucketful of huge hearts with their gaping, thick, white tubes.

'Which one is the lion, do you reckon?'

I knew he was teasing me, but I didn't know why. I blushed as red as beetroot and pointed to the nearest sheep. With his big hands, Mr Miller hoisted the sheep down and dumped it on his chopping block – a great slab of tree trunk on three legs. The block was worn smooth and gashed with cuts from his heavy cleaver.

Mr Miller held the sheep with one hand, his thumb hooked into the meat. The middle two fingers were missing on that hand. I stood on tiptoe to watch. He always chopped so close to his hand. He brought the cleaver down and in one mighty blow it split through the bone, which cracked apart. Then he dumped the back legs aside and dragged the row of chops to the edge of the block, and drew out a knife with a long curved blade. He rasped the blade against his steel sharpener and sliced through the meat, down to the bone. He held each cut open with two fingers, and chopped neatly through.

'How much have you got today?' he asked.

I held up Nan's little black purse.

Mr Miller unfastened it and took out two shillings and sixpence. 'Two bob should do it,' he said, and put the sixpence back in the purse.

He threw the chops on the neat pile of white wrapping paper and paused, looking up at the calendar on the wall. I was able to read the numbers on the calendar: 1946. 'A week to pension day,' he said, and from a tray in the counter he took out a handful of meat, which he dropped on my chops. He slid a hand under the big sheet of white paper and wrapped the meat. I held out my string bag, and he eased the heavy parcel in.

I stood there and looked up at him, my eyes pleading. Mr Miller tipped me a wink, and took a fritz from inside the counter. He cut a thick slice, and held it out to me.

'Thank you, Mr Miller.'

'And how's Mrs Robbins today?' he asked.

I put the string bag down on the sawdust and began. 'Well, she taught me a prayer to keep the monster away that comes every night when I'm asleep. Wanna hear it? "Now I lay me down to sleep I pray the Lord my soul to keep and if I die before I wake I pray the Lord my soul . . ."'

The bell tinkled and somebody strode to the counter, heels clumping. 'Good morning, Mr Miller.'

I froze. I knew that soft, commanding voice. It was the Reverend Mary Ariola. Last Sunday Nan took me again to a service at the Reverend Mary Ariola's Spiritualist Church, a little building in her back yard at Taylor Street. Branches from her mulberry tree stretched over the church, giving shade for people to stand in and leaves for children to carry home to feed the silkworms in their shoe boxes.

The Reverend Mary Ariola stood at the church door to welcome everyone. She was tall, powerful, with a big bust and clothes cut from expensive cloth. 'She is a statement,' Nan would say, and nod to herself. All I knew was that Reverend Mary Ariola had eyes that went right through me, and there was a ghost at the end of the third pew. It was an old lady in a brown overcoat and she wore a black scarf over her hair. She felt my eyes on her and turned to nod and smile at me. It was Grandma Evans come back to sit in her favourite seat.

Nan and I went into the dim church and put our flowers on the wide, silver dish out the front near the piano. Nan had to sit in the front row because she was too fat to fit between the pews. After some boring prayers and songs, Reverend Mary Ariola went to the silver tray of flowers and lifted a blue daisy – not one of the white roses Nan and I had nicked from over the Scott's front fence.

Reverend Mary Ariola cupped her hands around the blossom and waited for it to send a message. Her face was calm, but emotions showed, as if she was dreaming. The church was hushed, and I could feel the suspense. Whose flower was it? What would it say? I stared at every flickering movement of her face, holding my breath and almost swooning with excitement.

Reverend Mary Ariola began to speak. 'You have lost a ring,

a ruby ring. But do not worry. I see an old man, perhaps your grandfather, who passed away many years ago. He will leave a sign for you to find the ring. No. He is the sign.'

She opened her eyes and asked in a loud voice, 'Whose flower is this?' I turned around and saw a man put his hand in the air. His face was shining wet. 'Do you understand the message?'

'Yes. He has come back to protect me.'

Sighs and whispers floated through the church. One by one the flowers brought hope, comfort, warnings, questions, and each person said they understood.

Then the Reverend Mary Ariola picked up a white rose. I felt the pain of my fingernail digging into the palm of my hand.

'I see a little girl. Her hair is flying in the wind. Wait. There are shining skates on her feet, and she skims across the ice like a bird.'

Oh, I could see myself, dressed in all the colours of the rainbow, my costume fluttering around me, dark pine trees far away surrounding the frozen lake.

'Whose flower is this?'

I waved my arm in the air, and then, with a great shock, out of the corner of my eye saw Nan lift her hand from her lap and raise it almost to her face, where it hovered, trembling.

'Do you understand the message?'

Now, in Mr Miller's shop, I felt those eyes on me, but I kept my face lowered as she spoke. 'Why, Mr Miller, you have a new assistant? Good morning, Mary.'

'I'm not Mary. My name's Patti.'

'Oh no, you're Mary.'

'It's not true.' I knew what she meant and the thought terrified and appalled me. 'I'm Patti. Not Mary.' I glared up at her. 'Mary is my Nan's name.'

Reverend Mary Ariola's smile was gentle and sad. 'One day you'll understand.'

Suddenly my eyes were full of tears, and I shouted in a rage. 'I'm not Mary. I'll never be Mary.'

I picked up my string bag and rushed for the door. The bell jangled and I was out in the street running for my life. The street and houses were broken and splintered by my tears. I would never be that huge, angry woman sitting on her bed in her dark house. Day after day staring out the window, all alone, with bitterness and hurt. Nothing to do but wait to die.

# *The secret*

---

*Rain drummed on the galvanised-iron roof. As soon as I woke, I* thought, Friday, Test Day: six times tables, mental arithmetic with our hands on our heads, spelling, and the flags of England, Scotland and Wales. I sneaked a look at Nan, who lay on her bed, staring at the ceiling. I put my head back under the blanket. Time for a day off, to muck around at home and listen to the Phantom on the radio. What excuse could I get away with?

I flung back my blanket, bent double on the edge of the bed and started to retch. 'Nan, I'm going to be sick.'

Nan didn't move a muscle, except to roll her eyes towards her walking stick, which was leaning against the edge of the bed. I pushed two fingers right down my throat and ran, eyes bulging, no longer faking.

When I returned to the bedroom I was white-faced and shaking. Nan sat with her back against a pile of pillows. She reached out with her walking stick, crooked me around the neck and yanked me close to her side. 'I hope you're not trying to pull the wool over my eyes?' I gave her my sweetest smile, but she stared me down with her black look. 'Well, you might as well make yourself useful.' She pointed with her stick to the blue commode.

At that moment there was a hammering at the door. Nan and I looked at each other anxiously. Who could that be so early in the day? Strangers at the door, like telegrams, meant bad news. The knocking came again. Nan pushed herself across her bed and lifted the corner of the blind to glance out the window. 'Get me my stole,' she said. She struggled off the bed and snatched the long stole from me. Nan got in a tangle wrapping it around her shoulders, and her face got wild. 'Come on, help me! Don't just stand there gawking!'

Nan hobbled to the door and opened it. There was a man in a suit. He held a big black umbrella upside down and shook it, scattering raindrops on the ground. He had a narrow face and his thin black hair was slick on his skull.

'Mrs Robbins?' He pointed to the iron numbers 37, fixed to our front wall. 'How do you explain this?'

Nan peered at the numbers. Yesterday after tea I had painted them red, using an old brush and the gooey sludge in the bottom of a tin I found out in the shed.

Nan looked back at me, where I hid behind her legs. Then she leant forward on her walking stick and gave the bloke her look. 'And who do you think you are?' Her voice was not frightened now. I could hear the Irish.

'Let us say I am a concerned citizen.' He jabbed his finger at my art work. 'Red.' He looked closely at Nan, as though examining a strange animal at the zoo. 'Red. The People's Flag. You flaunt it for all the world to see.' He raised a skinny finger and shook it in Nan's face. 'Communist! I shall report you to our watchdog committee.'

Nan said, as cool as a cucumber, 'Just wait here, and I'll give you something to report.' She stomped back into the house. I knew she'd do something amazing, but I didn't know what. To play safe I held the door in front of me and put my head around it, looking into the man's face that sneered down at me. 'You'd better watch out, mister. My Nan's on the warpath.'

I heard her steps, I saw his face. He took one step back, an arm swinging the umbrella around like a shield, but he was too late. I saw the glint of eggshell blue and suddenly he was covered in a great splash of piss. He staggered back across the road, spitting and blinking.

'Wear that to your bloody committee.' Nan took a step out on the verandah, holding the pot high, and the man ran off. She turned back, and for the first time ever, she winked at me. 'Not a bad job, eh? But you'd better scratch around and find a bit of black for the numbers.'

I danced around and around under the verandah and yelled, 'My Nan, my Nan. She did it. Ow!' Her walking stick hit me on the shoulder bone.

'No need to make a spectacle of yourself. Inside, and get breakfast.'

I went to the kitchen and made Nan's 'compulsory slice of toast', as she called it. I spread the toast with apricot jam and hurried with it up to our bedroom. Then I raced back to the kitchen where the kettle was boiling.

When Nan had almost finished her breakfast, I said, 'Nan, could I wash you?' She shot me a glance. I kept talking. 'I'll make lots of hot water, and I promise I won't make a mess.'

Nan looked out the window at the grey sky and dingy street. 'Bit chilly,' she said, and gave a big sigh. Then she gazed at me with troubled eyes and nodded.

She took a Turf cigarette from the red packet, and lit up. I was as happy as a pig in shit. I put the kettle on, ran up the passage with towels and Nan's pink flannel, ran through the rain to the shed to collect all the bits of velvet soap from the dish near the copper, and picked up the huge preserving pan. From the kitchen I took a jug to pour the warm water. Whoops, almost forgot: I found the packet of Nurse's cornflour.

When everything was ready, Nan pulled down the blind and pinned up her auburn hair into bunches on top of her head. Then she took off her stole and nightie. She put a towel under her bottom and I watched the white flesh spread out wide as she sat back down. Nan packed towels tightly against the rolls of her back and stomach. I climbed up behind her and crouched on my knees. Her skin was smooth and glossy. I thought she was really old, maybe a hundred years old, but I had heard her talk to Aunty Jean about how awful it would be to turn forty. I put the hot flannel on her back and began to rub in circles. Her shoulders lifted as she gave a big sigh of pleasure.

'Where do babies come from Nan?' I tipped a little hot water on her back and watched it run down and collect in the groove around her hips where her bum stood out all the way around.

'Cabbages. Don't ask stupid questions.' I rubbed soap on my

hands and smoothed it over Nan's back. She seemed to sink down into herself. Her face was hidden, but I could feel her pleasure.

'How many kids did you have, Nan?'

'Little Miss Chatterbox.' Then, in a quiet voice, as though speaking to herself, she said, 'Sing to me.'

That was my Nan. Talking to her was like trying to listen to the radio with somebody turning the knob all the time. I longed to ask about the children she never mentioned, about the husband she never talked about, and whether it was true she was once rich and owned half a town. But I didn't want to risk her getting angry.

Instead I washed her back with a hot flannel and sang, 'Danny Boy'. The song made me sad, and I sang my heart out with romantic longing. When the song was finished we were as still as statues.

Nan suddenly caught her breath – she was almost crying. Her voice was all soft. 'Patti, I'm the only true friend you'll ever have. But you don't know. You think I'm cruel and heartless, but the day will come when you understand.' Her back was covered in goose bumps. 'Come on, girl, I'm freezing to death.'

I jumped off the bed and soaked the flannel in hot water. 'Is it true you named me?' From the floor, I could see Nan give a little smile to herself. I knew the answer, but I loved to hear the story over and over.

'Yes. Your mother wanted to call you Rebecca. But I wouldn't let her. I named you Patricia.'

'I like my name. Rebeccas are snotty-nosed little brats.'

Nan chuckled. 'Yes, you're certainly no Little Miss Muffet. You keep me on my toes. You know, I wouldn't let your mother take you that night she ran off with that bastard.'

'Why hasn't she come back for me?' If I heard the click of a woman's high heels on the street I would hold my breath in longing that the woman would stop at our front door and knock. If I opened the door, there would be a beautiful woman in a pretty dress, and she would reach down with her arms and hold me close, kiss me, and say, 'Patti, I've come to take you home.' I remembered standing in a cot and watching a man and a women who rolled about in the bed beside me. My mother looked up and said, 'Don't worry Patti. I'm just playing.'

Nan grunted. 'There is no love without hatred and hurt. My arms now.' She held out her right arm for me to wash. 'Where do you get all these questions?'

'I've got a sister.' I felt Nan's arm twitch. 'She lives inside me, hidden away. A brand new me. One day she'll come out.'

Nan scoffed. 'More like a brother. You should have been a boy.'

Nan put her hand to her mouth, as though to stop the words she had just said, and a guilty look flashed across her face. Perhaps she was thinking how she tried to make me into a boy. I touched my hair, cropped in a basin cut, my beautiful blonde curls shorn off. I had no pretty dresses to show off like my best friends, Veronica and Big Pat. All my clothes were dull, drab and ugly. I looked stupid in the hand-me-down shoes. Why was Nan so dark? Why did she always wear a black dress? It was no good asking her why she was angry and bitter. Nan would never tell the truth, just say, 'It's best to let sleeping dogs lie.'

She took the soap from me and I held the basin of water while she washed her front. I stared at her huge bellybutton, as big as a football, almost as big as a watermelon. Tenderly she washed all around and underneath it, holding it out with one hand. The hernia wobbled and, when she let it go, it hung heavily like a balloon full of water. That thing on her belly was another taboo subject. What could make a tummy burst out like that? I had tried asking Aunty Jean, but she went furious and told me, 'You keep your sticky beak out of other people's business. Poor Nan. You just shut your mouth and think yourself lucky.'

Me? Lucky? As Nan said about things being unfair, 'It all started in the Garden of Eden. God gave Adam and Eve free choice and then told them not to eat the apple. So, up the lot of them for the rent.'

When Nan finished washing, I handed her the towel and she wiped herself. I took the packet of cornflour and climbed back on the bed. Very carefully I lifted the huge sac of hernia and dusted cornflour under it. Then I lifted each great roll of fat around her belly to wipe cornflour between them. I pulled apart the long flaps of fat on her thighs and patted them with flour. Nan held the pink flannel over her private part. To my surprise I felt her fingertips brush the top of my bowed head. I pretended not to notice, but my scalp tingled. Nan had taught me, 'Keep your feelings to yourself, or you'll only get hurt.' I was shocked at her touch. Her best sign of love was a good belting each morning, 'Just in case you get up to mischief.' If only she knew how I longed for cuddles.

I panicked, knowing this was my best chance to tell her. I sprinkled more cornflour between her thighs where the skin was rough and red from chafing. I opened my mouth, then clamped it shut.

'Well, what is it girl? Cat got your tongue?'

'What if – ' Then I blurted it out all in a rush, 'What if there's something you're really scared of.' I was glad she couldn't see my face.

'What do you mean?'

I couldn't say it, so I said, 'You know, scary things.'

'Good grief, child. You don't still believe in those things?'

I did. That man I had to call 'Uncle', waiting in the shadows behind the toilet. He pushed his horrible beard in my face and shoved his finger in me.

Nan said, 'Count sheep. Make the whole flock walk past you one by one and count them.'

I looked up in disbelief. How could I tell her? But I knew if I was ever going to, it had to be now. I handed her the nightie, wide as a tent, that she had made from a sheet. When she had put it over her head I dumped all the bath things on the floor and got Nan's hairbrush. Then I knelt on the bed, slipped out the hair pins, and began to brush Nan's lovely Irish hair.

'A bit harder. Get right down to the scalp. That's it.'

A hard lump of fear grew in my chest. What would she do when I told her? The words wanted to come out, but I dreaded Nan's rage. When I was four, Uncle Mick smiled his crooked sick smile and caught me out the back, time after time, and put me on his knee. Smiling all the time, while his horrible big thumb with its dirty fingernail pushed inside my knickers, searching about. Then came the sickening pain. He took his thumb out and sniffed it.

I screwed up my eyes, as though Nan was about to slap me on the face, and whispered, 'Nan. Uncle Fred does things to me behind the toilet.' Her head jerked upwards and the brush banged her head. I saw the blood rush up her neck. I jumped for safety as she lurched around, her eyes black with hatred.

'You're speaking out of your arse.' She swung her legs around and heaved herself off the bed.

I backed towards the door. 'You never believe me. You are just as bad.' Tears filled my eyes. 'Yes. And Uncle Mick when I was just a little girl. For years and years and I could never tell you.' I put my thumb between my thighs. 'They did this.' I gestured with my thumb to show Nan.

That staggered her. For a moment she was as still as a rock, then her hand went out to her walking stick.

I yelled. 'You don't believe me, but it's true. For years.'

Her mouth was twisted, like my father's, as she shouted, 'You little slut. I bet you asked for it. Your mother's daughter all the time.' She tried to grasp the walking stick, but her hand was shaking and she knocked it down.

I held the door, ready to slam it behind me. 'You old bitch. My mother's not a slut. I hate you. I've seen you sit there while the bakery man puts his hands down inside to touch your ugly old boobs.'

Nan gasped for breath. Her eyes were shut, no, suddenly open and burning. She heaved herself up from the bed and reached for me with her claws.

I ran out into the rain and fled from Pickering Street. I screamed and sobbed like a mad girl. The houses and corners passed in a daze. Then I found myself on a swing, my fists tight on the cold chains as I swung with furious kicks, higher and higher, kicking the houses, kicking the sky, kicking all the world.

# *Scruffles*

---

*I was not completely alone. Since I was a tiny tot there was one friend* I could depend on absolutely. I remember that my father had gone away some place. I didn't care, as long as it was far away. Nan got a message there was a box waiting for us at the Railway Station. It was a puppy, for me. I did cartwheels across the back yard. I never got presents from my father, since my terrifying fifth birthday party. I raced like a mad thing up the passage to bounce on my big double bed. I went up and up, like it was a trampoline, trying to touch the ceiling. I did high somersaults and back turns. I got a clout on the shin from Nan's walking stick. 'Any more of that behaviour and I'll have the dog sent off to the pound and you'll never see it again.' I hugged my bruised bone and bawled with pain and rage.

Uncle Frosty took his truck to get the dog. I swung round and round the front verandah post, my hand in the smooth part I'd worn in the post. What did the puppy look like? Would he love me or run away? I would feed him Weetbix and milk, like I'd seen Aunty Maggie do with her pups. Where would he sleep? Nan would never let him in the house where I could take him to bed like a baby and cuddle him under the blankets. No. The poor thing would have to sleep out in the shed where the rats lived. I caught my breath. Would the rats bite my puppy? Ha, my dog will be a fighter. He'll hunt those rats right out of the shed. He will get them by the back of the neck and scruffle them to bits. I laughed. That's my dog's name, Scruffles.

Uncle Frosty's truck turned the corner and rattled to a stop right beside me. I ran to the back and looked in. There was a wooden crate with chicken wire on top. Uncle Frosty lifted it down and put it on the footpath. Inside the box, cringing in a corner, was a little terrier with baby brown eyes that looked up sadly. He looked like I always felt, trapped and waiting for a smack; or for someone to love him. Scruffles was mine.

Uncle Frosty carried the box around to the back yard. He got a claw hammer and lifted the nails holding the chicken wire. I knelt by the box and crooned to my dog, 'Don't be frightened, Scruffles. He's just taking off the wire. You're safe now. I'll look after you.'

When the wire was bent back far enough, Uncle Frosty put his hands in and lifted Scruffles out. He put the little puppy on the ground, where he stood on wobbly legs, his tail tucked under his bottom. He whimpered and my heart melted. Tenderly I picked him up and cuddled him against my chest. He looked up with such sad eyes I could have loved him to death. He was soft and warm and smelt like the sawdust in the bottom of the crate. He was my best friend for life.

'He's an Australian Terrier,' said Uncle Frosty.

I sat on the ground to inspect him. His nose was soft and damp. Wiry whiskers stuck out from his top lip. The skin inside his ears was grey. He twitched his ears when I touched them. Then I held him up to look at his tummy. Yes, he was a boy, and there were faint brown freckles on the bare skin. My Scruffles was perfectly adorable, right down to the hard little pads on the bottom of his feet.

Nan stood beside me. 'You be sure not to spoil him.'

'Yes, Nan. He'll be good, I promise.'

I swivelled around on my bottom and crouched over Scruffles so Nan couldn't see him. Why did she have to put her bib in? Scruffles was nothing to do with her. She didn't even want him.

'Well, just see to it. Animals are like children. You've got to break their spirit before they can be any good. Show you're the master, or they'll turn on you.'

From that day Scruffles followed me everywhere. He played ball with me in the alley. He stood guard while I sneaked a pram load of mallee stumps from the wood yard. He waited for me on the corner of Port Road every day after school. He gulped down the lumps of squashy white tripe I hid in my pocket at tea-time. He sat with his head on my lap when I told him my secrets.

Each morning I hurried to the shed. Scruffles lifted his head from his paws, stood up to stretch and yawn, then trotted up for a cuddle. I scooped him up, turned him over and held him tightly, his arms up like a baby. He wriggled once or twice and looked up as though to say, 'What are you doing to me, Patti?' I stroked the fur of his tummy and swayed from side to side.

Sometimes I dressed Scruffles in my old singlets or frocks. He rolled his eyes and tore at the clothes with his paws. Some days I'd sing to him. My favourite was 'The Donkey's Serenade'. Any words I didn't know, I made up. 'Senorita, dog is bitsa, song is sweeta, dum dum deeta, you're the dog for me.' While I sang, I tickled him inside his back legs, and he kicked wildly like he was scratching fleas.

Scruffles was my baby, my friend, my playmate. He was the only one in all the world I trusted. The day I fought Joe Visconsi, Scruffles backed me up. Joe had called out, 'Your Nan's an eighteen stone lump of lard with a football belly button.' I flew at Joe and Scruffles bit his leg.

That night his big sister stood at our front door to complain. 'Your dog should be shot.'

Nan roared at her, waved her walking stick in the air like a club, and Joe's sister went away with a flea in her ear.

One afternoon, on the way home from school, Scruffles was not sitting on the footpath at Worthly's corner. I saw a shape in the gutter, but my brain refused to register. It was the right colour fur. My heart stopped. Scruffles lay on his side, his back legs twisted sideways, his tongue sticking out. I fell beside him. 'Scruffles, oh Scruffles.' I crouched over him, weeping with terror and confusion. My body heaved with sobs. Scruffles tried to move, but he couldn't stand up. He just scratched at the ground wildly with his front paws. His eyes were scared. He tried to lick my hand, his head over on one side. He panted with short quick breaths, his side rising and falling.

I didn't notice the crowd gathering until a man knelt beside me and said in a quiet voice, 'Poor little chap. Looks like his back is broken. You must get him to a vet.' He stroked Scruffles between the ears. 'Go on girlie, run off home.'

How could I leave Scruffles lying in the gutter? He might die while I was away. I tried to lift Scruffles gently under the tummy, but he cried with pain. I gave him a kiss on the nose and ran home as fast as the wind. Uncle Mark, from across the road, hurried back with me and carried Scruffles home on a hessian bag.

He put Scruffles by his water dish in the back yard. I lay stretched out on the dirt beside Scruffles and pushed the water right under his nose. He sniffed it, but his head fell back. I put my face next to his and whispered to him that he would be all right.

'It's a bad business,' I heard Uncle Mark tell Nan.

'We've got no money for a vet,' Nan said. 'They charge a small fortune just to put a dog down.'

I cringed at Nan's words. Scruffles was a fighter. He wasn't going to die. How could I live if there was no Scruffles? How could I even look out the back door into the yard, if there was no Scruffles to prick up his ears and trot over for a game? I stroked his rough back and tickled him behind the ears. Scruffles must fight. Just like the day he took on the Alsatian and I had to pull him away. I ran my finger over the scar on the back of my hand where Scruffles, fighting like mad, had turned and bitten me when I tried to pull him off the Alsatian.

'I've heard of an old German couple in Halifax Street who are supposed to be good with dogs,' said Uncle Mark. 'What do you reckon? Worth a try?'

I didn't dare look up as Nan thought. After a while she said, in that voice that meant this child is more trouble than she's worth, 'I suppose we'd better.'

My heart jumped for joy. I looked up, pleading. Nan looked at me and frowned. 'No, Patti. It's better for everyone if you stay here.' I didn't dare protest in case she changed her mind and wouldn't let Scruffles go.

Uncle Mark backed his old blue buckboard up the lane and

put Scruffles in the back. When he returned there was no Scruffles. Uncle Mark stroked my hair. 'It's okay, Patti. They've kept him overnight. It's a broken pelvis. You've got to ring them tomorrow and see what's going on.'

Next morning I had to wait until nine o'clock before I was allowed to phone. It was agony waiting. I watched the kitchen clock. The big hand crept up towards the top. I dreaded the news that Scruffles might have died. But I had to know. I kept telling myself he'd be all right. The German couple were good with dogs. They'd done this hundreds of times. As soon as the hand reached eleven, I bolted out the house, ran to the phone box, climbed up on the shelf to put the two pennies in, and dialled the number I had on a bit of paper. 'Hello. Is that the dog people? Is Scruffles all right?'

I hung up in disbelief. They wouldn't talk to me. It had to be an adult. I ran back to Uncle Mark. They told him to come and collect Scruffles. I danced about. He was alive.

My dog came home wrapped in white all around his legs and waist. When Uncle Mark lifted him down and gave him to me, Scruffles rolled his eyes as though to say, I look really stupid like this.

Nan put her hand on my shoulder. 'Just this once, he can spend the night inside. Put him in your father's room.'

All day I nursed Scruffles. I tried to give him some Weetbix with warm milk, but he wasn't interested. I held a teaspoon of milk to his mouth and tried to tip it in. Most of it went down his chin. For hours I sat in the dark room, sometimes cradling Scruffles in my lap, sometimes lying stretched out beside him. I watched every breath, willing him to live.

When it was bedtime, Nan made me leave Scruffles alone, shut his door, and I had to climb into my double bed. I lay stiff with resentment and fear. I strained to stay awake and not desert Scruffles by sleeping. In the middle of the night I was woken by a bang, bang in Scruffle's room. I leapt from bed, then froze as Nan yelled at me. 'Stay here. He's all right.'

'He's not. I can hear him.'

Nan reached out and our door banged shut. 'Just let him be. Let nature take its course.'

31

I stood in the dark, and shivered with cold and terror.

'Just for once, try to understand that I know what's best. I'm trying to help you, you silly child. Now get back into bed. I forbid you to look at Scruffles until morning.'

For hours I lay in my bed. I listened for Nan's breathing to go slow and deep, but she would not fall asleep. For all those agonising hours, Scruffles kicked his wall. He was trying to run. A long time later he must have got tired. The noise stopped and the house fell silent.

The sound of a magpie singing woke me. I crept past Nan, who lay with her mouth wide open, her toothless bottom gum showing, her lips loose and flappy as she breathed. I went in to Scruffles. He lay against the wall, his eyes like glass. He was stiff and cold.

Something broke inside me. I buried Scruffles in a corner of the back yard and made a cross from bits of kindling. Every morning I put a dish of water by his grave. That little mound of dirt reminded me each day what love meant.

# *School*

*I crept from bed quiet as a mouse and knelt on the floor. From under* my double bed I pulled out the cigar box. I slipped back onto the bed and sat cross-legged, the cigar box on my lap. What jewellery would I wear to the grand ball? I opened the lid. With a fingertip, I quietly poked about among my treasures. An autumn leaf, bits of green and red glass, small lumps of lipstick. I held a chip of green glass to my left ear lobe, frowned into an imaginary mirror, and shook my head. The red would go better with the ball gown. Then I picked out a piece of scarlet lipstick and pretended to do my lips, my chin tilted back so I could see properly in the mirror. If one spot of make-up touched my lips, Nan would throw the lot out.

'Scarlet woman. Jezebel,' Nan had shrieked at the pretty woman who lived up Pickering Street. Nan had dragged me bawling to the lady's front fence. 'Throw it back at her,' Nan screamed. 'Throw it!' The words were bullets which shot the woman. She stepped back from the fence, and clutched her heart. 'Prostitute,' Nan yelled. She grabbed my fist, which was closely curled around the two shilling piece the lady had given me. Nan pulled my fingers apart and flicked my hand so that the money flew out, hit the fence and rolled back on the footpath. Nan pulled me away. 'You're never to speak to her, or have anything to do with her again.' I looked back at the woman, who gazed at me with horrified eyes. All the way home Nan held me by one arm and belted the backs of my legs. What was a prostitute to cause such crazy rage?

Anyway, I would wear scarlet lipstick to the ball, and Nan could go and suck eggs. I looked over at Nan on her single bed beneath the street window. She was awake but lay with her eyes shut. My box of treasures was full of all the things she hated. Speckled shells from the day we went in a truck to Semaphore beach. A baby red rose bud. Mrs Barry's lace hanky. I smiled to see hidden under a leaf my baby tooth, creamy white, smooth and cool. Nan only loved black. She wore black dresses. She made me wear black shoe-laces. Her mind was black, filled with anger. Colour was her enemy. In a rage she gave away my first doll with a sweet china face and eyes that closed as she lay down. 'Stupid thing,' Nan snorted. 'What good will it do you? Fill your head with foolish notions.' Nan also gave away the bright green pixie rag doll to some other girl. 'There are no such things as pixies.' But I ran down my enchanted alley next to Barry's Bakery, the ground a carpet of golden and red autumn leaves, and I searched for fairy rings.

The cigar box rattled as I shifted my legs on the bed. Nan grunted. I closed the lid, clutched the box, then fled down the passage and out to the kitchen table.

After a while I heard a dull thump, thump, thump from the bedroom. It was Nan's walking stick, that she banged on the floor. Time for morning chores. I closed my box, returned to the bedroom and hid it back under my bed, right over near the wall. Then I lifted the stinking chamber pot from the blue commode chair. Nan went to the toilet on the pot every night. There was beetroot stuff in it and my stomach churned as I hurried out to the back yard dunny. More sickening than the pot was the fear of 'Uncle' hiding behind the toilet, or in it.

Automatically, I sneaked sideways towards the shed so that I could see behind the toilet. He was not there. I stood far back to push the toilet door open with one foot. Safe for today. I tipped the pot down the hole in the wooden seat. Then I ran over to the tap to wash out the pot.

After I had made Nan's tea and toast I hurried to get dressed for school. I only had one school dress, the second-hand uniform. Nan sat up on her bed, settled in for the day with her Bex and her fags. From the jumble under my bed I dragged out

34

Veronica's green shoes and put one on.

'You're not wearing those to school.'

I pouted. These were my best shoes. My friend Veronica had worn them only a few times before her mum, Aunty Elsie, gave them to me, just as if I was her own daughter. I idolised Veronica and thought Aunty Elsie was the most wonderful lady in the world. Fancy having so much money you could give away a pair of new shoes and then go to the shop and buy more. They were the only beautiful shoes I'd ever had. I needed to wear them that day because I was giving a concert to my class. Deliberately, I put the other shoe on.

'How dare you defy me, you little monkey.' Nan shifted her grip on her walking stick.

Old bitch, I thought. You get my endowment money and spend it on cigarettes and Bex. If my mum knew, she'd come and take me away. I'd live in a real family where people are kind to each other, and talk about things and laugh. My mum would take me shopping and I'd have more than one old dress.

'And pull your lip in. It's sticking out like a doorstep.'

Just for once, Nan was not losing her temper. Her voice was almost kind. 'When I tell you what to do, it's for your own good Patti. Grown ups know what's best, and I know you'd look silly wearing those green shoes to school. The children will laugh at you.'

Pig's bum, I thought. They'll love my shoes and all want to wear special shoes to school. You grown ups think I'm just a bag of flour. You put me in a bowl and beat me up and mix me around. If I don't turn out like a good sponge cake, you'll be ashamed and throw me out.

Slowly I took the green shoes off and felt around for my school shoes – Aunty Jean's old high heels.

My feet flopped about in the shoes as I clopped along Pickering Street to collect young Jane and walk her to school. Her mum worked, so Jane had to get herself and her younger brother ready for school. Jane was in my class, Grade Four, and she was a ratbag. She had one eye turned in and wore glasses. If she wet her leg, she still had the dusty stain down her leg the next day. This morning when I called in, smoke poured from the kitchen. 'What's that terrible stink?' I asked, holding my nose. Jane opened the oven door. 'Snowy had kittens and they were all wet so I tried to warm them up.' On the tray were shrivelled hard black things with no eyes.

On the way to school I played games with Jane. 'See that lady coming towards us. Let's make out we're big girls going out tonight with boys.' Jane gasped and put her hands over her face. 'As she passes I'll say to you, "See you tonight at seven, and wear your best dress." And then you say in a la-de-da voice, "I do hope it's a good film."' By the time the lady got close we were too shy and scurried past with lips tight and faces down. Then we burst into giggles and ran for the gate of the Hindmarsh Primary School.

Mr Phelps closed the roll book. He inspected the nib of his pen to see how much red ink was on it. Then he peered through his glasses at the class. 'Patti Robbins, you may come out here now.'

An excited whisper followed me as I stepped up onto the teacher's platform and stood by his table. Mr Phelps looked down at my high-heeled shoes, and I saw the shiny bald bit on top of his head. His brown hair was parted on the right-hand side and smelt of California Poppy hair oil. He held up his hand for absolute quietness and said, 'Today, children, Patti will present another of her little acts. I expect your behaviour to be perfect, or I shall stop this privilege straight away. You understand me, Greg Shipway? Good. You may begin, Patti.'

I was fuming at his words 'little acts'. Little? Fat lot Mr Phelps knew. When I was grown up, I would sing and act to huge crowds. Hadn't my mum been a singer and dancer? 'Voice like a nightingale,' said Aunty Jean. In my mind was the flickering memory of a woman who held me in her arms and danced round and round a kitchen. Her voice was warm and her hair tickled my cheek.

I stepped to the middle of the low platform along the front of the classroom. 'This is the shop,' I told the class. I drew an imaginary wall with my hand. 'Here is the window. There's a puppy in the basket in the window.' Kids covered their mouths with their hands and whispered the name of the song.

I went over to the classroom door, took a deep breath, strode up onto the platform, stopped with surprise and sang, 'How much is that doggy in the window?' Then I crouched down like a dog, 'Woof, woof,' and continued right through. I acted all the parts in turn, lost in the music. My heart burst with the words 'true love'. Away in my fantasy, I hardly heard the laughter and clapping of the class.

I went back in a dream to sit with my best friend, Big Pat, who at every morning assembly stood behind me in the line-up, her arm out straight and her hand on my shoulder. As I sat, Big Pat gave me a grin. For the next few minutes I went over and over the act in my mind, until Mr Phelps asked me the answer to a sum I hadn't heard, and the horrible Shipway twins sniggered behind me.

Big Pat came from a good family, so she was never allowed to visit 37 Pickering Street and play with me. Nobody was allowed to play in our place. In Grade One, I brought young Scotty to our front door to show Nan he'd filled my nickers with the chook wheat. Nan went troppo, picked him up and threw him across the verandah. There was blood on Scotty's knees and he ran off crying. Nan held me by the shoulders, shook me, and shouted in my face, 'Don't you ever play dirty sex games in my house.'

I screamed back, 'You grown-ups have a lot to learn,' and took off to hide in the pepper tree. From that day I was forbidden to bring a friend home.

At recess-time Big Pat and I hung round the shelter shed and watched the boys play footy. There were two groups, and they booted the ball back and forward. Big boys went for high marks, and the little kids sharked the rebounds. Big Pat and I both loved Ray Hanrahan, the captain of the footy team. We couldn't tell him and so suffered agonies of longing and terror. What if he found out and chose only one of us? I ground my teeth with jealous rage. I knew what I'd do if Ray chose Big Pat. I'd let his bike tyres down and never speak to Big Pat again. But it was hopeless. What chance did either of us have against Mary Alvaro, who was in Grade Seven and already had breasts.

While we stood, seething with desire, I pestered Big Pat for gossip about her family. She kept her eyes on Ray's muscles and answered me as though she was a sleepwalker. We often had this conversation. 'What do you do when you get home? What do you have for tea? What do your mum and dad talk about at the table?'

Big Patti had everything I wanted. A mum, a dad, love. Her mum took her shopping for new shoes. Her mum came to watch her at school concerts. Her dad held her hand and called her 'Honey'.

The next lesson after recess was boring old Social Slops. The only good bit was colouring in a blue edge all the way round the coast of my map of Australia. Writing notes was stupid. Rules, rules, rules. Rules about how to sit, how to hold a pen, exactly where to put a date on the top of the page, how wide a margin must be, the finger space between words. I pushed too hard with my pen so the nib crossed and ink sprayed up the page. While Mr Phelps wrote on the blackboard, carefully forming each letter, exactly between the lines ruled on the board, I sawed away at the long wooden seat with my ruler. I had already made a deep groove between Big Pat and me. When the ruler was good and hot from the rubbing, I shoved it under the desk behind me to get one of the rotten Shipway twins on the bare leg. They kicked their legs about and got told off for making a noise. 'But Mr Phelps, it wasn't us it was ...' Mr Phelps stared at them and reached for Stinger, which hung on a nail from the bottom of the board. The Shipways shut up like clams.

Mr Phelps was giving us a lesson on Captain Sturt's journey into the Stony Desert. I reckoned Sturt was a loony to take a whaleboat up there. Mr Phelps talked on and on, then turned his back to write more notes. My eyes wandered to the picture above the fireplace. It was of a marvellous white horse with wings who flew through the sky. I slipped into a dream that I was Pegasus. I soared over mountains and rivers, free to go wherever I wanted. When I grew up, if anybody tried to keep me in a barn, I'd kick the door down and fly on my strong wings up among the clouds. Any man who held my bridle must let go or be pulled so high he would fall to his death.

Smash. The Shipway twins behind me had lifted the lid of their desk and crashed it down again. Mr Phelps spun round and pointed to me. 'Was that you, Patti Robbins?'

'No, Mr Phelps.'

Greg Shipway waved his hand in the air. 'It was her, Mr Phelps.'

I turned round and smashed Greg in his froggy nose. Blood poured over his mouth. Kids yelled and screamed. Mr Phelps charged towards me. I leapt to my feet, kicked off my high-heeled shoes and ran. Mr Phelps chased me so I jumped onto a desk and leapt from desk to desk while Mr Phelps weaved among the aisles. The door was shut and Mr Phelps too close for me to have time to open it. I set off again across the class-room. The class cheered. Mr Phelps made a detour to grab Stinger off the nail. That gave me my chance. I made a big leap to the floor, dragged it open, and headed for home. I glanced back over my shoulder. Mr Phelps stood at the door. 'Patti Bloody Robbins,' he yelled after me. I kept going, even though I had glimpsed the grin on his face.

I went to the Port Road lawns and hid in the rotunda until it must have been lunch-time. What would I do about my bare feet? Nan would be expecting me home, as usual, to make her lunch. I decided to sneak in and pretend my shoes were out-side. Then I would wag it for the rest of the day.

When I got home, Nan was dressed in her going-out clothes. She sat at the kitchen table. Her face was white and worried. She nervously tapped the ash off her cigarette, hardly bothering to notice me. She heaved herself to her feet. 'Come along Patti. Get your good clothes on. We're going to Veronica's.' My heart fluttered with fear. Veronica went to the convent school. What had happened to her?

'Why do we have to?'

'Never you mind, Patti. Just give me a hand with these laces.'

I knelt and tied up her shoes, which looked so funny at the bottom of such huge legs.

'Now run along and get ready, and don't forget to brush that hair.'

All the way to Veronica's I was sick with anxiety. What if

Veronica was dying? Nan refused to talk. She concentrated on swinging her hips because her thighs stuck together.

Veronica's mum opened their door. Behind her was Veronica's blind dad, in his suit. His face was serious as he listened to our names. We followed into the front room. Veronica sat in an armchair and cried. There was a long box on the table. I stared at Veronica's tears. 'Never cry,' Nan used to say. 'It shows other people your weakness and they'll take advantage.'

I looked in the box, wondering what it was. I opened my mouth to scream but no noise came. Inside, on his back, was Veronica's brother. His face was white. His hair was brown. Somebody had dyed his blonde hair. I staggered back, my mind filled with that dead face. In that instant I was terrified of dying. Somebody would comb my dead hair. I would lie in a box, looking asleep, but the life gone. I shut my eyes, but the dead face would not go away. It was there in my mind like a ghost to haunt my days and nights. One day I would be like that, my spirit gone into the air like a puff of steam that floats up and disappears. Patti would be gone forever. Put in a box. The lid put on. Total darkness. What if I wasn't dead and woke up when I was buried deep in the grave?

# *Attempted murder*

*When I was young, Old Pop used to take me to the Central Market.*
I went delirious with the excitement of mountains of colours:
bright apples, white and brown onions, red watermelons and
yellow rockmelons split open, piles of golden bread, huge
buckets of violets, the hot dusty smell of chicken shit and the
pong of fish just in from the boat – trays of slippery black eels,
huge snapper, silky gar and tommy rough with pretty spots on
the skin.

'Look at their eyes,' said Old Pop. 'If they stick out, then the
fish is fresh. Never buy a fish with sunken eyes.'

The air rang with the cries of the vendors. 'Half a case of
bananas for a bob . . . Come on, how can you go past . . . Just
look at these lettuces, feel that heart.'

All around me were legs, long frocks, kids pulling dinky-
carts piled with vegetables, kids with bare feet and the arse out
of their trousers. There were the high wooden counters where
Pop bought a little bag of his favourite black-and-white striped
peppermints, which scraped the roof of my mouth if I sucked
too hard. The air was filled with the sound of voices like soft
summer rain on the roof.

One night, when I was about ten years old, I sat with Old
Pop on the old wooden sofa in our front room. Old Pop hung
pairs of bright cherries over my ears. His hands were as dry as a
lizard's and twisted into claws from when he was electrocuted.
The cherries tickled and I squealed with laughter. It was safe to
laugh because Nan was away at the doctor's. Her belly button

had burst out some more. I crushed geranium leaves and smeared the juice on my mouth as lipstick.

Old Pop was related to us somehow. Every now and then he lived with us. I didn't care if Old Pop was a monkey's uncle, he could stay with us as long as he liked.

'Now, one of these carnations for your hair,' he said. His bent fingers struggled to snap off the red flower from its long green stem.

My father stumbled through the front door and stood swaying in the passage. He glared at us. 'Take those damn things off your ears.'

Without thinking, I yelled, 'You're a drunken old bastard.'

There was dead silence. My father's face went into a blank stare. Old Pop tried to get to his feet. My father staggered towards me. I grabbed one of the long cushions stuffed with rags and hid my face in it. The pillow was torn away and a hand slapped my cheek. I couldn't see for the tears, but I sobbed, 'You only hit me because you can't hit my mum.' Then everything went black as he pushed the pillow in my face. I couldn't breathe and panicked. I thrashed my body about, kicked up with my legs, but he shoved more pillows on me and then fell over me, pinning me under the pillows. My nose and mouth were blocked. My throat made a high whining noise. There was thundering in my ears, my heart hammered wildly and I went berserk with terror. Then a black whirlpool formed just above my face. Its point touched my forehead. It whirled faster and faster. My fingers dug into something. My eyes filled with flashing dots of light that were sucked up into the enormous whirlpool that spread out to fill the sky. Then nothing.

A long time later I heard Old Pop's voice calling, 'Patti, Patti, wake up. Don't go. Come back.' A dry hand brushed my mouth. Old Pop had come to get me. I opened my eyes and saw his mouth oozing with blood. His eyes overflowed with tears and he knelt beside me to stroke my hair again and again.

# *The*
# *lunatic asylum*

*Two women hung screaming on the wire fence of their cage. Their fingers* were cat's claws, their eyes wild, and their long gowns were dark where they had wet themselves. One shrieked at me, 'The kettle's boiling. Where's my baby? I want my baby.' She pushed her fingers through the wire. 'My baby. Come back, my baby.'

'Don't talk, keep walking,' said the nurse. She stopped at the end of the corridor and searched through the keys that jangled on the heavy metal ring. Hurry up, I silently begged her, glancing back at the cat women.

At last the nurse opened the door. 'Nearly there,' she said, and locked the door behind us. I looked along the empty corridor. The lino floor shone in the weak sunlight that came through the windows. All along one wall of the corridor were cell doors. The nurse smiled at me, and said in a cheerful voice, 'Do you want to look?' She slid aside a small wooden flap on a door and I stood on tiptoe to peer in. There was a filthy striped mattress on the floor. A teenage girl crouched in the far corner. She gnawed at the edge of a hard brown sheet she clutched to her chest. The nurse, her face next to mine, said, 'Leather sheet. So she can't strangle herself.' I shuddered and wanted to get away, but the nurse's body was pressed against me. The cell stank like the men's toilets at the back of the pub. There was no bed, no table or chair, nothing but floor and walls. The girl tugged the sheet into the corner of her mouth so her big teeth got at it. Her eyes stared vacantly. Her brown hair was in tangles. She looked about fifteen. 'Suicide,' whispered the nurse. Just like my father, I thought. 'And how old are you, Patti?' the nurse asked. 'Ten.' The mad girl looked up and for an instant our eyes met. I shuddered with horror that her spirit would jump from her eyes into my soul. The nurse slammed the wooden flap shut.

I shut my eyes. I remembered the kids' voices in Pickering Street. 'Your dad's in the nut house. Your dad's a loony.' I hit out. Hit them or be trodden under.

'You must visit him,' Nan said.

'I hate him. It's horrible there.'

'He's your father, that's why. He deserves that much consideration. While you live in my house, you'll obey my orders. Unless you want to leave. Go to the orphanage.'

The nurse unlocked another door. This time we went outside. I saw a man sitting hunched on a park bench underneath the long verandah. His head hung down almost to his lap.

This was the man who staggered into our kitchen, his face twisted with rage as he reeled drunkenly towards the table, eyes fixed on my birthday cake, hands outstretched. In a slow terrible nightmare his fingers plunged into the cake, ripping it apart. He smashed down my five little candles. The cake exploded, and I felt lumps spatter on my face and dress. The air was filled with screams. I saw terrified faces of children and my father's mouth wide open, roaring.

'Hello, Bloke.' The nurse went over to my father and put her hand on the back of his head. 'How are you feeling today?'

My father lifted his face. He gave a weak smile. He must have been handsome once, with his curly brown hair and strong face. He gave me an empty stare, as though he didn't know me. He avoided my eyes and looked down at my hands. I hid them behind my back.

I looked away from him, across the empty paddocks to the high wire fence, and through to the hills where I yearned to be living a different life.

'Your present, dear,' said the nurse, and took me firmly by the hand close to my father.

I held out the parcel. As he leant forward, I saw that he had two red scars high on each side of his forehead.

'Isn't that nice,' said the nurse, as my father took a block of Cadbury's milk chocolate out of the paper bag.

'My mate, George,' he mumbled, and pointed with the chocolate to a thin man who knelt on the cement path and held a cat down cruelly while he stroked it hard along its back bone. The cat twisted its face back and hissed silently at its tormentor.

'The menagerie is coming along fine,' said my father. He pointed to a wire cage along the verandah. 'George was in Borneo too,' he said. Then he got to his feet and called out. 'George. Got a present for yer.'

The thin man let go of the cat, which raced up the nearest tree where it crouched on a branch and switched its tail.

'Come and see,' called my father. Then he said to the nurse, 'George is my mate. Best mate a man ever had. He knows what happened out there.'

George shambled over and snatched the chocolate. He held it close to his face and sniffed the blue paper. 'Glass and a half,' he said. Then he broke off the end and held it out to my father. 'Here, you have some, Bloke.'

My mouth watered. Nan had to raid my money box to get enough for the fares and chocolate. I caught sight of my father's fingers tearing at the silver paper, and I suddenly felt disgusted. I hurried away to the cage under the verandah.

Inside were two pigeons pecking at the seed scattered on the tin floor. The feathers on their necks glinted bright blue and when they turned their necks they flashed with all the colours of the rainbow. I poked my little finger through the chicken wire and hoped a pigeon would peck at it. 'Here, pij, pij,' I cooed.

I wondered if there was ever a time I had loved my father. It always went wrong. The day he came back from the war every-one but me was excited. Who was this man they talked about? I had a new dress, Nan tied my hair in curling tongs, which hurt because they were so heavy. We went to a hotel, and a man came in, shouting. He was in a soldier's uniform. He grabbed me and flung me high in the air, past his chest with its bulging pockets, past the soldier's hat way up where I looked down at all the upturned laughing faces. Then he let me down, but scraped my cheek against the sharp badge on his hat. I screamed with fright and pain. I saw blood fall on my new dress. My father went stiff and thrust me at Aunty Jean. She dragged me out to the toilet where she smacked my bum and hissed at me, 'Stupid girl. Why do you have to spoil everything?'

In the middle of one night my father fumbled and bumped his way in the front door. He stood, unseen, in our bedroom doorway. I lay in fear. No light came in the street window, so I knew it was past the time they turned the street lights off. I saw the darkness move where Nan lay. My father stomped in, whispering to somebody, 'Sshh, Shoosh, Don't give it away.'

From the pitch black hole that was the bedroom door came a sudden screeching nightmare. I sat bolt upright and screamed. I felt the nearness of my father. Nan bawled, 'What is it? What are you doing?'

'Shut up, shut up the lot of you,' my father shouted at the top of his voice. A match flared. A bald galah gripped the back of my father's arm. Beak open, it shrieked like a banshee. Its huge eyes bulged. There was a white wobbling abdomen, wings out, and a knobbly tongue that rattled in its open beak.

'Shit,' said my father as the flame burnt down to his fingers. Out of the darkness came his enraged voice. 'Never do the right thing for you. Just like your fucking mother.'

My father did the right thing when he went away. Sometimes, after drinking stuff he stole from the chemist shop, mixing it with metho, he screamed at the huge spiders and lizards that dropped on him from the ceiling and crawled onto his face. Then he'd be taken off to this mental hospital.

Other times he'd spend the night in the lock-up, because he got excited at his preaching and went berserk. 'Come to Jesus.' He stood on a fruit box on the corner of Russell Street and yelled at people, who put their heads down and hurried past. 'Come unto me,' he yelled abusively at their backs. 'I am the way, the truth and the life.' He whipped himself into a frenzy of Scripture verses, took a few swigs from the bottle under the fruit box, then went round and chucked a brick through the window of the Hindmarsh Police Station. 'Come out and fight you gutless bastards. I'll take the lot of you. One hand tied behind my back.'

Bloke Robbins loved a fight. I'd lie in bed and listen to the adults drink and argue while they sat around the kitchen table. I liked those nights because I heard things I wasn't supposed to.

One night it started when somebody said to my father, 'Ah, bullshit, Bloke. You never volunteered to fight the Japs. Not until you found the white feather in your letterbox.' That got him going. There were smashings in the kitchen, a lot of yells, footsteps up the passage and out the front door. My father ran onto the road and flattened a neighbour riding home from late shift. Neighbours poured out onto the road and there was a ding-dong battle – this side of Pickering Street against the others. It was a great barney. It was a perfect chance to settle old grudges about whose husband was flirting with whose wife, and who threw rubbish over the fence or stole flowers from the front garden. Fists flew, men rolled wrestling on the ground, women tore at each other's hair, the dogs raced around and snapped at feet, and all the kids jumped about and cheered for their side. I even barracked for my father. 'Go on, Dad, put in the boot.' He was squared off against Charlie, who reckoned my father put Herbert the private detective onto a bit of Charlie's hanky-panky.

As quickly as it started it stopped. Men with bleeding noses shook hands to show there were no hard feelings. Women got to their feet and straightened their skirts. The adults straightened their hair and belted us kids back to bed.

I lay awake, and waited for the sound of the aunties feeling their way along the passage wall. Drunk as skunks they fell onto my big double bed, flung arms around me and cuddled me, beery breath in my face, wet belches and damp farts: 'If that's not out, I'll take me bat and go home.' In the morning I'd fix the cold vinegar compresses and put them on their foreheads. I mixed their hangover cures of Salvital, Bex, and a hair of the dog. I'd mop up the spew. Then I went outside for our kids' brawl. We fought for the honour of friends and relatives who were injured in the night. For the rest of that day we stuck our noses in the air to the best friends of yesterday.

When my father went away for a long time to take a job where nobody knew him, Nan and I folded up his bed, threw out the bottles of cough mixtures – twelve per cent alcohol – and shut his door.

I celebrated by cleaning the house from top to toe. First I twisted the lid off a tin of Nugget shoe polish and did the front step. Then I got the bucket and rags and the long wooden scrubbing brush with hard bristles and rubbed away at the green lino in the passage. I scrubbed in circles to make sure I got the Velvet Soap suds over every square inch. And so I went through the whole house. I even washed the legs of chairs and tables, loving the smell of wet wood.

With my father away, there was no need at night for Nan and I to sit in terror waiting for him to roll home from the six o'clock swill at the Brompton Park Arms. No longer did we wait for the sound of his curses as he blundered along the road. We sat all cosy at night and listened to the radio. We loved the quizzes, like Jack Davey's or Pick-a-Box. When my father was off in the bush, Nan and I had the money and the box. We didn't have to walk the streets to escape his rages. We slept safely tucked up in our own beds, not bunked down in Aunty Jean's spare room, where Nan took me to escape the bashings.

We had many months of peace when he actually managed to hold down a job in the pine forest at Nangwarry in the South-East. Just once, he told me to come and visit. Uncle Frosty had to deliver a new truck for the mill, and I felt safe with him. There was no room for me in the truck cabin with Uncle Frosty, another woman and Aunty Jean. So I crouched on the running board and hung onto the door handle. It was uncomfortable facing into the cold wind, but I loved the rush of the air and the danger of clinging to the side of the truck. It was about two hundred miles to Nangwarry.

My father lived in an old prisoner-of-war camp, in a long wooden hut. The pine trees crowded round, dark and sinister, and they sighed in the bitter wind. On the first night I made a cigarette of rolled strips of newspaper.

'Hey, look, I can do the drawback.'

My father whacked me over the head. 'Don't let me catch you smoking again.' And this from him, who smoked like a train, drank like a fish and fought like a bandit.

I stood back and shouted, 'You never tell me what you want me to be. You only belt me for what I can't be.' I ran outside and hid in the evil trees. I was frightened out of my wits that a goblin would leap out and drag me away. But anywhere was better than inside with those liars who beat me for doing what they did. Why were they so frightened? Why did they make a million rules for everything and then break them? Never, never open your heart an inch, I told myself, or they'll push in and bash you.

A mental hospital patient had wandered to the pigeon cage and was talking to me. 'Pretty, aren't they?'

I resented her intrusion and said nothing. She bent down and scratched the wire with her fingernails. She was so ugly. She had no chin, her eyes bulged, and her cheeks hung down like Droopy Dog's. Her fingers had square tips and the nails were cut straight, like a man's.

'I've got some good news for you,' she said in a sickly fake voice. 'Your dad is leaving hospital soon.'

Good news? I went hard with anger.

'And guess what?' She waited. I shrugged and inspected the pigeons closely. 'Your dad's going to be with me, and I can look after him.' She paused for the great news to sink in. I looked straight at her and produced an enormous grin. She breathed a sigh and clapped her hands. 'I'm so glad you like the idea. Now we can be friends.' As she spoke I decided to name her Godzilla.

She shuffled closer and put her hands on my hips. She turned me to look at her watery eyes. 'You see, Patricia, your father and I love each other, and want to be together.' Patricia? Nobody called me that except Nan when she lost her temper. I clenched my lips. 'We'll move into a place just down the road from you. Won't that be nice? Then you can visit us or even stay with us if you like. Just for a few nights at a time, until you get used to things.' I waited, my face blank. Godzilla tried again.

'It means that your father and I are engaged to be married.' Oh yeah, I thought. Join the queue.

I looked at her and wondered, Should I tell her? The last girlfriend bribed me with a new dress and a pair of shoes, which Nan gave to the Salvos.

# The coat
# and the convent

*I plunged the broom handle down into the boiling water. I pushed* it under a sheet and heaved it out. Steaming water poured out of the sheet and a hot cloud of steam washed over my face. My wrists ached, so I rested the broom handle on the edge of the copper to take the weight while I grabbed at a loose end of the sheet to put it between the rollers of the wringer. Ouch. The sheet scalded my fingers. My hands were already pink and wrinkly from the washing.

As usual I went off in a dream while I worked. That day I was a famous ballerina. The back yard at Pickering Street was too ugly and sinister for me. I lived in a secret back yard of my mind. There I was centre stage under a single spotlight. At the end of my dance, the audience, spellbound, rose to its feet in rapturous applause. A handsome man watched me from the wings, a huge bouquet of flowers in his arms. Over and over, as the wringer turned, I replayed the fantasy. I knew each scene by heart, but turned the handle, forcing my story to the same climax; then I started all over again. I added new refinements of torment and ecstasy, my teeth clenched with rage, my brain hot with suspense and fierce glory.

I heard Nan's voice from the back door. 'Get a wriggle on. We're going out.'

You could have knocked me over with a feather. Nan going out? I squinted at her through the steam. Her face was cross. That meant I had done something stupid, or she hated herself for doing something nice for a change. She banged her walking stick on the ground and growled, 'Move yourself. We haven't got all day.' She bustled inside and slammed the door behind her. I cranked away at the wringer.

I poked my tongue out at her and went on with the wringing. Now my mind switched from fantasy to curiosity. Where were we going? Not to Aunty Jean's. My father was up bush, and there was no need to run for shelter. Aunt Maggie's? But why get dolled up to go across the road? Not that it mattered. Anything to break the monotony.

When I had finished hanging out the washing, I ran inside. Nan sat at the table. She was all ready; even had her hat on. I stood and waited. My face ran with perspiration, my arms ached. Nan tapped her fingers in exasperation on her black handbag. 'Your father's coupons.' I looked blank. Nan scolded, 'War coupons. Now run along and make yourself presentable. We're going into town.'

My hands shook so much with excitement I took three goes to tie the bow at the back of my dress. What if Nan was to buy me something? I was eleven years old and had never been shopping in the city like Veronica and Big Pat. The city was a fabulous place only a few miles from Pickering Street, but as far away for me as another planet. The city was where rich people sat in restaurants and took tea and cakes. There were escalators, racks with hundreds of dresses, and a lady made you hold your arms out while she put a tape measure around your waist. Big Pat had looked down from the top of the Shell Building on North Terrace. It was so high the people on the footpath looked like ants. When her mother wasn't watching, Big Pat dropped her hanky over the edge. The wind swept it across North Terrace, dipping and floating, until it fell on the roof of a drop-centre tram and was trundled away towards the Museum where, so Big Pat said, there was a whale as long as her house, and shrunken skulls with shells for eyes, and an Egyptian mummy that had leaked goo in its coffin.

I put on my sensible brown school shoes. Veronica's green shoes lay under the bed. They were too small now.

Nan and I stood at the bus stop on Port Road. I leaned

out to look along the road that was so long it faded into the distance like a stretched-out letter 'V'.

I hoped it wasn't a trolley bus with poles going up to the electric wires. I wanted a double-decker bus so I could sit right at the front upstairs. But Nan couldn't climb the stairs. I resigned myself to sitting downstairs. Why must I always do what Nan wanted? This day, however, I was on my best behaviour.

We got off near the Beehive Corner on King William Street. The city was a whirlwind of people and noise. Tram poles spat and crackled with blue fire on the wires. Cars tooted, news-boys cried, 'Read all about it.' My head spun as crowds swirled past. Then we were swept into Rundle Street, away from a window full of chocolates, past Balfours with its cream cakes, kitcheners, chester squares, yeast buns with tops of white icing, and then on to the big stores.

Nan tugged my arm. 'In here.' Down we went into Myer's bargain basement. Customers clustered around racks of clothes that went way back into the store. Nan went up to a counter and asked a lady in a black uniform, 'Girls' coats, please.' I went hot with surprise. A coat? For me? I had never owned a coat. I grabbed Nan's hand and squeezed it. Her lips tightened and she snapped, 'Enough of that. Just keep close to me and don't get lost.'

We found the rows of girls' coats by a wall and Nan started to lift up sleeves and examine labels. I watched in a torment of anxiety as she lifted each label. Please God, not that black one. Or that dowdy brown one. I began to feel angry. No. Not that navy blue coat. Way down in the pit of my stomach I felt the horror of being dressed as a little Nan, all in dark.

A flash of green caught my eye. I broke away from Nan, went to the bright colour and pulled out a vivid green coat. It was my kind of colour. Green was for elves and Veronica's dancing shoes. Furtively I slipped the coat off its hanger and tried it on. The lining of the sleeves was cool and silky on my skin. I looked down at the hem of the sleeves. They were exactly level with my wrists. Perfect. I hugged the coat around me. It was meant for me. I put my hands into the pockets. Then, all in a panic, I did up the buttons. Would it be too tight?

No, it was lovely. I smoothed my hands down the collars, and danced around in circles. The coat tugged at my shoulders and swung around my legs. It was the most beautiful coat in the world. It had a pleat at the top of the back that got wider all the way down.

'Put that thing away.' Nan's words were a punch in the stomach. She charged towards me, holding out the navy blue coat. I felt sick as it came towards me and I hugged my arms across my chest.

'You heard me.' Nan flapped the coat. It floated in the air like a ghost. It was something dead to suffocate me. I stood, my breath panting in and out in quick, shallow gasps. My head was so dizzy I thought I'd faint.

Nan narrowed her eyes. She realised. 'Take that stupid thing off. You look like a cucumber.'

'No,' I whispered.

Nan blinked. 'What's that? What did you say?'

Very slowly, with deliberate defiance, I shook my head. The blood thundered in my head at the enormity of what I was doing. This was a declaration of war.

Nan's forehead turned bright scarlet. She raised her walking stick, paused, then quickly looked behind her at the other customers. She pushed her face close to mine and whispered, 'How dare you make a scene. Take that silly thing off, this instant.' A speck of her spit flew onto the collar of my coat.

I was terrified, but the words came out. 'Why can't I have this one? What's wrong with this one?'

'I'll decide what's best for you, young miss. Take it off.'

'But why? It fits perfectly.'

'How dare you "but" me. Ungrateful. After all the trouble I went to bring you here. Selfish, selfish, selfish,' she said, thumping her stick on the floor each time she said 'selfish'. 'Getting too big for your boots. You'll have the coat I choose or none at all.'

All right you old bitch, I thought. It'll be none. This fight was slipping out of control. 'Ungrateful?' I replied. 'After all you've done? All you've done is turn me into a little Aunty Maggie. Work, work, work.'

'Keep your voice down,' hissed Nan. She glanced nervously around in case somebody was watching.

I sensed her weakness, and felt a rush of power that I had never known. I must win, even if I lost the coat I loved. I reached out and grabbed the navy blue coat from Nan.

'What are you doing?' Nan looked frightened. She snatched at the coat. 'Give it back.'

We began a tug of war. I knew if I raised my voice Nan would simply walk out in humiliation. So, through clenched teeth, I said, 'Let me have it. I'll put it on then.'

Nan let go of the hated coat. She was confused. Had she won?

I held it up in front of me. Dark. Ugly. Nan hated my green one because she was scared of it; scared of me. She always called things bad that frightened her. I went on in a calm, quiet voice, sensing victory. 'If this one fits better than the green one, I'll take it.' This was a risk, but I knew that even if I carried the navy blue one home, I'd never wear it. This was a fight to break Nan's stubbornness. One way or another I was sure to win.

Nan watched closely while I showed her the exact fit of the green coat. Then I took it off, fearful I would never put it on again. Slowly I pulled on the navy blue coat. It felt rough and hairy and frumpish. Nan grabbed my hands in hers and yanked them hard to make sure I wasn't cheating by bending my elbows. Still holding my hands tightly, she stepped back and examined the length.

'See,' I said. 'Too big by miles.'

Nan licked her lips. 'But you'll grow into it.'

That was it. I felt the dam wall break. A flood of anger poured out. All I wanted was Nan's surrender. Nothing else, not coats, nor love nor anything mattered as much as feeling her break. I lashed out. 'And I'll never cry for you again.'

Nan stared at me, and swallowed as if she had a big lump of food stuck in her throat. Then she turned her back, went to the counter and flung the green coat on it.

We walked up the stairs towards the sunlight and the noise of Rundle Street. I carried the big brown paper parcel tied up with string. I felt sick. Nan looked old. Her bottom lip trembled as she struggled up the stairs, one step at a time. She was a lonely, suffering old woman, not the huge black creature who squatted in my mind. I felt ill because I had never been so far away from her. Nan was a stranger I passed on the stairway. I looked down and saw the brown spots on the backs of her hand wrapped over the top of the walking stick. My eyes filled with tears, and I reached over to stroke the back of her hand. Nan flinched and twitched it away as though a spider was crawling on it .

From that day things were different at Pickering Street. Life seemed to go on as usual. I continued to drudge away at the chores. Nan sat on her bed and stared out the window. But we knew, without saying it, that something had gone. Never again did I ask to wash her back. Now we were silent together. We moved past each other on our separate paths through the house.

There was a cold tension between us; a turning aside of the eyes. It was not the old battle of wills. We lived like two armies who fought without heart because neither side could win.

I was still, of course, at the mercy of Nan's demands, because I had nowhere else to live. There was a hard lump of resentment in my chest. For Nan to love me I had to surrender to her mindless authority. In Nan's rules, love meant destruction. The hardness in me was also a longing for love. The more we drifted apart, the more I clung fearfully to my duties. The floors were never so clean, the knives and forks were polished until they shone, the hankies were ironed into faultless triangles.

Repetitive work was an escape into a dream world. My secret life was, however, changing. Day by day the hidden Patti altered her costume. The childhood ballerina was still there, but fading away. One day her tiara was gone, and on another her swan's costume became a peasant's skirt. The ballerina continued however to dance with me in the street. As always, I sent around a message that there was to be a concert out the front of Number 37. The Pickering Street boys made a circle of their bikes. They slouched over the handlebars, smoked cigarettes, laughed and threw stones at my feet. Imperious, tyrannical, I bullied Mary Tarcento and Elaine O'Neill to dance with me. The boys' taunts and insults drove them away in tears of humiliation.

'I'm too old for those horrid boys, and your silly concerts,' sobbed Mary.

The Patti of my fantasies gave up on childish games and slum boys. She had a much better idea. Her peasant skirt became covered in a design of flowers, her long black hair was tied up in a red scarf. She no longer danced in a street but held her arms curved over her head and danced around a campfire to the strumming of guitars and the click of castanets. On the edge of the darkness, their paintwork flickering in the firelight, was a circle of gypsy caravans, a bit like those I'd seen on the poster for a film called 'Gypsy Girl'. I danced for the swarthy man who sat, dagger in his belt, dark eyes burning into me.

Soon after I brought home my green coat, I was taken from school and sent to St Joseph's convent school. No matter how I raged, how I cried at losing all my friends, how often I threatened to run away and live under the railway bridge, I obeyed. Nan had her revenge.

So I wore the horrid uniform and dragged my feet to the daily battles with Sister Bernadette, as Irish as the day is long, who carried a knobbly chair leg to crush our knuckles. My poor little gypsy girl stared up at gruesome statues of the man hanging on the cross, a cold ceramic smile on his face. The garish colours frightened me. Even Our Father which art in Heaven let his only child die. The ugly crucifix was meant to make it look all right. But it could never be all right, with its cruel spikes pushed hard down on the head, and blood pouring out of the heart. I stared for hours at the soppy smile on Jesus' face. 'Look at what I suffer for you,' he said. 'Why aren't you good enough for me?' Jesus and my Nan would have got on like a house on fire.

Every Sunday I was supposed to go to Mass. I knew what Nan and Sister Bernadette were up to. The church was supposed to do what Nan had failed to do: pull me into line; make me tread the straight and narrow. By now, I was ready to leave Pickering Street and do something spectacular. Nobody was going to stop me. I fought for what I wanted. When Aunty Jean told Nan lies about me being in the alley with boys, I flew at Aunty Jean and hit her. Nan had to pull me away because I

57

went right off my trolley. Jean ran shrieking out of the kitchen. Nan let go of me and gave me a strange, terrified look.

My only escape was the playground on Port Road where I sat on the swings and watched the boys who hung around the fish and chip shop. The Pickering Street boys were a pain in the arse. The Port Road boys were different. I began to wear the bras I pinched from Aunty Jean's place and kept hidden in the gas box. My breasts were growing, but were not big enough for the bras, so I stuffed socks in the cups.

While the rest of my class were at Mass, praying for salvation from sin, I sat on the swing and hitched up my bra.

Each Monday morning after Mass, Sister Bernadette questioned the class. 'Who was the priest?' Every hand rose, stretching for the sky with enthusiasm. Not to know the answer was a sentence of death. 'What was the Holy Scripture?' A forest of fingertips waved high in the air. Sister Bernadette pointed to the victim with her chair leg, and a great sigh of relief rose from those spared the inquisition.

My friend, Joan Hannaford, was my spy. She went to Mass and told me the right answers just before class report. So when Sister Bernadette asked, 'Who was the priest?' I raised my hand as wildly as any, and bravely kept my eyes on her.

Then one day, as I thrust my hand high with zeal, the leg of the chair pointed to me.

'Patti Robbins, who was the priest?'

'Father Donovan.' I gave Sister Bernadette a wide smile.

The room went as silent as the grave.

'Patti Robbins. Come out the front.' I stood in a daze of fear, at Joan Hannaford's treachery. I had trusted her. She was my friend. Joan Hannaford stared down at her desk. Had she lied to me each week, waiting? Like a puppet, I tottered to the front and stepped up onto the platform. I focused on the crucifix hanging on Sister Bernadette's chest. I heard the brush of her clothes as she raised her arm. I screwed up my eyes in anticipation. Her open hand slapped me across the face. It was just like home.

I felt my arm lash out as I slapped her face. She reeled back, shielding her face with the chair leg.

Before she could say it, I turned upon Joan and shouted, 'You can get your things too, and come with me.' Joan went white. A hand pushed me violently in the back and I stumbled down among the front row of desks. From behind me came Sister Bernadette's voice, 'Joan Hannaford, don't you move a muscle.'

I leant on a desk and called, 'If you don't come, you'll get a belting too.' Joan looked from Sister Bernadette, to me, and back to Sister. The class was breathless. Joan's eyes went blank. Then she burst into tears, flung both hands over her face, and stood up slowly, trembling. I sprang for the safety of the aisle and sprinted to the door at the back of the room. Joan rushed screaming after me, crowding past me in the doorway, crazy with panic.

I ran for the safety of the rotunda on Port Road. My chest heaving, I told myself, See, you can do it. You can stand up for what you want. I looked around at the road, the houses, the gasworks, the factories and thought, Nobody's going to stop me. I wiped my face with my hand, and looked around in confusion. What could I do about school?

Nan found out when the priest called round to the house. 'Mrs Robbins, I understand that Patti has enrolled herself at the State School. I have come to ask you to reconsider your decision.'

Nan didn't bat an eyelid. In a quiet voice she replied, 'If that is her choice, then wild horses wouldn't drag her back to your school.' In that moment I thought I would love Nan forever.

When the priest had gone, Nan called me to her. 'If you've got the courage, tell me the truth.' I saw the flicker of a smile before she hit me.

# *Boys*

*They fascinated me. The whole Heinz variety. The Pickering Street* gang were like their fathers. They smoked, swaggered, swore, spat, sneaked drinks, and anything they didn't understand they belted up. They rode their Malvern Stars and Super Elliotts around the streets and over to the pugholes where they played their John Wayne games. I had grown up with them, fought them, gone to school with them, been teased by them and so they did not deserve my favours. Anyway, their long gangly legs looked stupid in school shorts. The cleverest thing they could do was punch each other on the biceps to see who got a dead arm first. Their teeth were scummy, their ears stuck out like jug handles, and their tough voices kept breaking into squeaks.

Nan didn't approve of any boys, except those who lived across the railway line in the better part of Bowden, where kids' arses didn't hang out their trousers. 'Always marry above you,' Nan said. 'Get a man with a clean collar and a steady job. You don't want to end your days like me.' Absent-mindedly, she squeezed the ring-finger of her left hand, where once there was a wedding ring.

One day, I was annoying Nan by bouncing on my double bed. I loved that bed. It was where I did my dreaming, and where, if I was bored, I practised somersaults.

'Stop that nonsense,' Nan said, in a weary voice. I pretended not to hear. Our only communication seemed to be when we argued.

From outside came the sound of a motorbike, which slowed

down, then stopped outside our front door. I leapt over onto Nan's bed and we peeked out the window. There was a lad rocking the motorbike back on its stand. It was John Wright, with his red hair and freckles like Ginger Meggs. I was dressed like a bag of potatoes and my hair was not done. I jumped back on my bed and sat with my knees tucked under my chin, terrified of the knock on the front door. 'You answer it,' I whispered to Nan.

Out of the corner of her mouth, Nan whispered back, 'Who is it?'

'John Wright.'

Nan gawked at me. The Wrights were rolling in money.

There was a knocking on the door. I hid my face in my hands. The knocking came again. I heard Nan move off the bed, stand on the floor and walk out of the room. I sat hunched up on my bed, listening, my heart filled with despair. Nan never let me go out with the other kids. She was a prisoner of Number 37 Pickering Street, and my jailer.

When it was picture night at the Hindmarsh Cinema I would sneak off and sit on the cement steps outside to watch people go in, all dolled up, their faces excited, talking about the stars: Humphrey Bogart and Lauren Becall, Spencer Tracy and Katherine Hepburn, Fred Astaire and Ginger Rogers. I looked into the bright foyer at the posters of Lucille Ball, Bing Crosby and Bob Hope, Charlie Chaplin, and my favourite, seductive Mae West, dressed in a glittering gown with a split right up the thigh. I watched my friends go past with their mums and dads. They went over to the counter and stood for ages deciding whether to get Fantales, or chocolate eclairs, or Jaffas to roll down under the seats. My longing was more agonised because Nan did take me once. I loved the smell of the cinema, the thrill of the curtains opening as the film began, the music rising. But the day I won the battle of the green coat, I lost any chance for special treats.

Some of my friends would stop and talk to me where I sat on the steps. 'Why doesn't your Nan let you come?'

'I don't know.'

'I reckon she's cruel.'

I'd run back home before the music started and yell at Nan. 'Why won't you let me go?'

'If I say no, I mean no.'

'But why?'

'Just because I won't, and that's an end to it.'

'I hate you.'

'And I never wanted you.'

'I hope you die.'

I had discovered hatred. Not anger, not dislike, but something deeper and murderous. Nan had the sixpence. I didn't.

But on this morning it was Johnny Wright, in his Sunday suit. Johnny was known all round Bowden-Brompton as a boy with a big future. Why had he come to our place?

'Good morning Mrs Robbins. I've come to ask your permission to take Patti to see "Gone With the Wind", at the Hindmarsh Theatre.'

I flung myself back on my bed and grabbed two fistfuls of hair, pulling hard to stop the screams that tried to come. I waited for Nan's roar and the sound of running feet. Then I heard her say, 'Would you like to come in?' I panicked. What did I look like? My hair was a mess, my bare feet were filthy. Nan took Johnny into the front room across the passage. I flung off my old dress and put on my school uniform. In a frenzy I combed my hair, licked my fingertips and smoothed down my eyebrows. A boy, at my place. The first boy to ask me out. And on a motorbike. Veronica and Big Pat would curl up and die with envy.

The next Saturday night I was ready hours early. I sat on a kitchen chair with my dress spread out so I wouldn't crease it, and waited. Nan had given me a shilling to spend. 'You can't expect the boy to buy everything.' Nan was almost as excited as me. 'He's the right kind of boy,' she said. 'Tidy hair and clean shoes.' She put a hanky to her mouth and spat on it. Then she held my chin and rubbed the damp hanky against my chin to clean away a mark. I twisted my head aside. I hated the smell of her goozie, and it was humiliating being scrubbed like a baby.

Johnny was to pick me up at seven o'clock. I sat and watched the big hand of the clock creep up towards the twelve. Seven o'clock came, but Johnny didn't. At first I was cross. Stupid kid, probably got greased to the elbows fiddling with his motorbike. But if he hurried up, we could still make it on time. Then I got anxious. What if he had been run over on the way, and even now was lying in agony on the road, his blood trickling away. I imagined myself dressed all in black, following his coffin to the grave, where I stood, a tragic figure, casting a flower down onto the coffin.

I watched the clock. Come on. If you don't get here by quarter past, it'll be started, and we will have to sit down the front in the bad seats. I wanted to sit right in the back row, where the big kids smooched, and wait for Johnny to touch my hand, then hold it tight in my lap, and put his arm around my shoulders.

At twenty-five past seven I was in a torment of disappointment and rage. How humiliating. I'd told all my friends that a boy was taking me to the pictures. Big Pat was green. She was only allowed out with her big brother.

Then a horrible thought sneaked into my mind. What if he was right now with another girl, a beautiful rich girl, at the pictures, and they were in the back row, and at this very instant she was tossing her long hair with her fingertips and laughing about me: what then? As the clock ticked over and touched seven-thirty, I began to shake with fury. I fled out of the kitchen so Nan couldn't see my tears, ran up the passage and flung myself on my bed. I bit the pillow like a mad dog, snarling and roaring, all my pent-up passions raging around me.

Eight o'clock came and went. A sound broke through. It was a motorbike, then a hammering on the front door. I leapt from my bed, rushed at the front door, flung it open and charged out upon the terrified Johnny, my fists raised to strike. He backed into a verandah post, his arms held up to protect himself. 'I'm sorry, Patti. I was learning for a test.'

Bullshit. He had stood me up. As I closed on him he turned and ran across Pickering Street, and stood with his back to Scott's front fence. I stormed over. As I got near I saw a pile of bricks on the Scott's front verandah. I vaulted the fence, and took a brick in each hand. Johnny gasped and sprinted for his bike under our verandah. He dragged it away from our wall and leapt on it, but couldn't get it going in time. I ran over and hurled a brick into the fuel tank. We both looked in amazement at the dent and scratched paint.

That motorbike was the love of his life. His eyes went mad and he screamed at me, 'Look what you've done, you stupid kid.' I raised the other brick. He panicked and kick-started the motorbike. I yelled, 'Wrong side of the tracks, eh?' He stared at the brick, and took off along the footpath. The brick hit him on his left shoulder. He squealed, ducked and rode off into the night, hugging his dented fuel tank.

I strode back inside, flung the blankets off my bed, dragged up a sheet and began to bite it, frantic to tear it to shreds. Nan stood in the passage, her hands on her hips. 'Let this be a lesson,' she said. 'The educated class know how to tell cleverer lies.'

# The
# welfare lady

*Not long after Johnny decided not to come back to my house, I was* woken one morning by the sound of whimpering. I rolled over and saw Nan lying curled up like a baby, cradling the huge hernia on her belly. Her eyes were shut tightly, but tears trickled from under her eyelids. I watched spellbound.

Nan's eyes snapped open and she saw me. 'Stop gawking at me,' she said. 'Wake your father. Hurry. Something's busted.'

I ran to my father's stinking room, praying, Don't let Nan die. Please don't let her die.

Nan had to go to hospital for an urgent operation. I swung around a front verandah post and watched my father help Nan into an ambulance. I didn't know what an operation was, but from her face I knew it would hurt. Nan winced as she bent over to get into the ambulance. I clenched my jaw to stop the tears.

When the ambulance had moved off and turned the corner, I stood staring blankly at the empty street. What if Nan never came back? I drifted back inside to begin packing my suitcase. Who would have me? Not my father, for sure.

Another car pulled up outside. I heard a woman's high heels. My heart stopped. My mother! Somebody knocked on the door. In a total panic of hope I went to the door and opened it. There stood a pretty woman in a beautiful blue suit. Behind her was a new car. She held the car keys in her hand. I gazed at her, desperate to find any resemblance to the half-remembered photo I had seen as a small child. She had brown hair, so did my mother.

'Patti Robbins?' Her voice was gentle.

I nodded.

'Get your things, dear. You're coming with me.'

I leant over against the door frame and, in a dry, terrified voice, asked, 'Are you my mum?'

She smiled. 'Oh no, Patti. I'm from the welfare.'

I shut my eyes. There was a terrible crying in my head.

'What's welfare?'

'It's my job to help people. Just pop inside and get your things. We're going to find somewhere for you to stay while your grandmother is in hospital.'

I went to the bedroom like a sleepwalker, put more things, I didn't know what, in the case, shut the lid and snapped shut the locks. I went into the passage, shut the front door and turned the key. Then I walked down the dim passage, my case bumping against my leg, locked the back door, and went over to the shed to hide the key under the box at the back. I walked around the side of the house and out to the car.

The lady took my case and put it in the boot. She held the back door open for me. I stared in, but didn't move. The car was from an alien world. That empty back seat looked as dangerous as the inside of a flying saucer. If I got in, would I ever come back? For so many years I had planned escapes from Pickering Street. Here was my first real chance and I was terrified. The only things I knew were in Pickering Street. All I had to face the world were my fists and fantasies.

The woman from welfare said, 'Oh, you like to ride in the front seat? I suppose it's all right.' She shut the back door and opened the front. Helpless, confused, mortally afraid, I crept into the car and sat hunched over like Nan was in the ambulance

As soon as the car started, I raised my head to look. How quickly we were out of Pickering Street. Brompton was so small seen through the window of the car. I was in a time machine, watching my childhood whizz by and disappear. The future was as empty as a black night sky.

I turned my eyes to the lady. I could smell her soap, cool and sweet. Her hands on the steering wheel were strong, with sinews showing along her fingers, but there were no bruises or cuts from hard work. She was so relaxed and in control of the car. Would I ever be like her?

She kept glancing at me out of the corner of her eye. We came to the railway line in the parklands. The tall buildings of the city were over to the right. We went up the hill into a suburb full of trees and mansions. I sat up straight. Maybe the lady was taking me to her place, and I would sleep in a bed with starched sheets, and a servant would bring me breakfast in bed on a silver tray, with gleaming lids over the plates of bacon, eggs, and buttery toast. Just like Shirley Temple. I would stay there for a while, then go back to look after Nan.

The lady cleared her throat and said, 'We'll just pop along to Wellington Square. What do you think?'

I stared ahead dumbly. I knew her words were important so I tried to understand. What was Wellington Square? My mind in a jumble, I said in a timid voice, 'Is Nan at that place?'

The lady laughed. 'Good heavens, no. Your Nan is in the Royal Adelaide. She's a bit long in the tooth for a girl's home.'

A bomb exploded in my head. Girl's home. That was for orphans or bad girls. They were getting rid of me. I flung myself against the lady and gripped her around the waist. 'Not a girl's home.' I burst into wild sobs.

'Careful! What are you doing? You'll have us into a tree.' The lady tried to pull my arms off with one hand, but I hugged her with all my strength. She cried out, 'Stop. You're hurting.' I let go a little bit, my head buried against her side, my tears soaking her suit.

While she drove round and round I babbled at her, 'I'll be good. I promise. I'll never run off. I won't swear and hit. Please. Give me one more chance. I'll do anything. But don't make me an orphan.' All the time I hung onto her while she tried to drive with one arm over me.

Then the car slowed down and stopped. We were there. I dug my fingernails into her clothes and pushed my head down into her lap, bawling. But she didn't try to pull me away. She sat still, and with one hand quietly stroked the back of my head. It was such a lovely feeling, my head went all tingly and I stopped yelling.

At last she said in a quiet voice, 'Isn't there anybody in all the world who will have you?'

Not Aunty Jean. Not since I hit her when she told lies to Nan that I was up the alley with boys. Not Aunty Maggie Mulligan. She was not a real aunty, and Nan kept me away from her place since one of her girls got fat and went away on a special holiday for her twelfth birthday. Only my father, who made my flesh crawl. The thought of being with him sent my mind away, out of my body, and I felt like a zombie.

I loosened my arms and looked up at the welfare lady. 'Why can't I go home, and look after myself? My father comes home some nights.'

The lady frowned and chewed her lip. 'It was your father who signed the order to have you taken away.' She gave a great sigh. 'I don't know what the world is coming to.' She took a hanky out of her sleeve and I sat up while she wiped my cheeks. I burst into tears again, not in terror, but at her kind touch. After a while, she reached over and took out the ignition key. 'We'll give it a try. But I'll have a talk to the girls' home matron first.'

And so I stood behind her while she knocked on the door. A stern lady opened the door. Behind her was a big room, its floor so shiny you could see your face in it. While the women talked I imagined huge dormitories full of hard beds where sad girls slept in rows, while a spiteful nurse watched to make sure that nobody talked. Then some words filtered into my mind. 'We're full up.'

And so I was forced to stay with my father, whose only kindness I remembered was to hold me up when I was a little girl and show me the fairy lights flying among the leaves of a palm tree. In a soft voice, full of wonder, he said, 'Fireflies. I saw them in Borneo.'

# *End of childhood*

*When Nan came home I stayed away from school to nurse her. I was* worried about her at first because she didn't have the strength to lift her walking stick to belt me. Then, one morning, I spilt her breakfast cup of tea on the blanket and she managed a good hefty swipe. So life returned to normal at Pickering Street.

One morning I was in the bathroom cleaning my shoes with brown polish. When I stood up from the stool I saw, to my horror, that I must have left the shoe brush on the stool, because there was a stain on it. When I looked on the back of my skirt and knickers the stain was there. It had even soaked through onto my skin. I quickly ran some water in the bath, stripped off and sat in the water, scrubbing away like mad at the stained clothes. Then my eye noticed the blood. Feathers of blood spread out in the water from between my legs. I was bleeding from inside. What was wrong with me? There were stabbing pains in my stomach.

I scrambled out, clutched a flannel between my legs and ran crying up to Nan, where I stood, dripping wet and wild-eyed. 'Nan. All blood's coming out.'

Nan eased herself up on the pillows and scowled at me. 'Get one of the old sheets.'

In a panic, I dragged out a sheet. Nan made me shove it between my legs. Then she grumbled, 'Stop your caterwauling.'

I was doubled up, more in terror than pain. 'What's happening to me?'

Nan looked out the window, and said in a strained, sad voice,

'You're growing up.'

'What do you mean?'

She set her mouth in a hard line and half closed her eyes. 'Stop pestering me, girl. Just for once in your life, stop bothering me about things that are best left alone.' She blushed and turned her back on me.

All the rest of the day I was in a cold fear of dying. The pains got worse and more blood came. I knew that if I kept on bleeding I would surely lose all my blood and die. That night I lay awake, too scared to sleep in case I didn't wake up.

Not until I went back to school and talked to Big Pat did I learn what a period was. As soon as I knew, I felt a great surge of resentment against Nan for keeping me in such stupid ignorance.

For a few months after my first period, I detested all boys, not just because they were stupid and immature, but because they all seemed so physically disgusting. If I looked at their hands, I remembered all those years of the 'uncles' hurting me behind the toilet. No. Boys were not romantic; they were grubs. I spent hours on my bed, no longer dreaming of gypsy princes, but re-reading the tatty Little Golden Books of my childhood. *Sleeping Beauty, Snow White, Tuffy the Tugboat.*

I dug out the old cigar box I had forgotten about and examined my childish treasures of broken glass and dry leaves that crumbled to dust as I touched them, and the hard lumps of lipstick. Oh, and there was the Freddo Frog wrapper from Shirley Kranz's birthday party. I counted back the years. I would have been eight. I smiled as once again I heard the birthday call on radio 5AD. 'Clip, clop, Ghandi is coming . . . There are frogs under the pillows for Shirley Kranz who is eight today, and her friend Patti.' I was in heaven. I had been allowed to go to a real birthday party, and I had heard my name on radio.

My childhood, however, had passed away, with rare moments of innocence or joy to remember in all the long years of imprisonment and drudgery. My thirteenth year was a strange and disturbing time. I was no longer a child, but I lived a weird, hidden life with Nan, which made the world outside a faraway place that I had no power to enter, only observe.

# *Sex*

━━━━━━

*I was rarely at school, and when I was I had to cheat off Big Pat in* spelling and arithmetic. School seemed like an unreal world that got all excited about things I didn't want to know. The Queen was coming to Adelaide, and we had to go to Wayville Show Grounds to practise the hoop dance. The Queen couldn't give a stuff whether the buttons were straight on our white dresses. While Big Pat and I waved our hoops about I said, 'Sure, you wait and see. The Queen will stop and point and say, "There's Patti Bloody Robbins with her buttons lopsided."' Bit by bit I fell so far behind in school that it was a waste of time going and, during my last year, Grade Seven, I was given permanent exemption to look after my Nan.

More and more I hurried through my chores at Number 37, and wandered the streets to escape the dark life of watching, but not belonging to, the world of other people. I hung around the fringes of the Port Road gang. They were a lot older than me, about sixteen or seventeen. My eye was on the tall boy. I remembered him from primary school. From a distance I had watched him putting green almonds on the railway line. His name was Graham.

He was so big, maybe six foot two or three, and solid as a brick wall. He was as ugly as the rear end of a cow but, for all his height, moved with a smooth confidence, almost gracefully. The other members of the gang were all bravado, fighting each other in mock battles, jeering at police cars then running off across the lawns, over the other lane of Port Road, and away up

71

alleys. Graham didn't run, was never challenged by the others, and had a self-confidence that fascinated me.

One day when his gang had done their usual pathetic trick of running from the police, Graham stood and waited while the cops reversed their car and got out to talk to him. I drifted over from my watching place in the rotunda and wandered past. I stopped at the fish shop and pretended to look in at the widow display of white fillets laid out on cold wet steel trays.

A policeman got out of the car, but Graham showed no sign of bolting. The policeman went right up to him, and said, 'I don't know why you waste your time with those no-hopers.' I moved so I could see them reflected in the window. I was amazed. The police weren't arresting him. They were his friends.

'Yeah,' said Graham. His voice was quiet, unafraid.

I could see how he towered over the policeman. The policeman tipped his hat back and scratched the front of his hair. 'They're drongos. Will never amount to anything. But you've got a future. Don't throw it away by mixing in the wrong company. One day, if you put your mind to it, you could be another Polly Farmer, or Lenny Fitzgerald. Win the Magarey medal. Jesus, the way you got that goal from the pocket last Saturday. Magic, pure magic.'

For a while the policeman and Graham talked about tactics, coaches, freak goals, and I realised he was some kind of champion, one of the youngest in the footy league. A star. My heart missed a beat or two. When the policeman turned to leave, I wanted to run, but my feet refused to move. I stood, my back to him, and willed Graham to notice me.

'G'day.'

I turned around and looked at him but was too awed to speak. He tilted his head a bit to the side, and slowly moved his gaze down over my body, stopping to look at my breasts. Then he stared straight into my eyes, sure of himself, grinning, and said, 'I've seen you hanging around.' I sensed what he meant, and blushed, hating myself for showing my feelings, wildly excited because a real celebrity was interested in me, and suddenly afraid, because he knew what he was doing, and I didn't have a clue what I was supposed to do.

'How about coming to a party?'

I had nothing to wear, but I'd worry about that later. Nothing else mattered. This man was asking me out. He must have hundreds of girlfriends, but he had asked me, and I was only thirteen. He was all of seventeen, a footy hero, and the leader of the gang. But he was actually asking Patti, who didn't know how many beans made five.

My body, however, knew precisely what was going on. Trying to be really hip, I flicked my hair out of my eyes, tried to look back into his eyes, but only got as high as his lips, and squeezed out one word. 'Where?'

He reached into his hip pocket and took out a packet of Craven A tobacco. He pushed his fingertips into the packet and tugged out some strands. Then he teased the tobacco apart, cupping it in the palm of his left hand. With two fingers he slowly rolled the leaves into a tube. His fingers were slow, powerful, sure. He slipped a white cigarette paper out of its little box, spread the paper over the tobacco, quickly tipped the lot over and rolled the cigarette. Finally he held the cigarette to his lips, winked at me, and slowly slid his tongue along the edge of the paper. While he reached for a match, he said, as though it was the easiest thing in the world, 'What's wrong with your place?'

My place! Nan? A party with all his grown-up friends? His gang sitting in our lounge. Stupidly I put both hands over my mouth.

Graham smiled, struck a match and cupped his hands from the wind to light the cigarette. He took a deep puff, and blew the smoke out above my head. 'It's simple. Just fix a night when the oldies are out at the pub, or somewhere, and that's it.'

My mind fused. Impossible.

Graham examined the end of his cigarette. His grin had just the hint of a sneer. My blood began to boil. I was not going to lose this chance of my first real boyfriend; and what a boyfriend! I would die before I let Graham laugh at me. My jaw clenched, I managed a smile, and said, 'Leave it to me.' As I spoke I thought, Patti, what are you saying? You idiot.

Graham spat out a shred of tobacco. 'See you round then.'

I walked the streets in a daze, pounding my brain to produce a miracle. Inside my head I saw imagined rows of locked doors. Behind each door was a secret Patti, and one of them would know what to do. The little girl of my childhood did not even show her face. This was nothing to do with fairies, ballerinas, or gypsies.

As I waited at the railway line, the signal bells rang loud and the red lights flashed. At the very moment the train roared past, I saw in my head a young woman who was me, sitting on the bare floor of a room. She stood slowly and turned to face me. She was strong, terrifying, and she gave me a knowing smile. The train was gone, the gate went up for cars, and I set my face for Pickering Street.

It was easy. I told Nan that Big Pat's parents had invited me over for a night, and I was going, whether Nan liked it or not. Perhaps it was the way I said it, meaning that I could walk out any time I liked, and take my green coat with me, or perhaps Nan was sick of being in the house after her operation. Whatever the reason, Nan fell for it hook, line and sinker. I was growing up fast.

'Well, if you're going gallivanting, why should I be stuck at home,' Nan said, defiantly, as though I should feel guilty for neglecting her. 'It's time I had a break. I'll arrange for Jean to pick me up in a car and I'll stay the night at her place.'

And so it was that I opened the door that night for Graham and his mates and their girls. They barged in, laughing and smoking, bottles of beer in their hands, and charged through the house. Straight away, before I even knew their names, they paired off and began to do it, on Nan's bed, on my bed, on the sofa. They ignored me totally. I stood aghast, horrified. Graham laughed, took my wrist and pulled me down on the front room floor, under the table. He was so big he covered me, and he pulled at my clothes, and then there was a tearing pain and he was in me and it hurt so much I cried out, but he didn't stop. When he took it out I looked down. It was as long as a donkey's.

From that night I clung to him. He had done that to me, which meant I belonged to him. I trotted at his heels like his puppy. I was by his side when he and the gang hung round the fish and chip shop. Whenever he wanted me, I took him into the stables behind his house, where the only witnesses were the gentle horses who scraped their hooves in the hot, acrid straw. Sex gave me no pleasure. It was something hurtful he did to me. I whispered, 'I love you, I love you,' but that was only a plea for him to say, 'I love you too, Patti.' But he didn't. I had no idea what love was but thought this must be love, and surrendered desperately to his needs, whichever way he wanted to take me, in those stables that stank of horse urine.

He didn't know, and wouldn't have cared anyway, that I was acting feelings I didn't have. But I cared, because I knew what I was doing to myself. I felt as if I was beside a river and was taking little kittens, one by one, and holding them under the water until they were dead. Sex was pain and duty and shame, but I had to pretend I wanted it like mad, or he would abandon me for any of the other girls who sniffed around for his affections. The more I gave in to his cravings, the nicer I was to him, the more I had to be numb.

The price I paid for growing up, in the dim light and wet smells of the stables, was to be once again an infant, helplessly at somebody else's mercy. My escape into adulthood had made me a slave.

# *Moving out*

'Scarlet bloomin' Pimpernel,' grumbled *Uncle Frosty as we hoisted* my double bed onto his truck. Then he hauled himself up and tipped the bed over on its side to make room for the sofa, kitchen table and chairs, and all the rest of our junk. I stood back, hands on my hips, grinned up at Uncle Frosty, and chanted, 'We seek him here, we seek him there, we seek him every bloody where.'

'Language, language,' said Uncle Frosty, but his voice was jovial. He was as annoyed as Nan and I that on the day we shifted, the one day of hard work, my father was not to be found. After all, it was his rotten idea.

'Since the operation, Nan just can't seem to cope. She's lost her spirit, somehow,' he had said, then put on his religious God-bless-you look that fooled nobody. He didn't give a tinker's for his mother, or anybody else for that matter. Always look after Number One, and let the rest of the world go hang. He had the gall to add, 'Nan needs a proper home, after all her sufferings.' Then, in a false voice, he pronounced, 'Time for a new start for us all.' He shot a sidelong glance at me.

'Time for him to get his dirty hands on the double bed, more like it,' Nan had muttered under her breath. We'd met a few of my father's new starts.

I knew, however, what he really meant. Graham's mum and dad drank at the Gas Works pub, one of my father's watering holes.

I'd miss that old bed. We'd had some good times. I remembered my gymnastics, which drove Nan bananas, and the days I had scarletina, when I gripped the iron side of the bed to stop floating away in my fever. I had cried for my mother. Where was she? If I died, would she know?

When Number 37 was empty, I went for a last walk through it, like a ghost haunting my own past. It was eerie seeing the shiny patch in the lino where furniture had been. In the lounge-room floor were the dents made by the sofa where my father tried to kill me. As I walked down the passage to the kitchen, I remembered the voices I once listened to from my bed at night. Now that I was fifteen, how far away those nights seemed. There was the kitchen window where I stood on a chair to do the dishes in the galvanised-iron dish. Bloody dishes; thousands of them; stretching from here to Oodnawoopwoop.

Outside, I looked at the shed where the rats ran along the rails and scared the wits out of the little girl. Funny, I felt like crying, even over the silly old rats and the stupid copper where I slaved away on wash days. To lose 37 Pickering Street was to lose all I knew, all I was.

I knelt by Scruffles's grave and ran my hand along the little mound. 'Well, this is it, Scruffles.' I knew I'd not come back. Ever since I heard we were moving, I had the same nightmare each night. I was walking down Pickering Street on a dark evening, all alone, the street deserted, quiet, threatening, and I knew what I'd find inside Number 37, but I had to go in. The terror grew as I got closer to the door, which swung open. I'd go into the dark passage of the empty house, turn left and there, not on a bed, but on the floor, was Nan, dead, stretched out, gone forever, cold, horrible, her lips slightly parted, eyes not quite shut, showing glints of the whites.

For the last time, I filled Scruffles's drinking dish from the tap, and put it beside his grave. 'Now don't you get up to mischief while I'm gone,' I told him in my severe voice that he always ignored. Well, maybe it was good that one of us in this place wasn't broken by silly rules. I stood and built up the courage to walk away. It's so hard to turn away for the last time.

The truck horn beeped. No good hanging around here with my bloody head in the sand and my arse in the air. I left the yard and climbed up into the front seat, squeezing in beside Nan. There was nobody to wave us goodbye. Neighbours had said, 'Keep in touch. Drop in if you're going past. See you next St Patrick's Day.' Bullshit, I thought. I hate false promises. If anybody who's been nasty to me turns up at my funeral with white flowers, I'll rise from the grave and shove the flowers up their arse. I realised too late that I had planned to touch the smooth patch worn by my hands on the front verandah post.

Uncle Frosty ground the gear stick into place, and we began to move. He looked at Nan quickly and said, in a quiet voice, 'Reckon you'll miss the old place?'

I looked at Nan. She seemed so old and frail despite her huge body. She stared ahead rigidly through the windscreen and snarled, 'Only the fights.' I wondered what had happened to her. Why was she so run down? Why didn't she get up and fight? She had all that courage, but had stopped fighting. Life for her was to sit around dying bit by bit. I knew that after I took off, she'd sit on her own. I felt a pang of guilt for her future. She would call my leaving a betrayal.

To rid myself of sad thoughts, I looked back along Pickering Street as we turned the corner. I couldn't stop the prickling of excitement. For years I had dreamed of escaping. Now I was on the way. Something was out there waiting for me.

Our new house, in Londonderry Crescent, Mansfield Park, was a temporary wooden place that stood on bricks. It had two bedrooms, one at each end, with a living area in between. The back yard was full of weeds. The street was mud and slush.

I thought the house was all right, correctly called a temporary home, because I would stay only until I arranged an escape. I felt like a prisoner of war. In Pickering Street I knew every pothole in the road, every bump in the footpath. I could have walked blindfolded down to the pub. At Londonderry Crescent, not knowing what else to do with my time, I borrowed a spade and turned over the entire back yard. I dug the spade methodically in the soil, loosened the roots of the weeds, pulled them out and turned the soil upside down. If the place looked like a prison yard to start with, all the better. I would make it pretty before I left.

I took to walking in the rain down to the shops on Hanson Road. It was a beautiful feeling to get soaked to the skin, my shoes caked with goo and my head racing with plans of my glorious future.

Londonderry Crescent was not a family as Pickering Street had been, with fights and everybody being sticky beaks, and the adults hopping in and out of each other's beds, so it was hard to know who paid the rent. In Pickering Street the kids and dogs grew up together. There was a sense that we all went back forever. My new street was cold and felt deserted. Nobody knew anybody. Neighbours were wary of getting too close.

The people on one side were Dutch migrants and so Nan tried to stop me having anything to do with them. Their nephew, Walter, fell madly in love with me. He had a big body, soft eyes, and spent all his spare money on gifts of chocolates and flowers for me. After the brutality of Graham, it was a strange, nice feeling to be really courted. It was doomed, however, to be unrequited love for poor old Walter. He was too tidy. His brain was as organised as his back yard, with the cabbages in neat rows, planted in beds that were exact rectangles, with dead straight edges.

Walter invited me in for afternoon tea. Despite all the huffing and puffing from Nan, probably because of it, I went in. Their living-room was astonishing. There were tapestries of hunting scenes and paintings of serious old fogies inside Dutch houses; a piano with brightly polished wood; a glass cabinet with huge mugs that had curly handles and knobbly faces; a row of clogs on the mantelpiece; shelves of books with red binding. I was in shock. We had no paintings, no books, just bare walls. Walter's aunty served special coffee imported from Africa, and a plate of butter biscuits that she had made. I was terrified by these people. They were so nice, so good mannered. They held their cups and saucers properly, and sipped their coffee without slurping. They didn't burp. Walter sat on the edge of his seat, anxious to impress me. But I saw the way he kept glancing at his aunty for approval. He could say or do nothing without her tacit permission. My heart sank. He was no good for me. At nineteen, he was behaving like a nervous six-year-old. Walter could never be my escape. I sighed. It was a shame. I could take lots of this special attention and New Australian food. Walter was good for me, however, in one way. He opened my eyes to another way of living.

On the other side of our house was a Scottish family with nine kids, including three daughters. The mother was a frump, worn out by life and kids. Her only way to handle so many children was like Nan's. Shout and belt them. The father, James, was a little cock sparrow. From out of the shambles of his home he emerged each afternoon, spick and span in a black suit, a pair of glossy black shoes tucked under his arm, as he stepped through the mud towards the bus stop.

His kids were my type – rowdy, uncontrollable, full of fun. One morning a girl popped her head over the fence while I was digging the last quarter of the yard. 'Hey. Psst.' She looked back over her shoulder and waved madly at me to come over to her. I stepped through the clods and went to the fence. She grinned at me. 'Hey. There's a gang I know. Do you want to come with me?'

I raced inside, shut myself in the bathroom, tore off my clothes and jumped under the shower. A bodgie gang. Visions of lots of Marlon Brandos, gleaming motorbikes, gang wars, chains, tough guys all, and me the leader's girl in a tight black dress and peroxide blonde hair (which I'd done a few months before and scandalised Nan). All the other girls of the gang would eye off my man. Eat your hearts out, girls, he's all mine.

I stood in front of the mirror dressed in my plain skirt, a white shirt, a cardigan, and a pair of hand-me-down high heels. I wanted to be a widgie, whatever that was, with a tight jumper.

Nan watched me suspiciously from her bed. 'What are you up to now?' From the wardrobe I took out my box of treasures. I picked out the green earrings I'd bought Nan years ago, and which she never wore. While I put them on I said casually, 'Just going for a walk with the girl next door. Heather.' Then I ran. 'See you, Nan,' as I slammed the front door.

Heather and I swaggered down Londonderry Crescent. She was a raver. 'And there's this real cool guy, he's so cute, and I just go crazy when he says, "Get on, baby," and I climb up on his BSA, and we roar off, and I grab him real tight and we all go up Torrens Road, the wind tearing at us, and old wrinklies in cars scared shitless when we pull up beside them at red lights and stare right at them and chew gum and act so tough they're too scared to look at us, but pretend we're not there and look up at the red light, praying for it to go green. Zap into Sigalases and have a Long John with a Cherry Coke . . .' Maybe Heather never got a word in at home, with eight brothers and sisters.

We turned a corner and ahead, in Coker Street, was a row of motorbikes parked near a telephone box, outside the fish and chip shop. The gang hung around on the footpath. They weren't all in black. The nearer we got, the faster my heart beat. I pushed out my chest, put my chin up. What was I worried about? I'd been belting up boys since I was a kid. My eyes picked out a tall lad. He was the most handsome, with curly brown hair, and he stood straight while the others slouched around, some leaning against the shop or the telephone box. The tall one wore a brown bomber jacket with wool lining showing where it hung open. He had brown jeans and on his feet were motorbike boots.

Then I was among them. They opened a path and closed around us like they were a school of hungry fish, and I was the sprat. 'G'day, Heather. Who've you got here?' Heather grabbed the hand of a chunky guy with bow legs. 'Hi, guys, meet Patti.' Eyes began to undress me. I pulled myself up to my full height of five feet nothing and stared down anyone who happened to look as high as my eyes. The creaking leather of their clothes, the growls and little wolf-whistles, the bravado of cigarettes, narrow eyes, curled lips, held no terrors for me. They were just kids, only a couple of years older than me, about seventeen. They didn't hold killer chains, they weren't animal degenerates with slobbery mouths and long hair, there were no knuckle dusters on their hands, although I saw the edges of a few tattoos on their wrists. The most lethal thing they held were bottles of Coke. The Beagle Boys were kids dressed up, ordinary kids, with Elvis hair cuts and the pimply skin of brats from Trust houses. They didn't crawl home to some drug addict's den and have satanic orgies. They went home to Mum, and got told off for not doing the dishes. My brothers.

I relaxed, grinned and, to establish my authority, concentrated on the tall lad, who I instinctively knew was the gang leader. There was something about his face. Then it struck me. He was Jeff, the rotten little mongrel from Grade Four. One of the few boys I didn't bash the shit out of because he wasn't worth giving the time of the day.

Jeff gave me a crooked grin. 'Howdy, Patti. Long time no see.' I went over, stood really close and gave him the full Mae West treatment. Jeff leant back, almost took a step backwards.

'Hey, Patti,' said a voice behind me. I turned around. It was the lad holding Heather's hand. 'You want to join us, you've got to be initiated.' I felt a twinge of fear, but I could see Heather trying to stifle a giggle.

I fronted him. 'Okay, I'm ready.' From all around came hoots and cheers of approval.

'All right. First you've got to get into the telephone box.'

I shrugged. Big deal. I went to the box, pushed the door, and stepped inside. Crash. A skeleton head fell on me. I squealed and jumped up and down, the sheep's head rattling around my feet, its horns banging my shins and laddering my only pair of stockings. The gang fell about. They laughed, bent double, pointed at me, and shouted really smart things like, 'Whooee, Come in Spinner. Did yer see her face? Bewdy.' Jeff had a silly grin on his face.

I stomped out and glared around. Heather stepped over and touched my wrist. 'They did it to me too. Don't let it worry you.' Then she snorted and burst into laughter. 'You should've seen your face.' My temperature began to go down.

Jeff said, 'Let's go.' The gang forgot me and went to their motorbikes. I stood around, uncertain, while they got on their bikes, rocked them off their stands, and turned on ignition keys. Boots stamped down on the kick starts and bikes roared into life. Heather swung herself up behind her boy, and sat there, cool, happy, tying her hair in a scarf. Jeff was on the best bike, a gleaming silver Triumph. He zipped up his jacket. Then he glanced back over his shoulder to the empty seat behind him.

I stepped over, but wasn't sure how to get on. What did I do with my long floral dress? Jeff reached back and pointed to a little footrest. The bike was so high. I had to grab his shoulders and pull myself up to get a leg over the seat, which was hard and cold on the backs of my legs. I grabbed my skirt and bunched it under and between my thighs. I was scared by the powerful vibration of the bike. What if I fell off? I sat with my hands down stiffly by my side. The bikes rolled forward, their noise almost deafening. At the first movement I wobbled on the seat. I looked over at Heather, who mimed putting arms around Jeff, and nodded at me to do it. She slid her arms all the way around and snuggled close to her bloke.

Jeff nudged the bike to the front of the gang. He shouted back at me, 'Hang on,' and took off. I whipped backwards, my fingers grabbing for his jacket. I dragged myself upright and forgot my pride. I slid forward and clung on like a baby koala bear. The bike roared, the ground flew past, and I was terrified and exhilarated by the speed and power. Then my dress began to flap up around my bum and stream out behind me in the wind. Jeff glanced back and got a flash of thighs and suspenders. I wasn't game to let go and waited for Jeff to reach the Hanson Road corner, where he stopped to let a truck go past. I grabbed my skirt and stuffed it tightly around my legs. Jeff turned around and I saw the look in his eye.

Then the lights changed. I panicked as the bike tipped, charged away, and I leant far over the opposite side to balance it. The bike skidded on some gravel and Jeff yelled back, as he wrestled the steering, 'Sit up! Sit up!' I obeyed and wriggled close to his back and held him tightly around the waist. 'That's right,' he called back at me. 'You stick dead level with me. Don't lean out.' I was sure I had to lean against the turn or we'd fall, but at the next corner I kept exactly with him, like one body, and to my surprise the bike didn't crash over, but glided around like a bird.

We reached Port Road and were heading for the beach. Now that it was a long straight road, I peeked over Jeff's shoulder at the world hurtling towards us and then rushing past. The rough bitumen flowed like a river. It gave me a fantastic sense of power. The wind made my eyes water and blew teardrops around to my ears, but I didn't care. I was Patti, roaring away to the sea, my back to Brompton, my arms around a bikie, my heart beating wildly with the rapture of speed, my breast hard against the body of my new man.

The next months were a rage of wild fun, total happiness. I rocked around the clock at the Semaphore Palais and danced like a dervish at the Palais Royal in North Terrace. I screamed myself delirious at Elvis films, jumping up on the seats while the ushers flashed torches at us and hissed vainly at us to sit down. I gave my body to Jeff, not caring that it meant nothing to me. All the years of imprisonment screamed out of me.

# *Two brides*

*On the few nights I was home, I sat with Nan, both of us sharing a* painful sense of guilt, loss and anger. At this time, my father continued to drag a succession of old bags home to my double bed. There was Marjorie, whose dentures slipped when she gave a desperate sloppy grin. Marjorie was perfectly prim. When she sat down, she compulsively tugged the edge of her skirt over her dimpled knees, and at the same time gave a little sideways nod of her head as though to say, See what a good girl I am. Marjorie sat crowded against the kero heater, her shins mottled with thousands of pink veins, and talked manically about the only subject she really understood: the weather. At the end of every infuriating sentence about how dry the summer had been, or about the wind going around, she added, 'What do you think?' Her head bobbed like a chook pecking wheat. It was more agony waiting for the 'What do you think?' than it was listening to her dreary nonsense.

I watched this charade, thinking, There but for the grace of God . . . Poor Marjorie must've been just like me, once upon a time. No glamour, no education, no money, no power, nowhere to run. All she had left were compulsive nervous habits to keep the pain away. I shuddered at what life does to people, washing them up like soggy bits of wood tangled in seaweed.

One night, to my utter astonishment, my father brought home a magnificent looker: or should I say 'lady'. She was far too grand for my haggard, alcoholic, violent father. Jessica swept into our house like Jean Harlow. She spoke in a strangled sort of way, as though the words had to come from the back of her throat, like some of the Pommy voices on the ABC. She delivered words like, 'so civilised', and 'absolutely', in a voice that said, See what an education I had at a school for rich girls, and don't you think it was an absolute waste of good money? I liked her. With all her posh words and accent, she wasn't taking the piss out of us working-class people, she was just being herself – a bit of a ratbag – and I identified with that. Jessica laughed, was bright, told fabulous jokes, went to the theatre, and knew all the wrong sorts of people. Even Nan warmed to her. What could Jessica see in my father?

Jessie, as she insisted on being called, because it got right up her Pater's nose, liked her glass of brandy almost as much as my father loved his beer. 'Well, just a sip,' she said while my father poured her another. 'Yes, thank you, John, that will be fine, just half a glass will do nicely, whoops, not too much now, you'll have me on my ear, and I simply mustn't get tiddlers, or I'm liable to do anything, you Casanova you.'

And so they drank on, until the brandy was almost gone, and beer bottles littered the sink. Nan and I had shandies, keeping the lemonade bottle on the table so that my father wouldn't try to force too much grog into us. By half-past ten, bed time, I doubt that Casanova could have had his evil way with Jessie. The scars on his forehead stood out angrily, he slurred his words, and he had to concentrate very hard to pour the brandy into her glass. He slopped some in her lap, then got out his old handkerchief to wipe it away. Jessie was distressed at the stain, and while my father grovelled clumsily, she tugged her hair with both hands, and cast her pained eyes on me.

'Gather ye,' she said, and burst into giggles. Then she roughly pushed my father's hands away from her lap. 'That'll do, John. Don't demean yourself.' I saw the angry spot on his cheek as she waved him away. Jessica swallowed and went on, 'rosebuds, while ye may. This same flower that smiles today, tomorrow will be dying.' Jessica gave a crooked smile and glanced at the bedroom door.

My father stood, legs apart, arms folded over his chest, and said, 'Well, time to hit the hay.' His smile was wide, but his voice was tight with anger. Once something triggered him, he would work himself into a fury until he was ready to hit anything, or anybody. His face was so aggressive that an ugly feeling spread through the room.

Jessie's knees locked tighter and tighter together, and she said, 'Tomorrow and tomorrow and tomorrow, creeps in this petty . . . dum de dah . . . last syllable. Tale told by an idiot, full of sound and fury, signifying nothing.' She gave a burp, and rolled her eyes at my father. 'Beg your pardon, Mrs Vardon, there's a chicken in your garden.'

A hand slapped her face. My father stood over her, quivering with rage. 'Who're you calling and idiot?'

Jessie put her hand to her cheek where already a bluish bruise showed. She gave a high, frightened laugh. Then she took a deep breath and added, as though talking to a servant, 'Calm yourself, my man.'

I started to move, but was too slow. He belted Jessie in the ear with a closed fist. Jessie teetered over, slowly regained her balance, like a ship in a typhoon, and stared about in a panic.

Enough of this, I thought. I'd been hit so often by him, I knew the terror Jessie felt. I got up, grabbed Jessie and pulled her aside, forcing myself between her and my father. He pushed his face right close to mine, his stinking breath on me. I snarled, 'Don't even think about it.' He stood, wavering, breathing hard, his eyes blank with rage. Quick as a flash his fist shot past my shoulder and hit Jessie.

She screamed and ran over to the sink, where she fell back, and slumped to the floor. My father brushed me aside and began kicking Jessie in the side, time and again. Out of the corner of my eye I saw Nan appear in the bedroom door, her dress flapping, her walking stick half raised, her face white with fear.

'Stop it, stop it!' she yelled. My father turned around to look at her and then very carefully, with a dreadful smirk, trod on Jessie's stomach.

There was a blur of movement, a dreadful smash, and my father fell, head bleeding. I stood, wild-eyed, holding a lemonade bottle.

I didn't hit him hard enough. Slowly he rolled over onto his stomach and got to all fours like a dog. He reached out to the table, got a grip on a leg and began to pull himself up.

'Run, Jessie, run!' I shouted, dropped the lemonade bottle and tried to lift her up. She was paralysed, staring stupidly at the bottle on the floor. Then, with a great roar, my father hurled himself at Jessie and grabbed her by the throat, digging his thumbs into her Adam's apple. Jessie was in agony, her eyes bulging. I dragged at his wrists. Nan was there, hitting him on the head with her stick, great blows meant to knock him out. The air was filled with screams and shouts. Jessie was going purple in the face, her tongue coming out. Then Nan stepped back, shifted her grip on the stick and brought it crashing down on my father's head. He buckled, and slumped, his hands clawing at Jessie's dress.

Jessie, gurgling in her throat, tore herself free and stumbled to the bathroom. Nan and I stood panting, and looked at each other across the groaning body of my father, her son. Then Jessie was back in the room. I saw a glint of silver. I drew in my breath, but there was no time to shout. Jessie slashed her left wrist with my father's razor, then swapped hands and slashed the other. Her mouth wide open, she gazed madly at me, blinked, and slowly raised her hands in benediction, two great fountains of blood spurting into the air.

After the ambulance had taken Jessie away I walked the streets, crying for Jessie, for Nan, for myself.

It was in April that I was bridesmaid for my childhood friend, Veronica, whose green shoes I still kept under my bed. Veronica was lovely in her bridal gown, and I walked behind, holding her train. I wore a little half-moon hat of fabric flowers and a coffee-coloured frock as I, who should have been delirious with fantasies and excitement, walked down the aisle with a dead heart.

I stood near the altar of Sacred Heart Church, where I had gone to Mass as a child at the Catholic school. I could not be happy for Veronica. I looked at the groom and tried to work out what he would be like in ten years' time, in twenty. A silly song, 'I'm always chasing rainbows', came into my mind, and

I couldn't stop the words going round and round in my head. But I had no rainbows left to chase. When the priest raised his hands to bless the couple, I saw the streams of Jessie's blood.

The reception was in the Hindmarsh Town Hall. I sat at the top table. I stared down at the food: sausage rolls, little pies and pasties, sandwiches of egg and lettuce, tiny packets of sugar-coated almonds, maids-of-honour cakes, bottles of beer and jugs of orange cordial. I sighed, and looked out over the room. Nan was out there, sitting with Aunty Jean and my father.

Nan caught my eye and put fingers on each side of her mouth, pushing the corners up, frowning at me to smile and look cheerful. I gave her a weak smile and reached for a cold, flaky sausage roll. As I picked it up, I suddenly and unexpectedly knew what I must do with my life if I was to have any hope left. It was weird to feel my life change forever, just in the time it took to move my hand for a sausage roll.

As soon as the last speech was over, when the formal reception was finished, I gave Veronica a quick kiss on the cheek, excused myself for a moment, and walked out, away from the little pile of yellow telegrams, my bouquet of frangipani and orchids lying among the paper plates smeared with tomato sauce, away from the florid, boozy, happy faces. Veronica was clinging to the arm of her new husband, the hall was full of sound and laughter, the trestle heaped with wedding presents where Veronica's mum bent over the little labels to make sure they would know who to send thank you cards. Somewhere in the heap would be the crystal butter dish Nan and I had wrapped in white wedding paper with sweet pictures of a bride and groom.

I walked to Coker Street carrying my court shoes, which gave me blisters on the heels. Jeff was outside the fish and chip shop with a couple of his mates. I stood and looked at him. Then I gave a command. 'I'm coming to live with you.' He thought for a moment, shrugged, and said, 'Okay.'

Jeff's mum, Shirley, who lived opposite the Coker Street shops, gave me a tight black skirt, silk knickers, black flats, and a bright pink bunny wool jumper with puffy short sleeves. Shirley was the most glamorous woman I'd ever seen, and I took her as my mother. One day I would make my fortune and own one hundred and fifty pairs of shoes and five wardrobes of beautiful new clothes, and Shirley would borrow dresses she could never afford.

I told Nan I would not return to live with her. She fell into a rage. There were no words of, 'Please stay', or 'Good luck', no words of love or a hug to remember the St Patrick's Day drinks. Just blind fury.

Jeff and I were married in Sacred Heart Church. Jeff's mate, from the Beagle Boys, was best man. Nan refused to attend. I was only fifteen, but Jeff and I pretended I was pregnant so the adults would have to give us permission to marry.

On the wedding day, it rained cats and dogs. Squalls scattered blossoms from the almond trees. My dress, on tic from a store, got splashed. My shoes looked silly where I had painted them white to make them look half decent. There was no money for a hairdresser, so I just ran a comb through my curls before plonking on the veil. My father was drunk, late, arrived by taxi, and in his anxiety to get the deed over, trod on my veil as he hurried me down the aisle.

The rain continued to fall as Jeff and I came out onto the church steps for photos. I saw a black figure sitting on the bench at the bus stop. The distant face was turned towards me, an indistinct blur. I caught my breath and tears flowed not, as everybody thought, for happiness, but for sorrow, longing, guilt and the dreadful ache of walking away from the silly old woman who wouldn't see me married because, 'You've done it by breaking every rule I stand for.'

Nan refused to come to the reception at Uncle Frosty's house. When it was over, Jeff and I got into a big black limousine provided by Jeff's uncle, who half-owned Black and White Taxis. It was the kind of car I decided to buy one day, when I was rich. Jeff's uncle also slipped us a ten pound note as a going away present. He drove us to Coker Street and let us out at the fish and chip shop. Jeff and I stood around for a while, then bought ten shillings' worth of chips and a big bottle of Coke and went over to his place.

*Married Life*

# Outback cook

*One morning, two weeks after we were married, Jeff and I were in the* kitchen doing our usual thing. He took his motorbike to bits and I watched. He stripped the motor down into tiny parts, each of which he held up to examine minutely, frowning with concentration. He polished pistons with a rag until they gleamed. He tinkered with bits in the carburettor, turning a screw a hair's breadth this way or that. Jeff looked cute. His brown hair was thick and curly, his cheeks were smooth and his fingers were grubby. He was like a little boy playing at being a big man. He was seventeen years old. I sat with my hand on my tummy, which had its pre-period swelling and hurt. I toyed with the idea that it was the beginning of morning sickness. I was fifteen, and longed for a baby. I wore my dress tight to show off the little bulge, and when I stood, I arched my back just a bit to push my tummy forward. A baby was all my heart yearned for. It was a mystery to think of a tiny life growing inside me, quietly nestled deep inside, a part of me which nobody could take away. My childhood fantasies of dancer and gypsy had disappeared to a back room in my mind.

Jeff wiped his oily hands on a cloth. 'You ever cooked for a big mob?'

Did he mean a party for the gang? I panicked. All I had ever done was potatoes, some vegies and meat for Nan, and sometimes a few visitors. I'd never done fancy cooking like pies and pasties. Nan had never taught me. But what the hell, all you had to do was follow a recipe. 'Yeah. I can cook.'

Jeff picked up a spark plug and peered closely as he pushed a strip of metal into the gap. 'There's a job going on a station.'

My heart flipped with joy. A farm. Miles and miles away from here. Away from Jeff's mum who tarted me up for her Friday night men. Far away from the narrow streets, from life going nowhere, far from my childhood, my prison; so far away I couldn't even smell the gas works, or have to visit my father. A long, long way from the houses that reminded me of the 'uncles'.

'They need a rouseabout and a cook,' he said. 'What do you reckon?'

What did I reckon? I squealed and flung my arms around his neck and kissed the top of his head again and again.

Jeff eventually pushed me off, and grinned. 'I guess that means you agree.'

I imagined myself as Maureen O'Hara, in a riding outfit, astride a fine horse on a wind-swept hill, my hair blowing in the wind. My hair was peroxide blonde, not O'Hara carrot red. At the bottom of the hill a man urged his horse up out of the river. He looked up at me. I knew my fantasy was goofy, but I indulged it.

Next day I dressed for the interview. I wore my blue jump suit, long brown boots, and tied my hair in a green scarf. Jeff looked scrumptious in his brown leather jacket with the fur collar, his tight slacks and bike boots. I tied a scarf around his throat and tucked it inside his fur collar. He grimaced a bit at my fussing, but let me have my way. We drove to the interview at Grange, where the station owners were on holiday in a spooky old mansion near the beach.

Mr Mepstead met us in the lobby and took us to their flat, into a gloomy old lounge-room, where Mrs Mepstead sat bolt upright, her spine so straight it didn't touch the back of the hard sofa. I sat beside her and we listened while the men talked about sheep, horses, bore pumps, fences and army jeeps. It was all right for Jeff. He had been a rouseabout. I had never done anything, and I felt so young and ignorant. To make myself look more mature, I made sure my left hand rested on top of my right to show off the wedding ring.

Then it was my turn. Mrs Mepstead, who looked like an army

sergeant, asked me where I had cooked. She gave me a severe smile, and I felt a bit rotten when I told her I had cooked for years for a big family. I began to feel worse when she nodded in approval. She had ten in her family. With a rush of fear I realised she believed me and that this was for real. They hired us.

Just before we were due to leave, I got sick. Not with a baby, because my period had started. For years I had pains in my side every time I had a period. This time it was so bad the doctor put me in hospital. 'You've got a grumbly appendix. We'd better keep an eye on you.'

Hospital scared me. Sickness made me powerless, which was worse than the pain. Jeff was angry because we were supposed to go straight to the station. I was angry and afraid at hospital, so he came to get me. He chucked some things in a suitcase, brought me a black miniskirt to wear on the bike, and we walked out of the hospital.

As he kick-started the bike I had a pang of guilt and fear. I must explain to Nan. I heard her voice in my head. 'How dare you go traipsing off without my say-so. And what am I supposed to do, here all on my own? You don't ever think, Patti, except about yourself.' It was a shock to realise I didn't have to explain to Nan. I was a married woman now. But her voice was so much a part of my mind I wondered whether I would ever live without her.

Jeff turned the bike to the north and we drove off. I sat, legs apart, a gale blowing up you-know-where. I wished Jeff had brought me a pair of knickers. The suitcase with all our things was balanced across my knees. For a while I was thrilled. This was my big escape. I watched familiar streets and buildings rush past: Port Road, the rotunda and playground, the roof of Barry's Bakery, then onto Main North Road and out to the Gepps Cross Corner, where the city ended and the country began.

To our right, the Adelaide Hills sank into the plains, and I saw distant lines of gum trees marking creek beds. The road signs were for me now, not just the lucky travellers off on a holiday. Crystal Brook 123 miles. Port Augusta 202 miles.

The sky was bright cold crystal. Young green wheat poked up in the paddocks. This was a morning ride from which I would never return to the drudgery of my old life. I felt a great weight lift off my shoulders.

Away across to the left, on the edge of St Vincent's Gulf, was the dark smudge of mangrove trees at St Kilda Beach. I looked across the plains to the coast and thought of the time I had gone crabbing there as a kid. I remembered my father wading out into the shallows between the mangrove swamps. A rope around his waist pulled along a baby's bath. He carried a home-made spear of a broom handle and sharp prongs of wire. On the beach, Nan and I collected driftwood and lit a fire. We filled a kerosene tin with water and set it to boil. Nan buried four bottles of beer in damp sand, their tops poking up so she couldn't lose them.

My father returned, dragging the baby's bath across the sand. 'Have a squizz,' he said proudly. 'Beautiful blueys.' I peeped into the bath and recoiled as though from an electric shock. The bottom of the bath crawled with huge spider things, eyes out on stalks, their hairy mouths blowing froth, huge nippers waving up to grab me. I backed away, tripped and fell on the sand. Nan and my father laughed. He reached into the bath, lifted out a huge crab and held it dangling by a soft flappy back leg. My father looked at me and I knew what he was thinking. I squealed and jumped to my feet, ready to run. He grinned and made one step towards me. The crab snapped its big spiky claws.

'No, no,' I cried.

Nan grumbled, 'Oh leave the sookie-baby alone.'

My father shrugged and dropped the crab in boiling water. The crab scrabbled against the sides of the tin. What a horrible death to be boiled alive. I put my hands over my ear. The crab took ages to die. I ran way over near the mangroves so I couldn't hear as the rest of the crabs were flung into the hissing water. When they were all done, my father tipped out a tangle of red corpses.

I refused to eat any of the crabs. Once they were cool, my father and Nan set a tablecloth of newspaper, and tucked in. They cracked the legs to pull out long cords of white meat. They dipped the flesh in a bowl of vinegar and sprinkled it with lots of pepper. They munched on white bread and butter, and swigged beer from bottles. Soon their hands were messy with flecks of crab meat. Their lips were glazed with vinegar and juice from the meat.

I nibbled at a piece of bread and butter, then lost all my appetite when Nan broke open a crab's belly, picked out strings of stuff, and to my horror and disgust, sucked out the yellow poo.

Now, on the back of the motorbike, I turned my face from the places of my childhood. The wind blew cold so I hunched as best I could behind Jeff. I concentrated on holding the suitcase with one hand and with the other hand clung to the bar behind me. I wished there was no suitcase so I could snuggle close to Jeff. I loved him just for taking me away.

By the time we reached Burra, a mining town about a hundred miles north of Adelaide, I was as sick as a dog. We pulled up at a deli and Jeff went in to buy a pie and a pasty. I dumped the suitcase on the footpath and sat down on it, too bushed to bother to open it and see what Jeff had packed. My back was against a round verandah post, my feet on the edge of the gutter, and my spirits were rapidly disappearing down the drain. When Jeff handed me the pie, I held it up to bite, but the vinegary smell of the runny tomato sauce put me off. So much for the grand adventure. I was ready to curl up and die.

We left Burra and went on, past Hallet, then Terowie, where some American general had stood on the railway platform and said, 'I shall return.' Then Peterborough and the long road north. The land became more desolate. By now, Adelaide was far beyond the southern horizon. The tall gum trees had gone, and beside the road were small, twisted, scrubby trees, with strips of bark hanging off as though they were shedding their skin. Out in the paddocks, scattered flocks of sheep, their wool a muddy brown, nosed among boulders and slabs of rock.

My side hurt more and more with all the jolting. I bent over the case, trying to ease the pain by shifting position. I daren't fall asleep but had to brace myself for every twist and turn along the road that stretched on for ever.

We turned off and headed into a dreary land. I gritted my teeth as I saw the long dirt track. We shuddered over corrugations and banged through potholes. Just as well I wasn't pregnant. The horizon widened out flatter and further away, where the world became a desert of saltbush and bluebush. I was vaguely aware of the afternoon sun low in the sky behind us.

We slowed to hammer over a grid of rusted railway rails. Then there were rows of pine trees each side of us. Ahead were two houses side by side. The roar of the bike stopped. My ears hummed and the sounds around me were muffled. Over by a shed, two brown dogs leapt up at the ends of their chains and barked like mad. They twisted around in mid-air as they tried to break loose. Their barking sounded miles away to me. From the front verandah of one house a black dog, part collie, ran towards me, slithered to a stop a few feet away, and then wriggled closer on his belly, grovelling for approval. I leant down to pat him and he jumped at my face to lick it but smashed his hard, wet mouth against my lips. I wiped my lips on the sleeve of my jumper, but the dog kept bounding up to my waist His sharp toenails scratched my legs and put red dirt all over my dress. I stepped back in fright.

'Gerrout, you mongrel,' Jeff snarled. The dog stopped, looked at him, then scooted back to the verandah where a woman stood shading her eyes against the low sun.

Mrs Mepstead waved and stepped out to greet us. Quickly I straightened my mini-skirt and combed my fingers through my hair. I must've looked like death.

'You must be worn to a frazzle. Come inside.' Her words were friendly, but her voice was military. All I wanted to do was go back to Adelaide. Mrs Mepstead took us into a big kitchen. The wood stove was as long as my bed. The heavy wooden table, its top scratched and grooved from years of use, had six chairs around it. I thought of the china fruit in Mrs Barry's living-room. The radio on top of the kitchen cabinet played 'Just A-Cryin' in the Rain'. Station 5KA. Right now Nan, who always listened to 5KA, would be on her bed, looking out the window, listening to this same song. I wondered if she'd folded my bed up and put it away, or if it was still there with its rough grey blanket.

We sat at the table and I almost put my elbows on it to rest my chin, but I heard Nan's voice: 'Elbows off.'

Mrs Mepstead waved at the kettle boiling on the stove. 'Make yourselves some tea.' She put a tin of biscuits on the table. 'Help yourself. But get into the habit of keeping count of what you use.' I looked around at the kitchen that must tomorrow be my workplace.

'I'm Mrs Jim Mepstead, as you know. Next door are the Robert Mepsteads. You'll live in the quarters out the back.' Mrs Mepstead opened a Kelvinator fridge, stacked with vegetables and food to feed an army. It was more than I'd eaten in a year at home. Mrs Mepstead took out a jug of milk with a lace doily over the top, weighed down with glass beads all around the edge of the lace. 'There you are.' She looked at Jeff. 'We kill twice a week.'

Mrs Mepstead sat with us and held out the tin of Scotch Fingers, holding it in mid air until we had taken one. 'Just what the doctor ordered,' I said, trying to make conversation. Mrs Mepstead smiled at me. 'That's my girl,' she said. When I had broken my biscuit in half, I waited to see if she dunked hers in her tea. Mercifully she did, and so I followed suit.

Then Mrs Mepstead took a sip, put down her cup, rested her elbows on the table and cupped her chin in her hands. 'Now, Mrs Cooper, or may I call you Pat? Thank you dear. Well, Pat, this is where you'll be doing the cooking. It's the usual routine. Breakfast cooked by 7.30; cakes for morning tea; lunch by 12.30; cakes or scones for afternoon tea; and then dinner – a three-course meal – ready by 6.30. For ten of us.'

I gaped at her, my cup half way to my mouth.

'Good,' she went on. 'If that's all right. There are a few other odds and ends. Have the meals ready on heated plates three minutes before time and carry them on those trays into the dining-room.' She paused and, for a moment looked slightly embarrassed. 'Of course, you and your husband are welcome to eat in the kitchen.'

Like negro slaves, I thought, but kept the polite smile going, as though I had done these things for years and all that cooking was as easy as falling off a log. I tried to catch Jeff's eye, but he was inspecting the plaster flowers on the ceiling. His lips were pursed in a silent whistle.

'Now, today is Sunday' – Mrs Mepstead picked up the pot of tea and topped up my cup – 'so tomorrow is wash day. I'll show you the laundry after we've finished our cup of tea. Have all the ironing done by mid afternoon, depending on the weather and how long it takes to dry.'

The radio began to play 'One o'clock, two o'clock, three o'clock rock'. I was back in the Palais a-rockin' and a-rollin' till broad daylight. Mrs Mepstead tut-tutted, left the table and turned the radio down. 'I don't know why they play such rubbish. And they call that music.' She looked at me severely. 'I hope you don't go in for all that Elvis the Pelvis nonsense. It's not decent.' She turned the radio down.

Jeff kicked me under the table. I dunked the last of my biscuit and put the soggy bit in my mouth.

Mrs Mepstead took my silence and innocent eyes to mean agreement with her. She sat back down and stirred her tea. After a bit of a think she said, 'That should be enough for now. Don't worry about cooking dinner tonight. We'll make do with left-overs. I'll let you know about the cleaning and your other duties when you've settled in. Now, have you got any questions, dear?'

I swallowed my biscuit and replied in a weak voice, 'What time do I get up in the morning?'

'Oh, I think about 4.30 should do it. No later than five. It takes the stove a while to get going.' Mrs Mepstead smiled brightly. 'Anything else I can help you with?'

'Yes, please. Mrs Mepstead, could you tell me where the toilet is?'

The alarm. I flung out a hand and fished around in the dark. Where's the bloody clock? Where the hell am I? The window's in the wrong place. Come on Patti, turn that racket off. There. The green hands on the clock. Oh, shit. That can't be right. Not already. I stared at the square window. Faint moonlight glowed through thousands of splinters of frost that covered the glass. I touched the end of my nose. It was freezing.

I punched Jeff on the chest, but he just grunted and rolled

over, dragging all the blankets with him. I gasped at the cold and dived under the blankets. I pressed against Jeff's warm back. No. Don't go back to sleep. Mustn't fall asleep. With a super-human effort I swung my legs out and put my feet on the lino. Holy shit. Where are Jeff's woollen socks? I waved my arms around in the air to find the cord for the light. Nothing. The generator wasn't on yet. No way could I organise my brain to light the kerosene lamp. I leant out over the bed and felt for some socks. I found one. It was as cold as ice. I dragged one blanket off the bed to wrap around my shoulders. I stumped around the room to get Jeff's fur-lined motorbike boots. The air crackled with cold. I thought the outback was meant to be hot. I opened the door onto the middle of the bloody night, closed it behind me and stood in absolute shock as I saw the stars. In awe, I turned my face up to the sky.

Never had I seen such stars. The Milky Way was a fire of a million burning lights. The sky glinted with blue, red and green. The new moon was tangled among the branches of the pines along the driveway. My breath smoked in front of me.

Somewhere behind the houses a dog barked. From the darkness of the home paddock came the bleating of sheep. I braced my shoulders and set off up the path to the dunny on the hill. As I stomped along, my feet loose in Jeff's boots, the sky lost some of its magic. The cold and loneliness of outer space seeped into my bones. I pulled the blanket around me.

All my childhood I had been chief cook and bottle washer for Nan. Marriage was supposed to be the big adventure. Here I was worse off than at Pickering Street. My dreams of freedom and romance had led me to just a different kind of prison. Maybe I should just take Jeff's keys and drive myself home.

'He didn't even warn me,' I muttered to myself. 'Not a word. Now I know why. The bastard. Husband or no husband, I'll kill him. Slowly. In ice. Wait for his doodle to freeze and hit it with a stick. Crack. Right over the fence. Six and out.'

The further I went from the buildings, the more nervous I was. I kept cursing Jeff in order to keep up my courage. 'Typical man. A gutless wonder. Too scared to tell the truth. To hell with him. Well, if he wants any, he'll have to come crawling.'

In fact I was more terrified with each step and wished Jeff was with me. I hated all toilets anyway. I could hardly bear to use one if a man had just been in. I knew it was stupid. But I could never lose my fear of my 'uncles' waiting to pounce on me. What if there was some mad farm worker waiting behind the toilet? I stopped and scuffed about with my foot until I felt a rock. I picked it up and held it ready in my right hand.

The dunny was a black rectangle against the sky. I saw it where there were no stars. I imagined huge spiders waiting for me. Great hairy huntsmen spread wider than my hand waited to drop on my hair and run down the back of my neck. Redbacks spent the night spinning untidy webs across the open toilet seat. Even now they hung there, rocking in the web, waiting.

I smelt the toilet before I reached it. Pah. What a stench. Perhaps I'd use the ground. But I needed the newspaper squares nailed to the back of the door. And how could I hide the evidence on the ground as hard as cement?

I gathered all my courage, driven by the irresistible call of nature, pulled the blanket over my head like a monk's hood, took a firm grip on my stone-age rock, and strode forward to meet my fate.


A few hours later I was proud of how I had coped with break-fast. Weeties, eggs and bacon, mountains of toast, pots of tea and coffee. The Metters stove was long enough for me to move frypans on and off the heat so nothing burnt.

Then I raced to the laundry shed and, moving with the speed of the Keystone Cops, ran to and from the pump with a bucket for the copper, pumped the handle like mad, set the fire, and ran back to the kitchen.

Panic. Morning tea. I'd never made a cake. I grabbed the old Green and Gold cookery book from the pantry shelf. What's easy? Quick, find something, don't just turn pages. Scones. Yes. They must be easy. Do the cake after lunch. Let's see. Flour, salt, butter, milk. Oh no, it says to sift the flour. What does that mean? Try another recipe. How about 'Country Scones (Very Good)'. Damn. That also says to sift. What the hell, leave that out and just throw the ingredients together. 'Electric Cooker,

550 degrees F. Gas cooker 450.' What in the name of sweet Jesus do you do with a wood stove? Fire it up at one end, and rake hot coals along. Smart girl, Patti, even if I say so. I'll show them I didn't come down in the last shower. If it ever bloody rains out here.

The scones turned out beautiful. Well, a bit sludgy in the middle, and perhaps lopsided, but cut and covered with melted butter they were heavenly. Not bad at all for a fifteen-year-old. The washing! Run.

I wrung out sheets, which weighed a ton, then pegged them on the line strung between two poles. I scrubbed the armpits of the master's white shirts with meths, to get out the yellow stains. That was a trick I had picked up from Nan. Then I galloped back to the kitchen to check the roast. I peered into the long oven. The baking dishes of potatoes, pumpkin and carrots seemed to be all right. The two legs of lamb bubbled away merrily, and smelt mouth-watering good. I looked at the clock. Ten minutes to wash the piles of breakfast and morning tea dishes.

It was the gravy that did me in. So, the soup wouldn't be ready on time, but that would keep for tea. On my first day the old girl would forgive me. And there was no custard for the pudding. In fact there was no pudding either. I'd face that when the time came. I thought only the evening dinner was supposed to be three course.

The gravy. I had seen Nan pour boiling water over the meat juice and mix in some flour. I cut the lamb, served all the vegetables and meat onto plates, put the plates in the oven to keep warm, cut an Empire State Building of bread slices to make up for there being no dessert, and then turned my mind to the gravy. I poured some flour out of the bag into a baking dish. Whoops, slipped. A mound of flour sat high in the dish. So what. In went a great slosh of boiling water from the kettle. This was a cinch. I was so pleased with myself that I gave long swirls with the wooden spoon and sang, 'Roamin' in the gloamin' wi' me lassie by my side . . .'

Something began to grow in the pan. The flour swelled and rose up. I squealed, jumped back, and dropped the wooden spoon. The streaky brown monster bulged above the sides of

103

the pan and kept on rising. It flopped over the sides and began to crawl across the stove.

There were running footsteps. Mrs Mepstead grabbed a tea towel and dragged the pan off the stove, away from the smoking mess. She lifted my chin with her cool fingertips and looked me in the eye. 'You can't cook, can you?'

I shook my head and tears flooded out. What had I done? Had I ruined everything for Jeff? Everybody would know I was totally useless, a complete failure.

I half-hoped she'd say, 'You can leave now,' but she rolled up her sleeves and said, 'Come on, lass. Bring that other pan over here. No time like the present to start learning.'

So over the next months and years, I become the best gravy-maker in the world. And, on stations of the far-north and south-east, I became an expert maker of bread, coconut ice, egg and bacon pies, kangaroo tail soup, rabbit casserole, sponge cakes yellow with duck eggs, sage and onion stuffing for shoving up chooks' bums, jam tarts so hot they burnt the roof off your mouth unless you smothered them with cold whipped cream. I made baked custards with thin brown crusts, sago meringue pudding that looked like frogs' eggs under creek froth but tasted divine, apple pies with cloves and pastry as light as thistledown . . .

But all that was yet to come. Soon after I began with Mrs Mepstead, my grumbly appendix played up more and more until one afternoon, while doing the dishes, a spasm of pain forced me to lean right over the sink. Sweat poured down my face. To my astonishment, the sink full of dishes began to tilt over sideways, then everything went black. I had a faint recollection of a long ride in the ute. We bounced about and trees jumped out like white ghosts in the headlights. Then there was a big building with a long verandah.

I woke with my father's breath in my face. Somebody pushed his fingertips hard and deep into my stomach. There was a flash of pain and my eyes flickered open. I saw a grey beard and bloodshot eyes. His face had deep gullies and his lips were as dry and cracked as a claypan. His breath stunk of cheap wine.

Above him was a white ceiling. He prodded away again, way down near my groin. I flinched with the pain.

'Where am I?'

'Where do you think? Just lie still.' His voice was furry and angry. Then he said to somebody I couldn't see, 'May be the appendix, but I think it's something else. We'll have to open her up straight away. Just look at that bloody pulse in her throat.'

'No. Not open.' I squirmed and struggled to sit up. He put both hands on my shoulders and forced me down. I thrashed my head from side to side. 'No. You're pissed as a newt.'

'Shut your fucking mouth and leave it to me.' I was back in Pickering Street. Somebody spoke my language. But where was Jeff?

The man growled, 'Get that fucking needle into her hand.' The ceiling moved, my feet were aimed at a door and when I woke up I was flat on my back with a wall of curtains around my bed. I lifted the sheet and looked down at my stomach. I was the Christmas turkey sewn up with yards of black thread.

A nurse poked her head around the edge of the curtain. She was only my age; still a kid. 'Goodday. Feeling all right?'

'What's he done to me?' I was amazed at such a long cut just to take out my appendix.

The nurse came to my side. She took a thermometer from the top pocket of her uniform, flicked the glass tube hard in the air, inspected the little red lines, and then slid the thermometer under my tongue. 'I'm not supposed to say, but you're lucky to be alive.' She lifted my wrist, found the pulse and counted to herself while she stared at the upside down watch pinned to her tunic. Then she went to the end of the bed, lifted up a board with papers clipped to it and wrote on a sheet of paper. She looked so professional, so smart in her uniform, for a minute I wished I was a nurse. Then I thought about all that blood and people dying.

The young nurse looked at me, leant close and whispered, 'I heard him tell Sister it was to do with your womb collapsing, or something like that. It had got tangled in other things.' She saw my expression, grabbed a steel dish and held it to my mouth. I was sick until there was nothing left.

Two days later Jeff had not come to visit me. Nobody visited me. I really needed Nan. I looked at the pretty Get Well cards and flowers the other women in the ward had beside their beds. When their families came, I turned over on my side and pretended to be asleep.

Whenever the doctor came into the ward I shrank back in bed and tried not to catch his eye. He was a monster. When the lady in the next bed complained of a sore throat – she was organist at the Methodist Church and President of the CWA – he snarled, 'Too much screaming in the orgasms.'

When he had gone, she hissed through tight lips, 'I'd rather travel a thousand miles and have a Jap doctor touch me.'

The young nurse adored him. 'You're so lucky you had him. Sister reckons if you had an Adelaide doctor you'd be dead. He abuses shit out of everyone, but he's a genius. When young Bert Cummings was run over by a seed drill, he had holes all in his chest and arms. Doctor Thompson fixed him. And little Jimmy Sullivan was standing by his mum when she was at the wood stove. She flicked aside the iron ring from the top of the stove and it slipped and went over Jimmy's head and got stuck red hot around his neck. You can still see the burn marks right close to the jugular. Doctor Thompson saved his life too.'

She pulled her chair close and said, 'Doctor Thompson's invented some gizmo with a table tennis ball and a battery that you put in your heart to keep it pumping.'

'Go on. Pull the other one. It plays "Annie Laurie".'

The nurse crossed her heart. 'No. It's true. He's actually three sorts of doctor. He's one of Greek, and another of Letters, whatever that means, as well as a real doctor. From some place in England. Oxford or some other posh place. He carries a little book of poems in his pocket all the time. He'll sit out in the sun and just read the funny-looking words.'

'But he's a booze artist.'

The nurse frowned at me, disapproving. 'Only since his wife died. Oh, she was so beautiful and sang like a nightingale. Then she started doing weird things, like putting the canary in the washing machine to spin dry it. She got a tumour on her brain, went batty and died. Doctor Thompson nursed her himself right up until the end.' The nurse's eyes filled with tears and she looked away quickly. She sniffed. 'Silly me. Anyway, at the funeral the coffin got stuck half way down because the ground around here is all rock. When the coffin jammed nobody knew what to do. Doctor Thompson climbed down in the grave, treading all over the flowers. Then he jumped up and down on the coffin. He looked up at us and said in choked kind of voice, tears pouring out of his eyes, "Just driving you home, my darling."'

Doctor Thompson came to take my stitches out. He lifted a loop in the middle, snipped it with his tiny scissors, and asked, 'How do you want it? Fast or slow?'

I looked down at the forty-three black knots. 'Fast please.'

He wrapped the two loose ends around his index fingers and ripped.

That illness sent me to Adelaide for a long recuperation. Jeff and I were separated for some months, and our juvenile marriage suffered. We both discovered we could get along without the other. Jeff had his rouseabout job, his mates, his weekends roo shooting. When I thought about it, we didn't see much of each other on the station anyway except some times at breakfast. I worked from starlight to starlight. In the city I lived in a small flat at the Hackney mansions. There I rested my battered body, under doctor's orders to take it easy. I walked in the Botanic Gardens, tried unsuccessfully to fend off a young Italian hairdresser who took a liking to me, and experienced the disturbance of being both married and single.

When I had recovered, I went back to a different station. If I had a rare hour to myself, a time just for myself that Adelaide had taught me was precious, I heated up a kettle of rain water and washed my hair. Then I walked up the hill and over the top where I stood. Me, the kangaroos and the crows. The cool wind wrapped my dress around my legs. I put my face to the wind and brushed my hair with long, dreaming strokes. The horizon was away at the end of the world, and there was no sound but the hiss of wind in the myall and tea-trees, or the grating cry of a crow.

One afternoon as I returned to my bedroom from my solitary walk, a young man stood timidly by the door. It was the manager's son, Kevin. He had olive skin and hazel eyes. Kevin was my age, sixteen.

He shifted from foot to foot and gave me a lopsided grin. 'Hello Patti. Thought you might like a game.' Kevin took a packet of cards from his pocket. His sleeves were rolled up and his arms were covered in fine black hair. They were strong arms, the bulge of his muscles visible beneath the roll of each sleeve.

'Why not,' I said, and blushed, not from shyness but panic. Had I fixed the loose button on my blouse? I rapidly ran my fingertips down each button. Kevin watched and went red as a beetroot.

We stood in silence. Each passing second became more charged with tension, more embarrassing. To break the pain, I walked past Kevin and into the room beside my bedroom in the shearer's quarters where Jeff and I lived.

Kevin followed me in and we sat opposite each other across an old kitchen table. 'Coo and Can?' he asked

'Okay.'

Kevin shuffled the cards. Then he dealt, counting aloud, 'One, one, two, two . . .' until we each had seven.

I sorted my cards. Two jacks and a run of three, four and five. Jeff and the other men would not be back for hours. I glanced over at Kevin, who chewed savagely at a fingernail. If anything spoilt his appearance it was his fingertips, especially the way he gnawed at them like a dog with a bone. But I liked his hands. They were the hands that loaded a twenty-two rifle and passed it to me for my first shot. I aimed carefully, the little bead in the 'V' on the barrel, and the barrel pointed straight at a bottle on a fence post. I squeezed the trigger, squealed, and dropped the gun. Kevin laughed while I jumped up and down screaming. He reloaded for another go. His hands were those that moved the gear lever the day he let me drive the old ute from my quarters to the main house. 'You just steer. I'll work the clutch,' he said. Kevin was close beside me, his thigh pressed against mine while he pushed down on the clutch. We yelled and laughed as I bunny-hopped the ute along the dirt track. My hands gripped the steering wheel like a vice as I felt the power of the vehicle.

'Three tens. That's a qualification, and thirty points,' Kevin said. He spread the cards face up on the table. He raised his eyebrows and tried to look over the top of my cards. 'Get out of it, you big cheat,' I complained in mock seriousness, and clutched my cards between my breasts. Then I quickly lowered my hands because I was ashamed that they were swollen and red from the washing. My knuckles were raw from scraping the hard ridges on the scrubbing board in the laundry. I had muscles on top of muscles from winding the clothes wringer and lifting heavy buckets of wet clothes.

'Who needs to cheat?' Kevin boasted.

'I can lick you any time,' I retorted.

'Oh yeah? You and whose army?'

'You just wait. You'll see.' I rearranged my cards to suggest I had a group of four.

We smiled at each other, honour satisfied.

Then Kevin spoke quietly. 'Tomorrow's it.' We both knew but pretended it wouldn't come. Tomorrow his father took him to town in the ute. Then he caught the train to Adelaide and the boarding house at college.

It took lots of courage, because I was a married woman, but I asked, 'Can you give me the address of the college?'

Kevin stared hard at his cards. 'Yeah.'

How do you tell someone you'll miss them like crazy, that you've met someone you can talk to like an adult, and you've just had the best two weeks of your life?

A truck pulled up. Kevin and I looked at each other with wide eyes. The men were back. We hadn't done anything wrong, but we both felt so guilty. My husband came in the door, and glared at us in surprise and rage. We froze in terror. Then, very slowly, Kevin folded the cards in his hand, gestured for mine, and packed the cards into a neat pile. He picked them up, pushed back his chair, and, in a strained voice that he tried to make ordinary, said, 'See you round.' I thought, 'like a rissole,' but said nothing, just stared ahead. Kevin walked towards the door and had to brush past Jeff's chest to get out.

I sat and wished the ground would open up and swallow me. The other shearers stood around, looked at us, and didn't know whether to leave or stay and pretend nothing was happening. A voice said, 'Hiya Cookie. Where's me cup of tea and cake?' Nobody moved or spoke.

Jeff exploded. 'Damn you. Damn you to hell.' He raised a clenched fist and I shrank down in my chair, cowering like one of his sheep dogs. He looked around, lowered his fist, stormed over to our bedroom door, wrenched it open and began to smash things about. Then my suitcase flew out and crashed against a table leg. Then my clothes, comb, make-up and shoes all went flying through the air. I scrambled to my feet and picked things up. I stuffed them in the case. The shearers stood and watched as I scrambled about on hands and knees.

Jeff came to the bedroom door. I saw with horror what was in his hand. I pleaded with my eyes. He sneered at me and threw two Modess right across the room. I made myself go over to them and pick them up. As I carried the white pads over to the suitcase I knew I would never forgive Jeff for the humiliation. The mail truck took me to Port Augusta.

We made a feeble attempt to patch up the marriage, and kept working on stations. Our first baby, Jack, was born in Adelaide. I took him back to the bush and he played in his cot while I worked. I ran back to our quarters from the kitchen to give him a feed or change his nappy. Back in the kitchen I bent down to the oven, with my legs splayed like a giraffe drinking. I was eight months gone with Blondie when Jack was still less than one year old.

# Death

_Jeff tired of being a rouseabout and returned to Adelaide to drive taxis._
We lived with his mother, Shirley, in Young Street, Unley. That
suited me. I was sick of working from sparrow fart as station cook
and general dogs-body. But before long we couldn't handle
Shirley's drunken violence and nagging for more money. So, I
got myself a trust home in Ferryden Park, just around the corner
from Coker Street. It felt strange to walk the streets where I
had lived before. Then I was a bewildered, trapped teenager.
Now, at the age of nineteen, I was a mum, whose husband was
away so much I might as well have been single. And so I settled
into a blessedly lazy suburban life; well, as easy as it could be
with two little kids.

One afternoon I was in the back yard, at the rope clothes-
line, hanging out the washing. Blondie crawled around my feet,
picked up a peg and sat back on her bottom to suck the peg,
her chubby legs sticking out from her nappy. Jack pushed his toy
car through the dirt, his cheek right down on the car so that
he looked ahead like the driver. Vroom, vroom, he ploughed
around a corner and headed out to the wide desert. The hot
sun burned down on us all. Another stinker of a day.

I heard the front gate open, and a boy on a pushbike came
down the side of the house and into the yard. He leant on the
handlebars, his face hot and wet. Who was it? That's right, young
Bill, Aunty Jean's step-son.

He stared at me. When he spoke, his voice was flat, almost
resentful, 'Your mother's dead.'

111

I stared at him, dumbstruck. I didn't know my mother. 'My mother? I don't have a mother.'

'I mean the fat one.'

I ran, one child on my hip, another clinging to my back. The streets were a blur of tears. How could Nan be dead? I had seen her only yesterday. I had kissed her goodbye, and said, 'See you when I come back later.' But when it was time to call in again, Blondie and Jack were asleep, so I didn't see Nan. While I ran, howling, I raged and cursed at my stupidity for missing the last chance to see her.

I ran in the back door of Aunty Jean's, calling, 'Nan, Nan!' but she wasn't in her bed, which was made so neatly.

'They've taken her away,' said Aunty Jean.

I stood, distracted, demented, 'What do you mean?'

'Pull yourself together.'

'Where's my Nan?' I clutched the side of my head, the blood roaring in my ears. I shook with terror because she was gone.

I stared around at the relatives, some from Gladstone and Whyalla, five hours' drive away. How could they be here already?

I turned to Aunty Jean. 'How did she die? When?'

Jean just shrugged, then said, 'In her sleep, about seven-thirty this morning. She was gone when we took in her cup of tea and slice of toast.'

'Seven-thirty?' I looked at the clock. Three-thirty. 'Why didn't you tell me this morning? Nan was my mother.'

'It was her heart, the doctor thinks.'

The funeral parlour was in Wakefield Street, in the city. I stood outside, looking at the building, clinging to Veronica's arm. Jeff was beside me, sometimes gently touching my shoulder. I was scared. What would I see in the coffin? I remembered the dead face and tinted hair of Veronica's brother. I remembered the blind eyes of Veronica's father.

'Do you want to come in now?' Tenderly, Veronica gave me the choice when I had none. We had to go upstairs. It was a big scary room with an open coffin.

I hung back, pulling against Veronica's arm. 'No. I don't want to look.'

'But you must say goodbye to your Nan,' Veronica urged.

I wanted to remember Nan as I last saw her yesterday, alive, sitting on her bed, utterly worn out, her hands nervously twitching at a thread on her tatty stole. At the thought of that stole I stupidly burst into another storm of tears. I saw myself as an infant in Pickering Street, putting the shawl over my head and prowling about as the big bad wolf. That was the stole she wrapped around her shoulders the morning she threw the chamber pot over the man at our front door. Now that aggressive, silly old woman was gone. No more glasses of stout down at the pub on St Patrick's Day. No more taking swipes at the world with her walking stick. I sobbed at the utter loss. What had she said? 'I'm the only true friend you've got, Patti. One day you'll understand that.'

She was gone. I felt her absence in the funeral parlour. It was a hot north wind that morning. Already she was blown away across the sky, too far away to find her way back.

Step by step Veronica and Jeff led me forward to the coffin. I took great gulping breaths, as though I was in the pains of childbirth. My chest heaved. In my distress, there flashed before my eyes a horrible sight I tried never to remember. I saw again the almost human faces of my twins, aborted, swimming red in the bottom of the bucket. All around was darkness. I opened my eyes and looked down into the coffin.

I went roaring down a tunnel to a terrifying mask. They had painted the face that never wore make-up. A mask of rouge; clumsy, garish, like a cheap doll. Bright blue eyeshadow on her closed eyelids. And the thin lips scarlet red. A grotesque mask of a false Nan more horrifying than death itself.

I was out in the street, stumbling. A car squealed its brakes. Jeff shouted and pulled me onto the footpath.

That night I ran from my house out into the darkness. I strained to take a breath, gasping, unable to breathe. My room was a coffin, and I couldn't push up the lid. The nightmare was of me, walking slowly up Pickering Street, towards Number 37, knowing what I'd find in the house, but the dream dragged me forward to find Nan waiting for me dead in her coffin, waiting for me. The mask stared up. I stood out in the street, awake, bewildered, somewhere between reality and nightmare. Why didn't I tell her I adored her? Why wouldn't she let me?

At the funeral I felt the snap as somebody floated out of me and became the watcher. My body was there, but I had lost myself.

# I find
# my mother

*'I feel like a bloody Mormon,'* I said as we walked up another driveway.

Veronica smiled nervously. 'You? A Bible basher?'

Our voices were bright, but we both had butterflies in the stomach. What if this was the house?

I had decided to find my mother. My marriage was in pieces and couldn't last much longer. I had three kids now that Cassie had come along, and Nan was dead. Nobody would tell me my mother's address. Her married name was not in the phone book. Bit by bit, I narrowed the place where she was most likely to live. Of all places, it was Ferryden Park, where I began married life with Jeff. Veronica came with me, riding shotgun.

I cradled Cassie on my left hip. Jack hung on the other hand, and he dragged Blondie along. All in our best clothes, but with our shoes dusty by now, we crowded onto the small square cement verandah by the front door. If we didn't find the house soon, we'd have to give up for the day. Cassie was getting testy and wouldn't last much longer without a feed.

Veronica leant forward and knocked on the green door with fly-wire on the top half. Somebody inside said, 'You get it, Perce.' I licked my fingers quickly and tissied Cassie's curl. As the door opened I put on my brave smile. I felt Jack and Blondie slip around behind me. They hung onto my skirt, almost as fearful of meeting their grandmother as I was of meeting my mother. A middle-aged man opened the door and peered at us uncertainly. 'Hello.' He glanced from me to Veronica and then down at the kids' faces peeking around my legs. 'What can I do for you?'

I'm looking for the Calvinos. They're supposed to be somewhere around here.'

The man examined my face closely. 'The Calvinos? Hang on.' He turned back into the house. 'Mollie, have you got a minute?'

His wife came to the door and stared at us. She had a keen glint in her eye, and I started to lose my nerve. I was so glad Veronica was with me. It was hard to believe that the little girl who gave me her green shoes way back in primary school was here to give me the courage to keep going.

The couple stared at us, uncomfortably, the man with a frown. The woman spoke. 'Yes, we know the Calvino family quite well.'

My heart did a back flip. After all the years of childhood fantasies that a beautiful woman would rescue me from darkness and brutality; then the bitterness and cynicism of youth as the fantasy withered and died; and finally the deep, disturbed longing of adulthood, I was about to find the one woman I needed to love but despised for abandoning me.

The man and woman looked at each other and he nodded to her. She said, reluctantly, 'Well, I suppose it's all right to tell you.'

Who did she think we were? The police? Debt collectors?

The woman pointed to the house. 'Until recently, they were there.' The blood drained from my face. I took deep breaths to stop the dizzy feeling. Dear God. I looked around and there was my own house across the playground, over in Coker Street. For three years my mother had lived within, literally, a stone's throw. We must have walked the same streets, gone to the same fish and chip shop, stood beside each other at the bus stop, and never known.

'Are you all right?' The woman put out her hand and touched my wrist. 'You've gone white as a sheet.'

I swallowed, and managed to speak. 'Mrs Calvino is my mother.'

The couple glanced at each other in alarm. Why did the mention of my mother make them look so guilty? I stood there like a gawk, unable to think of anything to say. For years I had practised the lines I'd say when my mother saw me. I had rehearsed my every move and her reactions a thousand times. Now the fear on the faces of these strangers blew my plans away.

I felt Veronica nudge me in the small of the back. In a weak voice, I asked, 'Has she ever talked about me?'

There was a long, embarrassed silence. The man and the woman each waited for the other to speak first. Eventually, the woman said, 'Well, yes, she did mention you once or twice.' She paused. Her eyes gave away the bad news while she tried to work out how to say it. 'Now, please don't take this the wrong way. I mean no harm. And it really is none of my business, but . . .'

I thought, irritably, Spit it out.

She wiped her hands on the front of her dress, as if she rubbed away something dirty and horrible. 'Your mother wouldn't take it well if she met you.'

Wouldn't take it well. The words boomed around in my head. I heard voices that shouted in a dark cave. Nan's voice: 'If she wanted you, she'd come. But she doesn't.' I cried out: 'I'll run away and find her.' Then Nan again: 'She'll never want you, never did.'

Veronica said something to the couple and got my mother's new address. I felt Veronica's hand on my elbow. We drove across the city towards the house. We found the number and stood outside it while I stared at the home that could have been, should have been, mine. I wondered which was the bedroom window I would have looked out of. I examined the neat garden of weeded flower beds and shrubs in exact rows. I would have picked those red hibiscus and floated the blossoms in a saucer of water. I felt a rush of tears and anger. None of the brutalities of Pickering Street, not even the 'uncles', were as bad as the rejection.

I handed Cassie to Veronica, and searched for a tissue in my handbag. 'It's no good, Veronica. I can't do it. I just want to get out of here.'

Veronica held Cassie to her chest and rocked from side to side. Tight-lipped, Veronica said, 'Don't you want to see why? Haven't you always told me you want to see what you've been bashed for?' Veronica glared at me. 'Well? Don't you?' She looked into the front yard of my mother's house. 'Have you come all this way for nothing?'

My feet wanted to run away, but I was in the front yard, walking towards the door. A voice in my head said over and over, 'Don't apologise to her. She owes you a life.'

A woman opened the door. I saw her once in a photo. She was a pretty woman with dark hair and a timid smile. Nan caught me holding the photo, and I never saw it again. Now I gazed at a hesitant lady with hair already turning grey. She looked at me quizzically. Then she looked at the tribe around me. Her eyes were brown, and had an expression I couldn't quite interpret. Was it sorrow or was it criticism? I remembered then the eyes that looked at me when she put me down in the cot. My stomach churned as I thought, 'I was your baby, inside your body.' All the time we stood there, her face was burning into my brain, etching a picture that could never fade.

'Can I help you?' Her voice was polite, well mannered. Her smile was strained.

My tongue was stuck.

Veronica asked, 'Are you Mrs Calvino?'

A shadow passed over my mother's face. 'Yes. What can I do for you?' This tense, controlled, everyday face was once that of a young woman driven by passions and terrors.

Then I said aloud, 'I'm Pat.'

Her hands fluttered up to her lips. Her eyes looked at me with horror.

I spoke again, more to myself than to her. 'You're my mum.'

She looked wildly past me out to the street, than back over her shoulder into the house. 'Pat. Yes. Well.' She licked her lips.

'This is my friend, Veronica, Aunt Elsie's daughter.'

Automatically my mother said politely, 'How do you do, Veronica?' She stared, bewildered, at Cassie who sucked her thumb noisily. I had cried all those years for this moment and we all just stood like idiots. I reached down and, for something to do to break the tension, ruffled Jack's hair. He looked up, eyes wide. Any second I would burst into tears.

'Well, I suppose' – my mother put on a smile, but her eyes were going cold – 'would you like to come in?'

The house was immaculately clean. Jack ran over to the lounge and tried to climb up next to an Alsatian dog which lay there.

'No, Jack.' I grabbed his arm and pulled him away. It wasn't the dog I was afraid of, but the buckles in Jack's shoes that would catch in the lounge and tear threads. The lounge looked as though nobody sat on it, except the dog. The apricot-coloured cushions stood up in a neat row; one at each end, one exactly in the middle. Jack started to whinge so I sat him on the floor and put Cassie on his lap. I felt stupidly ashamed that our dusty shoes made scuff marks in the thick carpet. I looked around in fear. Woodwork gleamed, the glass doors of the china cabinet were spotless. My kids would soon have fingerprints all over them. So there I was, on hands and knees, sorting out my babies. I wondered how much more of this charade I could take before I sobbed or lashed out at somebody.

My mother looked down at me, and said in a brittle voice, 'Would you like a cup of tea?'

'Yes please.' I spread the hem of Cassie's dress out in a neat circle. For some stupid reason I thought that would impress my mother.

'White or black?'

'White with two sugars, please.' Why did the two sugars make me sound greedy?

'And your friend?' My mother meant Veronica, but had forgotten her name.

Veronica said, 'Black please. No sugar. Just the way it comes.'

I blurted out, 'I heard you were a great basketballer. I was captain of the school team, and we won every trophy in Grade Six and Seven.'

I saw the panic in my mother's eyes. She pointed each index finger to the floor. One for black tea, one for white. She blinked at me as though I was unreal, a ghost who would evaporate. She fled to her kitchen.

I could have bitten my tongue for making such a fool of myself. I ground my teeth. Don't show your feelings. Nan's voice was in my head. Don't you ever cry in front of others.

This was becoming a nightmare. That woman who rattled around with cups and saucers in her kitchen didn't want to know. Out there, she fussed with her things and tried to think of how to get rid of me. She had made no move, no sign of affection. Only fear and dismay.

I looked at the photographs in frames on the mantelpiece. There was a wedding photo of her and the man she ran away with. He was nothing special. What was so irresistible about him to make a woman leave her two-year-old child? My mother and that man were the grandparents my kids had never seen. She hadn't even asked their names yet, or even admitted to herself that her grandchildren were in her lounge-room.

I thought of the one or two things Nan had let slip about my mother. She had been an orphan. Her mother had died in childbirth, and the baby was put into an orphanage. She was later adopted by an aunty and uncle who were members of some strict religious cult. It was strange that my mother and I had both been handed around like a slice of bread and butter. It suddenly dawned on me. Was my mother pregnant before she was married? If so, had my Nan forced her to get married, or tried to stop it? Why did my Nan hate my mother?

On the opposite end of the mantelpiece was a studio portrait of three boys and a girl in school uniform. My half-brothers and sister. I wondered what name she had given the girl. I liked the eyes of the boy in the middle. The others smiled out confidently at the world, but there was mischief in that boy's eyes. With a shock I wondered if they knew about me. What if one of them suddenly came home? Was that what made my mother so jittery?

My mother returned from the kitchen. 'The kettle won't be long.' She stood in the doorway, her feet just outside the line that divided the lounge-room from the rest of the house. She fidgeted with the string that tied her pinny on. Mustn't get a spot on the good dress. 'Would you like to look around?'

We were all relieved. Anything was better than sitting around looking at each other with nothing to say. Veronica picked up Cassie and I took the other two by the hand.

'And this is Karen's room.' I let out a gasp of wonder. This was a room for a princess. I had never seen anything like it. Her bedroom suite was white, with a lovely dressing table that had a big mirror. I saw myself as the a little girl in that room. I imagined standing in front of the mirror and picking up the brush with the silver leaves decorating the handle. Then I tried spraying the perfume on my wrist. No. Today I'd use the other bottle. I looked at the bed and suddenly I was Patti, my heart thudding away. I hadn't met the girl who slept under that beautiful bedspread of crimson satin. It was the same material as the curtains. Her photograph was there on the dressing table. She stood proudly in a ball gown, a sash around her shoulders with the words, 'Miss Wonderland'. That stranger had come from the same womb. We shared my mother's blood.

'I didn't want to go,' my mother said quietly.

We stood as still as statues, facing ahead into the room, not at each other.

'Why?' I whispered.

'Your father.' The tone said it all.

Had she abandoned me, would she continue to reject me because I was my father's child? At Pickering Street they hated me because I was the child of my mother – the slut who ran off with the soldier.

I knew my mother's sense of disgust, loathing. At first they must have been happy. I remembered standing up in my cot watching them rolling about in bed. Suddenly I realised how young they had been. I had always thought of them as old people. But my mother was only twenty-one, a bit older than me now, when she had me. My father was only nineteen when he went off to war.

'Was it the war?' I asked.

My mother shook her head. 'More than that. We had to get married.' Her voice was thick with regret, as though she thought, The day you were born I wanted to throw you out the window. You messed up my life. 'He forced himself on me. I had to get married because of you.'

Oh yeah, I thought. You let him into your room or wherever it was that you did it.

'You know, for years after he drove me out your father pestered me. He made my life a misery. He came here at all hours of the night. At three in the morning, stinking drunk. He stood out there and shouted at me, abused me, woke all the neighbours with his foul language.'

121

I was so shocked I reached out to hold the door handle. All that time my father knew where my mother was. When I lived in Coker Street he must have staggered past my house to stand in front of my mother's only one or two hundred yards away. He never told me. Nan never told me.

For the first time my mother and I turned and looked in each other's eyes. We shared the same horror of that man; the same disgust and heartbreak. It was a moment, just a tiny moment, when our eyes met. But it was recognition. Then the glance flicked away like a fish.

The shrill whistle of the kettle came from the kitchen. My mother tried to speak, but thought better of it. I saw the heartbreak in her eyes. Then she scurried off to the kitchen. What was it she couldn't bring herself to say? For a moment we had connected.

By the time she brought the tray into the lounge, the moment was lost forever. She glanced at the clock. Who was she afraid of?

'Nice weather,' said my mother.

The long silence was broken by Veronica, who gabbled, 'Need the rain though. It's been a dry winter.'

I balanced the thin china cup and saucer in my lap and looked down into the cup of tea I knew I would not finish. She wanted me to go away. It was all going wrong. Better for us all if I just went. I would use Cassie's feed time as the excuse. Before I left, however, I must ask the one question that had tormented me for so many years. I might never get another chance. My voice came out harshly, 'If you knew my father was so rotten, why didn't you come back for me?' I thought, but didn't say, Wouldn't any mother fight to rescue a kid from such a father? I'd rip the place to pieces. I'd never let another woman nurse my baby.

My mother looked at me in utter astonishment. 'But I did come back.' Her eyes went glazed. 'Don't you remember? I came back to visit you but that grandmother wouldn't let me see you.' My mother's face was filled with horror. 'Your grandmother screamed in my face.'

# *Hairylegs*

*As time went by, Jeff and I drifted further apart. After Nan's death,* Jeff gave up the taxis and went into the army. He was away at camp most of the time. Bit by bit he cut down on the money he sent for me and the kids. There came a week when he sent nothing, then another week, until the trickle dried up altogether. I had to get out of the Trust home, and moved into an old shed. That was impossible, and so I found a small two-bedroom place. Jeff's mother Shirley moved in with me. She brought her other son, his wife, their two kids, and two male boarders. All in a two bedroom house. Shirley had become such a tyrant and a vicious drunk that I dreaded her Friday and Saturday night violence just as I once cringed at my father's drunken return to Pickering Street. My stomach was always in a knot of fear and humiliation. I had to move again, this time to a small flat in Carrington Street in the city. One of Shirley's boarders, Sid, had become my lover. Sid helped me move into Carrington Street and stayed with me.

The day I settled in I heard loud fights from the next door flat. Noise travelled easily through the walls, and I heard some ding-dong rows. One morning they were at it more than usual. Something smashed against a wall. Then came loud shouts, doors slammed, kids cried. A woman's voice shouted for all the world to hear, 'I know you're screwing the fat cow.' Thump, and the sound of somebody running.

Then the fight spilt out onto the footpath. I couldn't resist a little peek. A fat man crouched on the footpath with his arms over his head and a woman was beating shit out of him with a broom. Blood poured down his face as he backed away, stumbling over the broken suitcase and clothes scattered around. He was fat and too slow to run from her. She shouted, 'You filthy rotten bastard!' and flattened him with a tremendous hit on the head. He rolled over and she kept on belting him. She was in such a rage she didn't know where she was, and I was worried she might kill him.

I ran out and grabbed the broom handle as she swung it right back over her shoulders for the knockout. 'Take it easy.'

She turned on me, eyes glazed, blood on her mouth. 'Mind your own bloody business.'

That diversion gave the man a chance to escape. He staggered to his feet, threw himself the few paces to his taxi, wrenched open the door and forced his body in behind the wheel. She leapt at the door, but he pushed the lock down and started the motor while she tugged madly at the door handle, screaming abuse at him. The taxi roared off and she ran after it, hurling the broom like a javelin, but it fell short and skidded along the bitumen.

The blokes who had come out of the factory across the road gave a great cheer. The young woman gave them the fingers up and walked back disdainfully, ignoring their whistles and shouts of, 'Bewdy, you showed him.'

She was about twenty-eight, tall, skinny, with long, thin, hairy legs. She wore a maroon check skirt, an old sloppy jumper, and men's woollen slippers with holes in the toes where her horny toenails stuck through. She looked like something the dog had dug up in the back yard.

As she walked towards me she lifted one hand to brush her hair out of her face. 'Hi,' she said with a cheerful grin, blood on her front teeth.

We looked at each other. She had a long face, jug-ears and fierce eyes that weren't afraid of anything. Looking at her was like seeing my own life from the outside. It was strange. I had come into the city to escape the bashings and abuse, but the same thing happened here. Maybe it was everywhere. Only this time, with Hairylegs, it was the man who got the hiding and the woman who swore like a trooper.

A bit uncertain, I said, 'Why don't you come in and I'll fix that lip? Bring the kids with you. I've got a few biscuits.'

She stared me in the eye and gave a lop-sided smile. 'Okay. My name's Liz.'

We made a cup of tea put her kids out in the back yard with my toddlers. Liz's kids rushed for the two tin trucks while mine went for the old pram to push around the outside dunny. Liz sat at the kitchen table and dabbed a wet flannel against her lip, examining the spots of blood. 'All men are dirty dogs,' she said, 'whether they wash or not.'

'Vampires,' I said.

'Arseholes.'

'Fuckwits.'

'Total complete dickheads.'

'Make them roll over and wave their legs in the air.'

'Make them do cartwheels.'

We laughed, raised our cups, touched the rims together.

Hairylegs looked at my wedding ring, and raised an eyebrow. I hesitated. I longed to pour out my heart to somebody who accepted me and didn't criticise.

'He's in the army.' I wasn't about to tell how Jeff wrote letters home boasting of his girlfriends, or how when I went to visit him he introduced me to his mates as a 'friend he picked up on the side of the road'. Perhaps we could have got through all that and still stayed married. After all, I wasn't exactly the Mary Poppins wife. And I was brought up in Pickering Street, where married couples regularly brawled over infidelities but, after the fur and feathers had flown, settled down once again in their nest, or a new nest a couple of houses from the old. I looked across at Hairylegs. It was impossible to tell her, or anyone, of the way he hurt me.

'Maybe it began to fall apart when he went kangaroo shooting,' I said. 'He was so restless he couldn't last two days at home.' I glanced out the window. 'Not that I blame him. Jack was a screamer as a baby. He must've cried eighteen hours a day for more than a year.'

'Tell me about it,' said Hairylegs. 'My second one drove me

nuts. There were nights I thought I'd kill him if he didn't shut up.'

'I suppose the crunch came,' I said, 'over a simple thing. One day a policeman came to the front door. Jeff was certain it was a summons to repossess his motorbike. He leapt in the wardrobe like a frightened child, and left me to answer the door. I reckon that ended it for me.

Liz nodded. 'That's it. One day a switch goes off in your head, you look at them, and know you don't love them, don't even like them. What do you do about it?'

I gave a weak smile. 'I stayed with him. It was all over, but it wasn't finished, if you know what I mean.'

'Well, come on. Don't leave me in suspenders. What happened next?' Liz leant across the table, her eyes sparkling. This slap-happy woman, who looked like something from a horror movie, was all the friends, mothers, aunties, brothers and sisters I'd longed for.

'One day I had to leave my kids with a neighbour while I went to the Relief Office. When I came back, the babies were gone. The neighbour told me, "Your husband and father came with the police and took them." I went demented.

'I tore around to his mother's place in Bowden, but she wouldn't let me in. I screamed at her from the front fence. My husband and father came out the door. I went totally berserk, leapt into the yard, grabbed Shirley by the hair, she grabbed mine and we began to tear it out. Jeff pulled me off and dragged me away. I wrenched my body around and spat in my father's face.

'My father wiped his face and yelled, "What sort of mother are you? You aren't fit to be a mother. Living like a prostitute with a man you won't even marry."'

I looked at Hairylegs to see if there was any sign of disapproval. She had winced when I said, 'Not fit to be a mother.' Now she just sat, wide-eyed, waiting for more.

'My father ran past and off to the telephone box. When the police arrived they told me to go. "But they're my kids," I said.

'The policeman said, "The father has as much right to them."

'I saw red. "Right? He abducted them. Him and that drunkard and that old prostitute."

'"That's enough of that talk. Go home or be arrested."

'I went right off my tree. Ranted and raved. My kids were in that house, and they wouldn't let me near them. But the policeman forced me to go. I couldn't believe this was happening to me.

'Soon after I got back to my empty house, a taxi arrived, and the driver gave me a note from Jeff: "Meet me in the park off East Terrace at seven." I knew where he meant. In the park was a metal elephant that the kids loved to climb on when we took them out as a special treat. I went to the park and waited. Jeff turned up in a taxi.

'We took the taxi to collect the kids from Shirley. Jeff asked me to wait at the corner, while he got the kids. He brought them in a pram. "You can have them," he said. "I only wanted to hurt you."'

Hairylegs reached over and patted the back of my hand. 'My parents bashed the living daylights out of me when I was a kid. I could never come up to their standards. When I got pregnant with Number One, they threw me out. Yet my mum had been up the spout when she got married.'

Hairylegs looked down sadly at the kitchen tabletop, and added quietly, 'And my mum has the neatest rose garden in the street.'

Hairylegs looked at the clock. 'Time to eat. Have you got any flour and carb soda?' I shook my head. It was two days to Relief Day, and all I had was four carrots and half-a-dozen potatoes.

'Tell you what,' said Hairylegs, 'let's have a cook-up. We can throw your stuff into a stew, and I've got a bit of mince. You can do miracles with mince. All we need is a couple of things from the corner shop.'

She ran next door to her place and came back with a battered black purse. 'Come on, Pat,' she said, 'get your purse.' Hairylegs tipped her purse up and shook a few coins onto the kitchen table. I up-ended my purse. We looked at the tiny pile of money, raised our eyes, and burst into laughter.

# Single
## supporting mum

*'Ring a ring a rosies, a pocket full of posies,'* I chanted, pushing the old pram down Carrington Street. Jack sat on the plank across the pram, his legs dangling down. He sang along, his eyes laughing like mad, 'And when your mother calls you, UP jumps Rosie.' Jack flung his arms in the air on the word 'up', pleased as Punch that he knew the song all the way through.

Blondie was tucked in my end of the pram, her back against the white wicker work, her legs under the pink bunny rug, her head covered in a woollen beanie with a yellow pompom on top. 'Up!' she shouted, copying her big brother who sat on the plank. Sheltered under the curved roof of the pram, probably buried by now under the rug, Cassie was fast asleep after her ten o'clock feed. I stopped, to check that she was breathing.

My new friend, Hairylegs, who I now thought of fondly by her real name Liz, was beside me, her brood of kids clinging to her, falling off, running about and, if they weren't careful, collecting a clip in the ear for being stupid. Her jug-ears stuck out, and she wore that same dishevelled maroon check skirt. I couldn't look at her hairy legs without dying to shave them. When I looked at Liz I thought there must be a God.

At the corner of Carrington and Pulteney, Jack waved at the deli and cried out, 'Ice cream.'

'Not yet, Jack. On the way home. When Mummy's got some money.' I looked at Jack's shirt, which I had made from an old sheet. 'Not a brass razoo for two weeks,' I said to Liz. 'I can't even clothe the kids properly, and that mongrel Jeff, living off the fat of the land, hasn't sent a penny.'

Liz hitched a baby onto her left hip, her arm under its bottom, its legs bumping her thighs. It's a wonder women don't have arms as long as a chimpanzee's, I thought. 'I wouldn't call men "mongrels",' Liz said with a crooked grin. 'I like dogs.'

Far ahead were the tall buildings of the city. I could see Cox Foys with the ferris wheel on its roof. We still had all that way to go. The nearer we got to the corner of Rundle Street, the more my stomach tightened. Relief Day came once a fortnight. Every time, without fail, I'd lie awake the night before, ill with worry, endlessly going over the scenes of humiliation. One of Liz's kids veered off to the side, almost running onto the road. 'Come here, you little bastard.' She grabbed it by the arm, yanking it savagely across the footpath.

'You're too hard on them,' I said. Earlier that morning she had clouted one of the mob with the wooden copper stick. Liz gave me the look. I smiled.

What a pair we made. Liz with her wild romantic fantasies of being swept off her feet by a Fred Astaire, while her partner on Thursday nights was the fat taxi driver who wore a toupee, and who she belted if he so much as looked at another girl. This was Liz, rough as guts, the girl who burst into tears at sad songs on the radio, tears dripping into the kitchen sink. Liz was the woman who made incredible wedding cakes with fantastic decorations of roses, wisteria and ornate lettering, and sold them to help make ends meet. And Patti, who had an absent husband, a jealous lover who got violent when he was drunk, three kids under three, an ulcer, and who, at nineteen years of age, and feeling more like forty, didn't know what to dream any more, but knew she'd never give up.

Liz glanced across at me. 'Tell you what. When we get back, I'll whip up a sponge cake. What do you reckon?'

Could we afford real cream? I thought. What about some pink marshmallows to put round the top, and a packet of Amgoorie tea? But the kids would miss out on clothes from the Salvos. I said, 'I reckon we make a detour on the way back. Go past Laurie Tredrea's and I'll pawn my wedding ring.'

Liz propped like a horse. 'Really?'

'Really. Let's splash out. Just for once, let's kick up our heels.' Besides, why should I hang on to a cheap bit of trash? I'd ask for three pounds and be glad to be rid of it. Funny how you measure your life. One marriage was worth a bag of groceries, with a few spare packets of cigarettes thrown in, and enough left over for an Amscol vanilla ice cream for the kids.

'Bloody bewdy!' Liz shouted and, carried away with excitement, cuffed her eldest on the back of his head.

We reached Cox Foy's corner and went into the Relief building. Inside was dingy and the air smelt stale. We waited in the queue for the lifts. 'Shit of a place,' said Liz. The woman next to me murmured, 'You said it.' Others stood like statues, staring at the lift doors, but I saw a few give little nods. I looked at the woman beside me. She dragged her trembling fingertips over her lips, pulling her mouth sideways. Her eye was puffy, the lids swollen and purple. She held a grubby little baby to her chest, its nappy ripe.

The lift doors opened and we crowded in. Somebody pressed the button. 'Going up: ladies' underwear,' said Liz in a toffy voice. Nobody moved or looked at her. 'Shocking, shocking, shocking,' she continued defiantly, 'a mouse ran up my stocking, when he got to the top . . .' The lift doors opened and I looked out to a refugee camp. We faced a hollow echoing shabby hall, the centre partitioned off with cubicles for interviews. Hard wooden benches were bolted to the walls. Liz and I raced for a bench with some room on it. Liz got there first and scattered children along it to claim the possie.

All around were mothers with haggard, frightened faces. We were like wrecked boats washed up on a beach. The place was full of wriggling, irritable kids with runny noses, spots, and dry harsh coughs. I watched one young woman try to cover herself with a white shawl while she undid her blouse to feed her baby. Another baby cried and turned its head aside to push out the teat of its bottle. The milk was probably cold and there was nowhere to warm it. Just as there was nowhere to change a dirty nappy, except on the dusty wooden floor at your feet. There was no heating, only a few dim lights, and the air was old with despair. A part Aboriginal woman with five kids had one area to herself, a space each side of her family. I thought of Aunt Maggie, caught the woman's eye and gave her a wink. She gave me a weak, tired smile.

We settled in for the long wait. I took out my knitting. I did long scarves. Although I could cut out and sew up a shirt in the wink of an eye, I could only knit scarves. Nan had taught me how to knit one and pearl two, but never how to knit around corners. Jack climbed up next to me and opened that battered Little Golden Book, *Dumbo*, which I had rescued from my childhood. There was Mrs Jumbo, her blue hat on, a blue shawl around her neck, smiling down at her chubby baby. She put her trunk around him, even though the other animals teased him for his long ears, which dragged on the floor. Jack started to read, Anne cuddled against him, thumb in mouth, eyes soaking up the page. Jack couldn't actually read, but he told the story, moving his head from side to side as though he was. When he got to the picture of Casey Jones pulling the circus train over the bridge I made him stop.

'How many carriages?'

He paused, took a deep breath and rattled off, 'One two four sebben.'

'No. Do it again. If you're going to count, get it right. No need to rush at it like a bull at a gate. Now, with Mummy, touch each one, slowly now, one, two, three, four, five, six, seven.'

An official who looked like a wasp in a suit, his hair slicked, nasty eyes that darted over us looking for a place to sting, called a name and the woman with the bashed face jumped up in a fluster. You'd think the money came out of his own salary. You had to tell him everything, down to the colour of your shit, just to prove you had a rotten husband and no money.

I wasn't going to be like Dumbo and forgive everyone who had been unkind to me. Why should I forgive that 'uncle' who had got hold of me behind the toilet when I was only four, barely a year older than Jack? I shook my head and tried to think of something else.

I thought of Jeff's telephone call to the hospital after I had Cassie. 'Goodday.' His voice was flat. 'So, I've got another daughter.'

'Yes.' I hated his word 'I've'. All he'd done was unload his lot then run back to the army camp and his drunken mates.

'Oh. Well. That's it then. See you.' He hung up.

Maybe I never loved him, only thought I did, in those early years on the stations. A pity. In the beginning we really liked each other, and could have been friends. There had been some good times, tearing about on his bike, getting zonked at the rock 'n roll nights. But hard work, sickness, money worries, his mum's violence, separation and our other lovers had proved too much.

After waiting donkey's years, Liz and I were called from one official to another, to a third. At last, boiling with rage, we collected our pittance and hurried off. We raced around to the pawn broker's and I got one pound eight and six for my wedding ring. I blew it on a bottle of Barossa Pearl, which rode home under Cassie's pillow. We got the kids an ice cream each and hurried home to get stuck into the bottle while it was still cold.

We shoved the kids out in the back yard. I showed them my wooden spoon and warned them, 'If you hang the dog just one more time in the tree . . .'

Liz slumped into a chair and slipped off her flatties. 'Oh, that's better.'

The wine made a satisfying hiss as I opened it and, because it was an occasion, I pushed aside the Vegemite glasses in the cupboard to find the two special glasses with a strip of gold around the lip. I tilted the glasses sideways carefully so that the bubbles wouldn't froth over the top.

'Here's lookin' at you baby.' I held my glass out.

'Up yours too.'

It was Liz and me against the world. I sipped the wine and wished expensive booze didn't taste like cheap vinegar.

I looked at Liz, and said, 'How's the job?'

Liz sloshed down half a glass. 'It's dough. Pity the boss is a groper.' She paused. 'What I really mean is, pity the boss is as ugly as a horse's arse.' Liz had a weekend job as a waitress in Victor Harbor. I tried, and failed, to imagine Liz swanning about being polite to customers.

'Look,' she said, 'I got that job when a friend offered me a drive in the country. So I took some of my cakes and touted them around, to pay for the petrol. A restaurant bloke liked them. You never know. One thing led to another. Next thing I was a waitress. Half the time it's not what you know but who.'

Sure. But Liz was a genius. Anyway, what job was I supposed to do with three babies? I ran my finger around the rim of my glass and said, 'I had a job at Paterson's before I was married. I saw an ad in their window for a casual, walked in and got the job straight away.'

'Good for you. How'd it go?'

'I lasted two weeks. I sold a customer chicken wire when he ordered mosquito netting. I didn't know the difference. He went right out of his tree, threatened to remove his account, and all that. He was a friend of the boss. I got the sack. It's who you know all right.'

'Typical. Give us a refill, Pat.'

I filled her glass. Liz held it up to the light to watch the bubbles. 'You know, Pat, half your trouble is you let the blokes rule the roost. Give them half a chance and they'll carry on like they're Lord Muck.' Liz must've heard Sid last night. The walls have ears . . . 'How'd you get mixed up with a bloke like that?'

'Sid was a boarder at Jeff's mum's.' I paused and thought how I had once so admired Shirley. It was she who gave me the bitter aloes and I sat bleeding over the bucket. 'Tell 'em you tripped and fell,' Shirley called through the door. I let her do that to me and my baby twins.

I gave Liz a grim look. 'There were ten of us jammed into that little dump. Sid slept on the settee in the front room. I lived like a reffo in my own house. I paid the rent, but Shirley ruled the roost. She was Queen B. During the day she'd pamper the kids – "Come to Nanna" – and at night lock them away with me in the front room, telling me, "They're yours; you put up with it." Only Sid showed me any kindness. He brought me flowers.'

Liz leant forward, and whispered, as though a parent might be listening. 'You mean, you did it right there with Sid, in her sitting-room?'

'My sitting-room.' I looked Liz straight in the eye. 'I'll never forget the night just after I'd first left home when I was still fifteen, that she dolled me up, made up my face. I looked a million dollars. I thought she was doing it because we were mother and daughter. No way. I was pretty, and soon to marry her son. Then the feller knocked on the door, and Shirley gave me the nudge.'

Liz stared at me. 'Did you?'

I laughed. 'No. I felt sick at the thought of being a prostitute. But years later I did it for free with Sid.'

'Hang on. You were pregnant with Cassie.'

'Seven months.'

Liz squealed, and looked at me in amazement. When she could get her breath, she asked, a wicked twinkle in her eye, 'How?'

'Very carefully. And you know what? I had my first orgasm.'

'You're joking.'

'No. For real. I'd no idea we had them. Three kids, a husband' – and a scrumptious Italian hairdresser – 'and I loved it, and wanted more, lots more.'

'That's one advantage of an older man. How many years between you?'

'Fifteen.' As soon as I said it, I knew what Liz was thinking. I'd thought about it often enough. Always looking for a father to protect me, a good man to rescue me from the one I was stuck with. Trouble was, after I was hooked, Sid put away his good clothes and good manners and began to behave like a father. 'I'll tame you, if it's the last thing I do,' he'd say. If I was helpless, that drove him mad, and he hit me all the more. If I tried to be his obedient child, it brought out his cruelty. If I resisted, that made him worse. He preached at me: 'I earn the money. You do as you're bloody told. I'm the man. Who else would have you? Where else will you live, eh? Tell me that. The least you can do is show a little respect, a little gratitude that I keep you off the streets where you belong. And don't worry, if I want to throw you out, there's nothing to stop me.' The sermons were followed by some stupid test of my loyalty. 'Why don't you just do what any other wife would do? Come on, come to bed.' I knew what that meant. Sid wanted me to sleep naked. I'd always slept in a nightie, because it gave me a shield against other bodies, a shelter of privacy.

Last night Sid watched me slip my nightie on over my skirt, and then take my skirt down, like I was dressing at the beach. He saw it as a signal that I didn't want sex. How true. The fight started that Liz must've heard through the wall. Sid leapt off the bed and grabbed the shoulders of the nightie, trying to tear it apart, but the seams were too tough and the cloth bunched up. The nightie was cutting me under the arms, and I cried out.

'Shut up! Shut up!' he screamed and punched me in the stomach.

Sid grabbed my nightie and ripped it up over my head, forcing it over my crouched back and over my folded arms that were too weak to stop him. Then he rushed into the bathroom. I heard the ripping. When he came back he held up the material, cut to ribbons with his razor, which he held up, triumphant.

I don't remember much of the next ten minutes, only the smashing as I picked up a stool and trashed the bedroom, Sid backed off, arms up, bellowing at me, 'You're mad. Sick. They should lock you up.'

'No, no, no,' I screamed while I smashed the stool into the mirror. 'I'm what you want. This is what you want, isn't it? A child. A child you can abuse. A naughty child. Well, I'm that child, so you watch out.'

My eye focused again on Liz and the kitchen. Outside the kids were yelling their heads off. I took a deep breath. Liz waited, silent, watching, knowing there was more to come.

I clenched my jaw, looked down into my empty glass, and said, 'It might sound stupid to you, but when he tore up my nightie, he was killing one of my rituals.'

I looked for support from Liz. She just nodded to show she understood and, after a long silence, said, 'We've got to get you out of here.'

Bitterly I said, 'Love is just a word that drops out of people's mouths.'

Liz poured wine into my glass. 'You know that friend I told you about, you know, the one who takes me in his truck to Victor Harbor, well, he delivers to an Itie club over at Paradise. He's a mate of the owner. I'll put the hard word on him.

Never know your luck. Maybe they want a waitress or something. Nothing ventured.'

She stretched her arm right across the table and stroked my
wrist. 'Come on, Pat. It's not the end of the world. Cheer up.
Let's drink to Paradise.'

# Little Italy

*I opened my new white handbag and fished about for the key. It was my* own key. I was thrilled at the thought that Joe trusted me so much. The door opened and I stepped in. The air was stale with last night's cigarettes. I walked around the billiard table and found the light switch.

Then I surveyed my little domain. My counter, the coffee machine, the fridge, the arch through into the club room, with tables for cards, and the jukebox in the corner. My secret world.

This was the hour I gave myself. First, as I did every night, I went through the archway, into the clubroom, over to the juke box, put sixpence into the slot and pressed the buttons K 12 for old chocolate-voice Deano to sing 'It's Amore'. Singing along like mad, I waltzed through my work. My high spiky heels clicked on the lino floor. My heart was as light as a feather. I sang at the top of my voice while I fired up the cappuccino machine. Then I polished the laminex table tops, cut up two plates of mozzarella, peperoni, and salami – not in neat thin slices, the Australian way, but hacked into lumps, the right way.

Through the front window was an Australian street, drenched with a red and gold sunset, but for me the sun was sinking in the Bay of Naples, the Mediterranean burnished like copper, just liked the picture on the wall. In my imagination I flew to the high mountains of Calabria to watch the range burn with the scarlet light of the setting sun; or I was in Rome, smiling as young lovers threw coins in a fountain, a flight of pigeons clattering into the sky, startled by bells ringing out from the towers.

When the club was spick and span, I tidied my hair, wriggled my new half shift around, checked that the seams of my stockings were exactly straight, then stood proudly behind my counter to welcome the first customers. The jukebox played 'Coma Prima', and I sang in my purest Italian. Was I not Patti, who had won the music scholarship when I was nine? Not that Nan had let me go to the lessons.

The door crashed open and in strode Mario, all swagger of hips, arms held wide, carnation in his button-hole, belly leading the way, bald head gleaming, voice crying out, 'Pattericia.'

'Come sta,' I said, and fried him with my sultriest Sophia Loren smile.

Mario sailed up to the counter, reached over to grab my hand and kiss the back of my fingers. 'Bene, bene,' he cried, his wide skull bowed, the ridges of bone showing. 'Why will you not marry me?'

'My husband wouldn't like that.'

Mario stepped back, one hand tapping his heart. 'Where is this husband?' He looked all around. 'I only see me and you. A good husband would never let such a pretty wife out alone.' He tugged the red carnation from his buttonhole, kissed it, and handed it to me. Every night Mario was the first customer, and every night he proposed to me.

'Why, thank you, Mario.' I looked around, pretending I didn't know what to do with the flower, then saw his eyes pointing to my hair. I slipped the stem into my hair, just above my left ear.

Mario clapped his hands. 'Yes, left side is for not married. I do not have to kill myself tonight.'

This was my Italy. Mario, and all the rest. These were the people my family called dagos, who would knife me, or worse. The Italians were everything my family could never be: charming, exuberant, passionate, lovers of life, outrageous flirts – eyes flashing with laughter as they competed to win my smiles. I pulled the lever on the coffee machine to make Mario his first cup.

The door opened and men crowded in. The club burst into noisy life. The older men sat at the card tables and played poker, slapping down their cards. They sipped wine from coffee cups; it was illegal to sell alcohol in the club. They bet with matches and paid up later because it was against the law to gamble. The law was as much a sour puss as Nan. If it was fun, it was sinful, and the wowsers had to protect us against ourselves. Bloody do-gooders in their twin sets and pearls, double-breasted suits, nice homes. Their morals were no better than the Welfare. They were afraid of us, afraid of losing control, afraid of wine, sunshine, happiness. They used their churches and Relief to keep us in our place.

In the Italian club, however, if a vice squad cop called in, I'd offer him a coffee and chat, while the card games went on and the young bucks glared at him from around the billiard table. The cops were happy. The Italians sorted out their own fights, looked after their own. The vice cops really called in to get a coffee, to break the monotony and grab an envelope.

During the night I served drinks and food, emptied ash trays, welcomed each visitor, and every hour collected the ten shillings' fee from each gambler.

As the night wore on the club became rowdier. The more tipsy the men became, the harder they played. The three old men who sat at the corner table talked loudly of sunlight in Florence, warm days in vineyards, and nights among the olive trees. Their stories were full of light, but they were night people, not leaving until two or three in the morning, when I would shoo them out so I could be home before Sid left for the bakery at four.

I never told the Italians where I came from. My slum life was as much a secret from them as my Italian life was kept from Sid. At Carrington Street I was abused and despised. In the club I was adored and given respect. The flirtation was mostly a ritual game. Occasionally, the men gave me looks that meant a lot more than they should. But I turned those shafts aside, laughing.

Except for Raphaelo. He was seventeen years, a virgin for sure, with puppy-dog eyes and beautiful long eye-lashes. Raphaelo hung around my counter, his soft eyes pleading, his face scowling and sulking when I teased the older men. Raphaelo was as weak as piss and twice as salty, but I fell for him. I couldn't quite conceal the glances I gave him. Whenever he noticed, his face flamed, he clenched his fists and turned his back to me to hide the blushes. I adored him just for adoring me. There's nothing like the exquisite anguish of unspoken love. If I didn't watch my step, I'd be dragging Raphaelo into the tomato garden behind the club and deflowering him.

Most nights, Joe, the boss, called in. I would have worked my fingers to the bone for him. The very first night, after we had finished, he took me in his car to Hindley Street, and we ate at an Italian restaurant. My eyes must've been as wide as dinner plates. Here I was in Hindley Street, the place Nan had drummed into me I should never go. The restaurant was classy, the table loaded with dishes of lobster, crusty bread, salads in oil, black and green olives, bottles of champagne. I had heard of these things but never seen them. I was bewildered by the atmosphere, the strange speech, the gaiety, the intensity of enjoyment. I was the foreigner and, if Joe hadn't interpreted what was said, I wouldn't have had a clue. I sat quietly because I didn't know what to say. Instead I gave the men shy smiles. My head was dizzy with champagne, but I would have been drunk just on the excitement, the strange language, the exotic foods.

As we left, Joe said to me, 'The men like you.' Then, with a smile, 'You never interrupted.' As he held open the car door for me he said, 'You did well tonight. I think you are an attraction at the club.' His words rang in my ears. How long since somebody had praised me? I kept repeating his words in my head as we drove to Carrington Street. I got Joe to drop me off on the Pulteney Street corner.

Whenever Joe called into the club, as he did this night, Raphaelo would shrink away into a corner and glare at him. Joe and I got our heads together and talked about the takings from the till, orders for food and wine, the behaviour of the men, any problems with the equipment. Joe treated me like a partner, took my suggestions seriously, and thereby gave me the highest respect I had ever received. He let me run the club.

I kept careful records, writing myself little notes which I kept in my handbag. When I opened it that night, Joe must've seen the card.

'What's this?'

I blushed, and quickly pushed the card deeper into the handbag. 'Nothing.'

Joe grinned and wrestled the card out. He opened it. 'You are twenty-one? When?'

'Today?'

'Ha. That is wonderful. And still you come to work. No party?'

If only he knew. There was just a card from Liz, and Aunty Elsie called in; the dearest aunt, who gave me coloured trinkets when I was a kid, and came all the way down from Queensland just to see me on my twenty-first.

Joe hurried over to the fridge, reached right to the back and took out a bottle of champagne. He held it aloft, and called out, 'A celebration. Patti is twenty-one today.'

Men crowded around, slapped me on the back, pinched my bum, laughed, then burst into song, 'Happy birthday to you . . .' When they had finished they gave me three cheers. Joe handed me a coffee cup of champagne, and cried out, 'Speech. Speech!' the cry taken up by the crowd.

I blinked at the faces, somewhere in the background the jukebox played 'It's now or never' and, not knowing what to say, I blurted out, 'It's not coming to work, coming here to you. It's like coming home to a whole street full of friends. I wish I was born an Italian.' Then I burst into tears.

# On the run

*At the same time as I tried to create an independent life through my job* at the Italian club, Sid increased his bashings. Where could I run? I didn't have enough money, yet, to be free of a man; Nan was dead; Shirley was an impossible bully. The most urgent problem of my life – a safe place to live – had no solution. My only friend, Liz, let me shelter in her house on the nights Sid handed out maniacal beatings, but there wasn't enough room for all our kids. Also, her taxi-driver boyfriend didn't like us cluttering up the place. Liz had got him to the stage where he was just about ready to propose and make an honest woman of her, respectable enough for her parents to speak to her again. I didn't want to mess up her chances.

One night I heard on the news that a body, washed up six months earlier on St Kilda beach, had been identified. It was my father. Actually, it wasn't a body, just some bones and stuff, because the crabs and fish had eaten most of it. None of my relatives had told me about the discovery. That convinced me it was a waste of time asking for help from them. And there was no way I could survive on the money from Relief. The people who made the rules for Welfare must've had no idea about the real world I lived in.

Then I discovered I was pregnant with Number Four. Although I'd aborted my twins as a last attempt to save my marriage, the backyard abortion was so terrifying that I couldn't face the thought of it. I'd heard of the women who died, and the babies who survived with dreadful deformities. The night I told Sid that I was pregnant, he went on a rampage, and even though I put my body between him and the kids, he clubbed Jack with a broom.

I packed a case, grabbed the kids and fled into the night. I was numb with despair and hopelessness. I couldn't even cry. Each time I tried to make a free life, I ended up a slave again. At twenty-two I was walking the streets with my babies, just as Nan had taken me out in a pram at night to protect me from my father.

There was only one place I could think of to run. I phoned Jeff, who had a place in West Street, Brompton, a few streets away from Pickering Street. I went back to him, who was driving taxis again since he left the army. Jeff took me in, on condition. I was to share the house, but he'd give me no money to look after the kids.

That worked fine for a little while, but the kids grew out of clothes and into measles, mumps and chicken pox faster than I could keep up with them. I had put a roof over our heads but run out of money. I slept with Jeff as a way of keeping the house; also, as an adult woman, I needed to feel loved and cuddled. I was giving out to the kids night and day, and I needed to have someone show affection to me. And, strangely, considering all the bad things between us, there was still a bond between Jeff and me. It was almost a friendship; disturbing, regretful, sad, longing, guilty; but there. It was good for us both that he was out so much driving the taxis. I must admit, I got pretty hot under the collar at the thought of Jeff wolfing down pies and pasties for lunch each day while I tried to scrape together something the kids would eat.

Nevertheless, Jeff refused to supply money, except for an occasional ten shilling or pound note, especially to a wife pregnant with some other bloke's child. Jeff insisted that if I was to stay in the house I have a blood test to prove the baby wasn't his. On the day when I had no money to buy tea for the kids, I phoned the only person I could think of. Sid. So much for my childhood fantasies of being Pegasus.

Sid hid a pound note under the gas box. One night we arranged to meet, and he handed two pounds over the back fence. I burst into tears. Then Sid said, 'Come back to me. We can't go on like this. Look. I won't hurt you or the kids. Promise. I've turned over a new leaf. Just come back. I want my kid with me where I can know he's got food and decent clothes.' Something fell on my head from the tree. I reached up and touched a squashy thing with lots of hard legs. I screamed in revulsion and terror, wildly beating my hair. Sid knocked it off. A huge black spider fell to the ground and dragged itself sideways, legs broken. It was an omen.

I returned to Sid, but in a new house in Croydon, knowing I'd get my head bashed in. But how else was I going to feed my children? The Welfare Relief was never enough. Sid was as sweet as pie for a few weeks. Then the old rages began. He wanted me to divorce Jeff. Then Sid's son, my fourth child, was born. It was a boy. I named him Ryan, my dead father's middle name. The name Ryan gave me some sort of history, some thin thread connecting me to the world. I hadn't just fallen from the sky.

But the sky had well and truly fallen on me. I had an ulcer, a kidney infection, and my weight was down to seven stone. My body was running on empty. At twenty-two years of age I had four kids under school age. I loved my children, but the thought of another one was too horrible for words. If a period was late, I dreamed of suicide. I walked the streets of Hindmarsh at night, my children padding along at my side or jammed in the pram. In the darkness we visited the Port Road playground and went down the slide or I sat Ryan in my lap, on the old wooden swing, and sang all the nursery rhymes. 'Hidey, hidey ho, the great big elephant is so slow.' My song soothed me, the gentle swinging rocked me into a trance of comfort. If it rained, we sheltered in the rotunda where I had played when truanting from primary school, just nine years before.

What had happened to all the dreams of my childhood? That other Patti, a spell cast upon her, slept somewhere deep in a cave of my mind, the doorway blocked by wild bushes of poisonous thorns that grew higher and thicker as each year passed. Each time I destroyed a part of myself, another thorn bush grew. I knew the other Patti was alive, waiting to be freed. Only if I gave up would Patti die, breathe out her last breath.

Sid wanted me to cry. I watched his face when he hit me. He wanted to break my spirit, just as Nan tried to, just as Shirley did. I was the wild animal which must be tamed. Why? They lived in rage at their own wasted lives. They beat me because they were driven crazy by the terror that I might do what they had failed to do. They beat me so that my screams drowned the voices in their own heads. They had to make me what they needed me to be: the obedient child who surrendered to their power, even to their right to bash her for grovelling, who surrendered up her dreams just as they had done.

Nan had taught me that love was always hurt and trouble. Love meant always playing a part to be safe. Love meant becoming what pleased somebody else. Love meant always walking in fear of disapproval. Love meant being good to the one who abused you, learning to accept cruelty as your lot in life. No way, I thought, swinging backwards and forwards on the swing in the dark. No way, I cried inside.

To resist meant an endless circle of beatings. To resist meant isolation, being driven out into the darkness. I ground my teeth. To quieten the endless thoughts that went round and round, I sang quietly to my baby as we swung backwards and forwards under the stars. 'Andy Pandy, come out to play, round and round the houses . . .'

My confidence was almost gone. Whichever way I turned there seemed no way out. If I gave in, they would make me into a rubbish bin. If I fought on, and insisted on being myself, I was at the mercy of my own mind. To survive I had to turn my heart to stone. Either way, by their power, or at my own hands, I might as well be dead.

The recurrent nightmare, in its own ghastly way, kept me going, even if it was just from sheer terror. In my sleep, I turned the corner and saw the verandah posts of Number 37. I knew with certainty what I would find when I opened the front door, and entered the room and went to the coffin. I woke in terror, sitting up in the dark, trembling at the monstrous, ghastly painted face.

The only way I knew to keep going was to make myself take

the next step, put my body between my children and violence. If I loved them hard enough, with a love more strong than all the hatred, if my will was so powerful, I might yet win, whatever winning meant. If anything, to win was to be unconquered in my kind love. And that was still possible. I had some strength to face and overcome them, because I had a secret.

Despite all the cruelties, all the debasements, threats, sermons, tests of love, tests of loyalty, grief and shame, I had known pure, overwhelming, sweet love. When my first child was born and I held his slippery little body I felt a rush that swept through me like a wave. My baby's face was like a squashed prune, his little legs were bowed like a monkey's, but he lay squalling in my arms, the most beautiful thing I'd ever seen. I called him Jack.

He was my first, and I had gone into labour not knowing how he came out. Nobody had told me. Did he come out my bum? When I saw the thick tube coming out of him, I panicked. 'What's wrong with him?' I asked the nurse and she stared at me, then began to explain everything. She cut the cord, and told me how to dab some meths on it. She sent a lady in to show me how to bath the baby, how to hold him behind the head. He squealed and fought not to be washed. From day one Jack fought me.

I fed my baby and kidded myself he looked into my eyes and knew who I was while he was at my breast. He was a mystery, a wonder, a fragile treasure. I held my baby in awe. He was all my childhood dreams, and somehow I had to save him from the horrors of the world. As I looked down into his eyes, I felt that I held the greatest treasure in the world. In sudden terror I would clutch him tightly to me. So it was with each baby. That vision of love never forsook me. I felt them grow inside me. I felt their little kicks. I took them to bed, whispering, 'There's plenty of room.'

None of the fathers came to the hospital. They were too busy. The love for my children kept me going: all the hopes and possibilities that they would have a better life than mine. When one of my kids gave me a cuddle, I felt like a soldier in the trenches who'd suddenly got a love letter from home: a gift to be prized, turned over in the mind time and time again. I lived in a battlefield of love. I was a pathetic refugee pushing my pram load of kids among the craters.

Then came the day Sid changed jobs to drive a truck. He scraped up enough money to put a deposit on a new home in Tea Tree Gully. He had good money coming in, and he promised we could start a new life in our new house. The kids would have a real home, the best they'd ever seen, brand spanking new, with a great back yard. He even let the kids climb up in the truck and sit in his seat, provided they didn't touch anything.

For me, Sid promised a garden for fresh vegetables and flowers; a new kitchen with a servery dividing it from the dining area; an inside toilet that flushed; unlimited hot water; and a beautiful view of the city. And we could never tell what handy little surprises might fall off the back of a truck.

I didn't believe him, but I needed to. I had stuck it out in the hope that I could love him into submission, shame him into behaving like a human being. It was hard, however, to get out of my mind the image of Sid chaining up the dog and kicking it mercilessly – like my father kicking Jessie. Those bad memories kept replaying in my mind. Still, the dog got his revenge one day Sid was bashing me, and I slammed the door so it caught Sid's hand and cut off the top joint of his little finger. Quick as a flash, the dog leapt on the bit of finger and ate it.

Despite all the broken promises, I had to believe that reform was possible. Sid did have his good side. I remembered the night he brought Cassie to the Italian club. He had bathed her, dressed her in the sailor frock, and tied up her hair in ribbons so her little ears stuck out.

'Look, Patti, she took her first steps tonight.' Sid grinned with pride in himself and in Cassie as he put her on the floor and said, 'Go to Mummy.' Cassie held out her arms and toddled towards me, lifted one foot too high, flapped her wings and plomped down on her bottom. I swept her up in my arms and the Italian men cheered and shook Sid's hands, not knowing Cassie was Jeff's child. Sid beamed and Raphaelo roasted him slowly on a spit in hell.

The one or two other times Sid had called in, much to my

embarrassment he had worn a T-shirt to show his muscles to the Italian men. A bit like sending a gunboat up the enemy's river.

Because no other self-deception was plausible, I kidded myself I could manage the new life with Sid. He would be out in his truck a lot of the time. There was one glint of hope. Sid had been brought up by a cruel mother. He hated and feared her. He also wanted, craved her acceptance. He wanted to be somebody in her eyes, and so he forced himself to be nice to her. Maybe, if I was lucky, he would need me that much.

At first, for a few weeks, life was good. I tested out the new stove, started a garden, loving the slide of the spade into damp soil. I got all hot and sweaty, then soaked in long steaming bubble baths, the water so hot I turned red as a lobster. My fingers and toes became wrinkled and soft, and I was dizzy from pleasure.

Soon, however, I regretted that our house was on a huge block at the end of the street, with no neighbours to hear my screams. The beatings were more vicious. He beat me at night, lining the children up in the hallway to watch. 'Cry, fuck you! Why won't you cry?' The children were sick with fear.

I appealed to Jeff for help. He brought his girlfriend out to the house, gloated at my appearance, for I was a washed-out, skinny frump, and said, 'You made your bed, now lie in it.' Sid, of course, put on airs and graces, and was the perfect host. The men got on like a house on fire. Who could believe Mr Innocent would give me a hiding as soon as the visitors were out of earshot?

My stomach was in knots each evening when Sid came home. As soon as I heard the truck I grew frantic that the house and children were not perfect. I'd give the children a last hurried inspection, shut in a bedroom anyone who was testy, race around straightening up the lounge pillows, and stand with my hands clasped until my knuckles were white. As soon as he came in, he'd look for some fault. The tiniest mistake and he would explode.

My ulcer pains increased. One night I vomited blood, and bent double. 'Stand up straight, damn you.' I couldn't. 'Then I'll have to hit you up straight.' On one of the awful Saturdays when we had to go and watch him umpire junior football, I nearly killed myself. We were going past the Greenacres shopping centre, when one of the kids began to grizzle. Sid just lashed back with his hand. I yelled. He promised to get me when we were home. I opened the door to throw myself out, but he grabbed me and held me in.

My head was hot with despair and fear. My brain could think of no way out. I had nowhere to run, no money of my own. I was sick for so long I lost my job at the Italian club.

I tried pitiful attempts at reconciliation with my mother. She brought some second-hand clothes for my kids, and posed for photos with the babies, her face scowling. I had taken elocution lessons to imitate her proper speech. We both sickened at the pretence. I was only acceptable on her terms.

Then, always restless, always needing a new start, never able to commit himself to anything, Sid moved again, to a house built on a steep hill at Banksia Park, about twenty kilometres northeast of the city.

This time, by a wild stroke of good fortune, I had a protector. Hairylegs had at last made an honest woman of herself, married her ballroom dancer and, by a miracle, lived just a few streets away in a house almost hidden by masses of rose bushes. By tying the knot, Liz was accepted back into her mother's life.

Like Nan, who took me to safety at Aunty Jean's, I fled with my kids to Liz's. My eldest struggled along with the suitcase almost as big as himself.

Another child was on the way, the fifth. This time nobody demanded a blood test to prove it was his. When my labour started, as with all my births, I got myself to hospital on my own.

During the pregnancy I developed an abscess on my bum. I was too scared to show it to the doctor in case he put me into hospital and so separated me from the children. The abscess grew to be as big as the top of a cup and went deep inside. When my labour started I was in so much pain I had to lie on my stomach in the taxi to the hospital. The doctor took one look at me and said, 'You poor little bugger.'

The day after Pepe's birth I had the operation to dig out the growth. The hole was inches deep, right where I sat. That night I was crying because I was afraid for my children. Sid's mother visited and said, 'Stop snivelling. Here. I've brought you a strawberry tart. It cost me one and threepence. I hope you enjoy it. You're not indispensable you know. If you died tomorrow, it wouldn't matter. The children can manage without you. They always do. There's plenty of families in a far worse state, you know.' Then she took Pepe away home. 'Sid has a woman to take care of him. The baby'll be well looked after. And you are in no state to nurse him. You can't even sit up.' I had to lie there and watch another woman hold my baby, then carry him away. I imagined the baby crying for his mother, and some other woman holding him, giving him a bottle. My mind was filled with hatred and outrage, a wild desire to get my baby back.

Next morning I signed myself out of hospital. While the nurse helped me hobble to the taxi, I asked her, 'What does "indispensable" mean?'

I arrived home unexpectedly by taxi, and dragged myself inside, looking like Death. To my enormous relief, Sid wasn't there. I snatched my baby from the young woman, who gave me a stupid, guilty grin. Manic with stress, I tried to breast feed Pepe, but the milk wouldn't come and there was an awful tension between us.

When Sid arrived home from the pub, he was amazed and angry to see me. 'Why didn't you let me know?' I was holding Pepe with my back to the floor-to-ceiling window that looked out over the city. When Sid hit me, I was flung against the window, broke through and fell down into the yard beneath, still clutching Pepe to my chest.

Next day, when Sid was gone, Liz helped me escape to the Semaphore Caravan Park. We had no car and when Eddy, the man who read the gas meter, came into the yard, I begged him for help. He put us in his car. Four children sat bug-eyed in the back seat, Pepe on my lap. I would rather live in some horrible little caravan, with shared toilets, and only Relief money, than stay another minute with Sid. I didn't care what life was like, as long as it was without him. There was no way he could trace me to a caravan park. For the first night in years, I would sleep in peace.

Sid had sniffed me out within three days. When I had just

stopped jumping at every strange sound, Sid pulled open the caravan door. Behind him I saw Liz, pleading with her eyes. In that fleeting glance a friendship was damaged.

Oh, Liz, how could you? What did he say to make you? Then, I remember how believable he was in his tears, grovelling, and false promises.

As soon as he had got me home and taken his eyes off me, I escaped again. On the run, I went to a cottage in St Peters, full of Sid's own relatives. I surrounded myself and my children with an armour of people. Sid moved in, sleeping in the next room. 'Don't leave me. I'll do anything you want,' he pleaded. I went out and picked up four boyfriends, the biggest I could find, and kept them in turn beside me and the children.

This insanity could not last. If I couldn't find a permanently safe place, I'd be dead. The only way out that I could think of, in my exhaustion and fear, was another man. Another turn of the wheel. Crazy. Hopeless. Who would take on a clapped out wreck with five kids?

# The Latin Quarter

*Some saint in heaven must have interceded for me, because it was not* a man, but a woman, who came into my life. She was called Charmaine. She was a soft woman, blonde out of a bottle like me, but with bigger boobs. Her husband had just left her for another woman, and she proved to be not all soft, but part animal, like all of us. Charmaine was on the lookout for a place to share, and we had known each other for years, without making real contact. Charmaine was Jeff's sister in law.

We decided to try life without husbands, without pressures. It was a new way of living for us. Charmaine found a house on South Road, and I pinched a sign off a Stobie pole: 'This way to the Telethon House of Hope'. I painted arrows along South Road to our place.

We were like sisters, sharing all our secrets. Charmaine's real mother had died in childbirth during a backyard abortion. Charmaine had taken Shirley as her own mum, and got hell in return. Charmaine was good for me, for whom every little thing mattered. She just said, 'What the fuck.' 'I love you, Patti,' she said, 'because you say it as you see it.' We shared the same big bed, in a room away from all the kids. If one of us brought a man home, the other looked after the kids through the night. We did each other favours, like I'd bash up her husband's girlfriends. Eternal friendship was sealed the morning after Charmaine had sent a man on his way. She drifted into the room where I lay in our bed, and said wearily, 'Can I borrow the batteries out of your vibrator? Mine's as dead as a dodo.'

152

Life with Charmaine gave me a chance to do my thing at the Latin Quarter, in Hindley Street. Adelaide only had one Hindley Street at night. It was spangles and glitter, beautiful clothes, laughter, music, the aromas of coffee, spaghetti, steaks; the cries of people greeting friends; the dazzle of cinemas, nightclubs, restaurants. In the swirl of people, you checked out the faces and clothes – not in case they were going to knife you, but because Hindley Street made us all a great big family. There were all kinds, from Billy Boggs out with his family for a night at Wests Theatre to dapper Donny Dunstan with some international big-wig. Where else to find excellent food and real entertainment? Doctor Charter was there with his cheque book hanging out of his hip pocket and two boys in tow. So was Christine the Contortionist, who bought the Baygenew Night Club – the strip joint. Drag queens floated along like bright comets in their stunning outfits we'd give our eye-teeth to wear. The air was filled with happy voices calling out in Italian, Greek, Yugoslav or some other lingo.

These were the golden years of the nightclubs. The Paprika Club was up steep, scary steps, and hard to climb in high heels. At the top of the stairs it was a Humphrey Bogart movie scene: palm trees, the stage brassy with the band and a trio of girls belting out, 'It was an itsy bitsy teeny weeny yellow polka dot bikini'. Waiters glided past with silver trays. Life was a spangle of diamonds, sequins, sex, laughter, seduction and happiness.

I worked as a hostess in the Latin Quarter Club, opposite the Baygenew. The Latin Quarter was plush, with red velvet curtains on the back of the stage and over the cloak room where I hung guests' coats.

'Good evening, sir, madam,' I said slinking up to the guests. I wore a long black skirt, split right up one thigh, a shimmering top glinting with sequins, and a tailor-cut jacket. My hair was Marilyn Monroe blonde, immaculately set by Nilia, the Italian hairdresser. I weighed eight stone, and reckoned I looked the ants pants. I lived on Duramine weight tablets, and never ate. Skinny was beautiful, although the tablets gave me palpitations. My make-up was no longer from Coles. With the tips left for me on the tables, I shopped at David Jones.

I was the hostess with the mostest. 'Hello, Patti. Nice to see you.'

'Good to see you again too. Your table is ready. This way, please.'

I'd settle them down, hand them the menu, light their cigarettes, spoil them rotten but not make too much fuss.

The Latin American band – maracas, guitar, piano, drums, clarinet – played not just for entertainment but for dancing. The polished wooden floor clattered and shushed to feet doing the Samba, Rhumba, fox-trot and swing.

Champagne was served in cups because of the wowser liquor laws. As the night wore on, I saw society dames turn into fuckwits. There were beaut fights among jealous rivals, the loser sliding on his back across the dance floor to crash into the stage. The men loved me to death. They flaked out with their faces on the table cloth, were carted out by the bouncers and, if anyone mauled me, Sandra, the manager, bounced them.

Clark from Myers Menswear fell for me. He was middle-aged, immaculate in his tailor-cut suit, grey hair and pencil-thin moustache. He lit my Kool filter cigarettes, drowned me in champagne, and when we danced the people stood back to watch as we flew around the floor.

Clark paid for the kids' clothes, groceries, and doctor's bills when the kids got whooping cough. I gave him sex. It was a strange feeling as I glided into the borderland world of mistresses and prostitutes.

Clark drank heavily. Which man didn't? When drunk he was violent, and my flesh crawled because his slurred voice and bad breath reminded me of my father and Sid. One night he got sloshed at the Latin Quarter and said in a loud, aggressive voice, in front of all the others, 'Call yourself a lady, Patti. You're just another prostitute.' I slapped him, and when Sandra threw him out the door, I followed and threw him out of my life.

I went home in a daze. I had done it. I had actually thrown a man out. The sense of power was like being drunk on French champagne. For the first time I had the feeling I could run my life. Trouble was, I was pregnant. Not to Clark, but to Eddy the gasman, who had driven me away from Sid, taken me to the

Semaphore caravan park, and moved me again when I was in trouble.

# *Abortion*

*I spread a single-bed sheet over the kitchen table, and tugged it this* way and that until it was exactly square on all sides. 'If you're going to do a job, do it properly first time.' Would I never get Nan's voice out of my head? Moving like a robot, I went to the sink and took two bath towels from the top of the pile. I could feel myself beginning to float away, as though I was a ghost standing in the room, watching. Frightened, I pushed my face into the cool towels, just brought in from the clothes line. They smelt like winter's wind and, in my mind's eye, I saw a little girl running down Pickering Street. She carried her beach bucket and spade and raced as fast as her chubby legs would carry her to find the end of the rainbow. With a great sigh, I took my face out of the towels and went to the table. I unfolded the towels and smoothed them flat on the sheet, where my hips would be. Then I positioned the pillow so it would raise my pelvis.

'For heaven's sake, stop fussing,' said Shirley. 'She won't be here for ages yet.' She leaned forward to the baby's high chair and aimed another teaspoon of Heinz apple jelly at Pepe's mouth. He twisted his head aside and clamped his jaws. 'You little bugger.' Shirley waved the spoon past his face and crooned, 'Here comes the aeroplane, vrrrooom.' Pepe glared at her and swatted at the spoon. I resented Shirley's presence, but she was the go-between for the abortionist. And I felt sorry for her. Shirley had cancer of the pancreas.

Along the head of the table I carefully lined up a new cake of velvet soap; a bottle of Solyptol disinfectant; the green hand basin for boiling water; and the bottle of gin. I heard Cassie push her doll's pram past the window. Ryan took his Matchbox racing car under the table and sat in his new cubby, created by the hanging sheet. He looked out with big eyes, and absentmindedly put the car in his mouth to suck it.

'The bath will be ready,' I said, and looked up at the clock. Ten o'clock. One hour to go.

Inside the bathroom, with the door locked, I leant on the hand basin and looked at myself in the mirror. It was somebody else who stared back: skin like raw dough, red puffy eyes, narrow lips. For an instant I glimpsed my dead face beneath the living, and jumped away from the mirror, shaking all over. Nobody would see the tears running down my cheeks. 'Don't you let me see you cry in my house,' my mother commanded the day I gathered the courage to return to her place.

This was supposed to be my wedding day. By rights, at this exact time, I should have been nervously getting ready for the taxi to take me to the church. Eddy, the gasman, who was so kind in helping me get away from Sid, had fallen in love with me – even with this clapped out twenty-five-year-old with five kids. He had proposed. Eddy was tall, good looking, and I felt such gratitude for his goodness to me that, as a special favour, I let him make love to me without using a contraceptive.

Besides, even with all I knew about men, and life, I thought that marriage to a sweet, thoughtful man would give me the kind of secure, peaceful, life I really needed after so many years of trauma. Hairylegs had done it. She had found her ballroom dancer, an older man who, after a few rough patches, was devoted. Liz also had a new home, her rose garden, and the best prize: she had got her mum and dad back. She was a daughter in a family; not an outcast to be walked past as though she was invisible. Liz was no longer a scapegoat for other people's disappointment.

The good life with Charmaine was fun. Clark from Menswear, however, had shown me another side of being the gay divorcee. What would I do in a few years' time when I turned thirty, and was past it? End up like Shirley? No thanks. Eddy offered me what I had sought for years. Kindness, rest from the heartaches and violence, stability, respectability, and maybe my mum.

Then, one afternoon, in a tizz of wedding preparations, I raced around to my bridesmaid's house to show her a new colour of nail polish which went beautifully with the dresses. Eddy's white Valiant, with its gleaming fish tails and spotless doors that must never be slammed, was parked outside. I walked in, found them, smashed Leah, turned on Eddy and king hit him. He snarled at me from the floor, 'Bitch. You can forget the wedding.' He looked at my stomach. 'And you might as well get rid of that. Who'd want your bloody baby?' Stupid with rage and grief, I contacted the abortionist.

Instead of walking down the aisle, I slowly lowered myself into the deep bath, so hot it made me gasp. I lay there and thought of the horror of contacting my mother and her children: my half brother and half sisters. Then there were all the relatives and friends who had received wedding invitations. They were pretty white invitation cards with scalloped edges and a raised picture of a bride and groom standing under an arch of flowers. I spent a fortune on them but didn't care. They were my last hope of respectability. More than anything in the world, probably even more than marriage, I wanted my mum. She represented what my step-brother and sister had – a family, a home to call in on, where I could sit and gossip over hot scones and cups of tea, where the kids would know that Nanna always had a little treat. I opened my eyes and stared down at my pink belly washed over with miniature waves.

Barbara's taxi arrived just before eleven. The abortionist, with her black bag, was a familiar figure in many suburbs.

I was ready in my nightie and dressing-gown. The kettle steamed on the stove. I listened to Barbara's footsteps crunch on the gravel path, and then the knock on the door. I opened the door and the first thing I saw was her big black bag. My other abortion had been done with drugs. What has she got in there to use on me? Knitting needles? Coat hangers?

'Come in, Barbara.' She was dressed in a pink floral dress with bright blue buttons. Her hair was tied back tightly in a bun.

She examined the kitchen. 'Where are the children?'

'In the lounge-room with Shirley. If they get restless, she'll take them outside to hunt for snails and have snail races. Jack and Blondie don't get home from school until half-past three.'

'That's no worry. We'll be finished in three quarters of an hour.' Barbara dumped her bag on the floor near the table and looked at the kettle. 'How about a cup of tea first?'

Barbara checked that the kitchen door was firmly shut and made herself at home by dragging a chair back to table and leaning her elbows on the sheet. I took two cups from the sideboard and Barbara said, 'Just one sugar and no milk. Don't bother to make yourself one. Your cup is for the gin, mixed with hot water.'

I turned to her and she shrugged. 'Gin makes you bleed more.'

She looked at my left hand and narrowed her eyes. Slowly I twisted the diamond engagement ring off my finger. It was my Italian ring – kept to reassure me – the only thing of value I had left. Barbara took it and held it to the light. Worth four hundred pounds, it should get enough at the pawn shop for her fee, one hundred pounds.

When the tea was drawn Barbara took a couple of noisy slurps, gave a long sigh and said, 'Well, up you hop.'

I took off my dressing gown and hung it over the back of a chair. Then I climbed up awkwardly on to the table, feeling stupid and afraid. The laminex table top was cold through the sheet. I lay on my back and stared up at the old brown strip of fly paper hanging from the light cord. I counted ten dead flies stuck to it.

Barbara was at my side. 'Up with your nightie. Good girl. Now, knees up Mother Brown, and wriggle a bit more on the pillow. Whoa, stop, that's right.'

My legs began to shake. Barbara put her hands firmly on my knees and held them still. 'It's all right sweetie, we'll get you through.'

She bent down and took things from her bag. I heard something rattle over at the sink. I closed my eyes tightly and began to pray. Dear God, please don't let her mutilate me. I had no idea what was going to happen, and in a panic wanted to tell her to get it over with quickly. But I remained silent.

159

'Before I do anything to you, why do you want to go through with this? Have you thought it through?'

My voice surprised me with its harshness, 'He said he didn't want it, and he called off the wedding.' I suddenly knew it was the shame of powerlessness, more than the failed wedding or any other thing, that I hated.

Barbara nodded, and said, 'I'll just disinfect these things, and we'll get down to business.'

I opened my eyes and saw her pink dress. In a dry voice, tense with terror, I asked, 'What are you going to do?'

'I'm going to do it with a douche.'

I had no idea what she meant.

'I will put a little tube inside and at the end is a nozzle. The nozzle goes right up against your uterus and I squeeze warm water down the tube with this rubber bulb.' She waved a black bulb over my eyes, just like the bulb on the hairdresser's sprayer. 'See. That's all. Simple. It perforates your uterus and that gets things started.'

Then Barbara stood by my knees. 'Just a bit wider, dear, you're too tense. How far gone are you? Three months.' She tut-tutted with her tongue. 'I don't like it. Two and a half months is my usual limit.'

I felt her open me and I gagged. Hot, acidic vomit was in my mouth and I swallowed desperately to get it back down.

'You'll get a little pain like a period pain while I prep you.' Then something hard went into me and I felt a sharp jab of pain. 'This is the part I hate,' muttered Barbara. 'If one bubble of air gets in, it could kill you.'

Oh God! She blasted a hole in the wall of my womb. I heard somebody scream. 'Don't move,' she hissed at me, and there was another screaming pain.

'Right. Rest a minute, dear. It's going well. All things being equal, you should go into labour later tonight and lose the baby soon afterwards.'

I tried to speak, but my lips were stuck together. I swallowed once or twice, licked my lips, and asked, 'What if things aren't all equal?'

'Then you'll haemorrhage. If that happens, you get yourself

160

to hospital quick smart and don't mention my name to anyone. Now, that's the prep done. Let's get down to work and have this over and done with.'

At eight o'clock that night we were in the lounge watching television when there was a ferocious battering at the front door. I heard Sid's voice, drunk, yelling, 'Let me in, you bitch. I know you're there.'

'Quick, Shirley, run and check the back door's locked.'

The children, lying in their pyjamas on the floor, looked up at me with fearful eyes. Cassie whimpered, ran over, pushed her face into my lap and wrapped her arms around my legs. That started the others, who began to howl. Even Jack, who was six, had tears in his eyes.

'Shut up!' I snapped. 'I want to hear what he's doing.'

Sid kicked and bashed at the door. 'Slut! This time I'm going to kill you.'

Shirley came back and stood white-faced. Something metallic was being dragged to the front door. I pushed Cassie away, rose unsteadily to my feet and stood facing the door. In as brave a voice as I could manage, I called out, 'Just piss off, Sid. You're not wanted here.'

Slowly, as in a dream, the glass of the skylight above the door exploded and showered down towards me, so slowly it seemed to hang in the air. Then glass brushed my face and shattered all around me. Sid's face, like a ghastly apparition, pushed through the skylight and his whole body slid through like a thick reptile. He dropped and crouched, his hands bloodied, glass crunching under his boots. He leapt past me and with a tremendous blow of his fist bashed Shirley in the face. She crashed back against the wall, blood flowing from her mouth and slumped down to the floor.

He turned to me. I heard the children screaming as he hit and I fell. A great gush of hot blood burst from me and flooded the floor between my legs. Sid stood above me, and clenched his fist to punch downwards. I was completely helpless. My belly shuddered as it pushed the baby out. The air was filled with confused cries. I shut my eyes for the punch. Nothing.

Sid was wrestling with the door. He looked back wildly at the spreading pool of blood. There was cold air on my face and he was gone.

I rolled over on my side and saw Jack, his arms rigid as sticks. Behind him cowered the other children, their eyes on the spreading pool of blood. I whispered to Jack, 'Run to the phone box and call the police. Remember what Mummy's taught you. Run, Jack, run.'

# Somewhere,
## over the bloody rainbow

*After that abortion I fell into a habit of fretting over every little thing.* The only solace was the bottle of pills. I had a sort of freedom, with no husband, no beatings, no knots in the stomach when it was time for the man to come home. But my moods were all over the place like a mad woman's spit. One minute I'd find myself at the sink, scrubbing away at a saucepan, and merrily singing along with the radio – 'We all live in a yellow submarine' – then a blasted advertisement jingle, say for Louie the Fly, would sneak into my brain and keep playing on and on, driving me nuts.

If I went to the shop, I had to have a list, which I worried over as I wrote it. Could I afford sugar, were loin chops too expensive this week, we were almost out of toilet paper, and should I get four rolls or six? Six would be better. If the cupboards looked full, I felt more secure. Then, at the shop, I couldn't find my list. I'd forgotten to bring it. I'd stand in the aisle of the supermarket in panic, my head dizzy with fear and despair, then I'd leave the shopping trolley in the aisle and run home with no shopping done.

After years of brutality and anxiety, I was fearful of losing control of any detail. My perfectionism drove the kids crazy. More and more I ran their lives as though they were in the army. The harder I tried to be the perfect mother, the worse I behaved. I screamed at them for things that sometimes really didn't matter, then crawled away to my bed where I lay and felt sick with shame.

Why couldn't I let go, just let things be? I nagged myself, and everybody else. It only made us miserable, and I hated myself. I had to do something or I'd end up in the loony bin, like my father.

I forced myself to go out with men, to have a good time. But they pissed me off. I had to doll up, be the brilliant woman of their fantasies. They'd get sloshed, belch at the restaurant table, pick their teeth and be complete yobbos. They didn't ask, or even think, about my feelings.

For years I had battled to escape my childhood, to find security and happiness out there, somewhere, over the bloody rainbow. Wherever that was, it was miles from where I lived.

Lying on my bed, blinds down, door shut, I tried to work it out. I'd lie there, and wear myself out with horrible memories, clenching my jaw until it ached. If I wasn't busy hating myself, I restlessly tried to reassure myself. One afternoon I was in my room, worrying away. I sat and stared at myself in the mirror. Were they crow's feet at the corners of my eyes, or just ordinary lines? I ran my fingertips over my cheeks, checking for dry patches of skin.

Bit by bit an idea came to me. All this make-up, all the glamour; really it was not to attract men but a shield to keep them away. Why? Because men didn't have the faintest idea how to love. How could a woman go to her husband and say, 'I've really stuffed up in this or that.'

What it all boiled down to was this. There is no safe place out there, or even in the home. The only safe place is inside. Unless I could become strong enough within myself, I had no hope. It was a matter of power.

I remembered when I was a little girl at Pickering Street and saved for months to raise ten and sixpence. I went to Worthly's and spent hours choosing Christmas presents for my aunts and uncles. It was a thrill just to pick and choose, then put the possible present back on the shelf again. What would they really love most of all? I took the trinkets home and wrapped them in brown paper. 'You're wasting your bloody time,' Nan said. I didn't care. On Christmas Eve, at Aunty Jean's, I put my presents under the tree. I looked and looked, but there were no parcels there with a label for Patti. When it came time to open the presents, the adults looked at mine, put them aside and went on talking. Only Uncle Frosty thanked me for my gift.

While I was battling against the tide of my depression after the abortion, Eddy, the gasman, came back into my life. He had the gall to knock on my door. But I let him in, cold as ice.

Eddy began to court me, as though it was the first time. He showered me with presents, apologies, attention, and just wouldn't give up, no matter how many times I gave him the cold shoulder.

I knew he was serious when he took me home to meet his mother. She had a blue fit when I walked in. Eddy just gave me a great grin, like a Labrador dog. It was so long since I'd enjoyed anything the slightest bit as mischievous as that lopsided grin of his that I felt my heart give a little jump.

After a while, I felt a thawing of my heart. When Eddy took me to the pictures I cried at the sloppy scenes, soaked up a fistful of tissues and leant my head on Eddy's shoulder. I even laughed during the funny bits. Not a huge laugh, just a giggle, but it was real.

Eddy proposed, of course. Proposals were two a penny. I had a collection of cheap engagement rings at home. When Eddy refused to be put off, I had a good think about it. He had been a total bastard, but he was also capable of genuine kindness. And, after all, there comes a time when you have to believe a person is telling the truth. Maybe, love didn't need to be a battle.

We had a beautiful wedding. My friend from primary school, Big Pat, whom I discovered only two streets away, made the dresses. It was a rainbow affair, with brilliant colours: pink, lilac, white pearls, and the two flower girls in blue. Charmaine was my matron of honour. It was a lovely day. There was a crowd of people. We had crayfish and prawns at the reception. I'd packed Jeff's three kids off to him for the day. Barbara, the abortion lady, had the other two. This was a wedding for a new start to life. I was twenty-six.

To my surprise, the marriage worked. I was soon pregnant with Number Six, and this time it was a love child. Well, the nearest thing to love I'd known.

I loved giving Eddy little signs of love, like a cup of tea in bed, or a naughty note packed in his lunch; or, if I was feeling stupid, a pair of my knickers.

Eddy babied me. At first I revelled in the attention, the sense of protection. But after a while it began to pall. How soon the honeymoon is over. Eddy was a heavy drinker. Mostly I felt embarrassed, or annoyed, when he was drunk. He'd stroke my hair and say, 'Hello my little Blondie.' His lips were wet and his eyes bleary. 'How's my little kootchie-koo? Dadda's got something for you.' A pile of smelly tommy ruffs wrapped in newspaper, sixteen of them for me to scale and clean. Thanks, Daddy.

Not long after we were married I got sick and we moved house again, back to my old stamping ground of Ferryden Park, just around the corner from where I once lived with Jeff. Because I was so ill, Charmaine moved in with her tribe to help look after my five. We shared my twelfth House of Hope since my first wedding, eleven years before.

Eddy was away all day, working a special long shift at a flour mill. More and more he was on the drink. He rocked up every night at eight, pissed out of his head, and I began to dread his return, just as I had my father rolling in stinking drunk after the six o'clock swill at the Brompton Park Arms. Eddy's weaving walk and sour breath reminded me, although I tried not to think about it, of Sid.

When the pains began for the birth, I phoned Eddy's work to ask him to come home and take me to hospital. Five times I had taken myself off alone to hospital to have my babies. This time, I wanted my husband with me.

The girl at the flour mill said, 'Oh, sorry, he's not here. He always leaves at two.' What had he been doing for those six hours every day until he came home?

Soon after Michelle was born, Eddy went off with his girlfriend. What is it in men that makes them unable to commit themselves? Is it some sort of fear that makes them Casanovas? I tell you, I was just about finished with the whole pack of them.

When Eddy left, I was ready to smash down walls.

166

Somewhere out there was the good life I saw on television. Money, a beautiful home, a new car, love, laughter, parties, kids who never had snotty noses, nights out on the town. I had seen glimpses of it at the Italian club, and at the Latin Quarter. But how the hell do you get it, if you've got six kids, no husband, no job, no money, no power, and the whole bloody shebang belongs to those who've already got the lot?

Michelle was a teasy baby, and so I asked Eddy to come back and help look after his daughter. We decided to make a fresh go of it. Eddy found a job in the railways, and was given the choice of the south-east or a place called Spalding in the mid-north. I remembered the dark pine trees, the evil winds of the south-east, and refused to go down to that cold place of gloomy closed-in forests.

We packed up and headed north into the wide lands of dry grass and gum trees. We lived in a tiny railway cottage, in a row of cottages beside the railway line. Eddy went off to work up the line on a little railcar with a handle to pump up and down to make it go. The kids loved to stand in the front yard and watch him go by. 'Wave bye-bye to Daddy, (the bastard).' He pumped his way past our house and up the line. As I watched him disappear, this stranger on a silly little cart, I knew that, like all relationships, it was finished before it actually ended.

Eddy met a bloke in the front bar. Kasey wore cowboy boots, no socks, tight shorts, a T-shirt, and had huge biceps from hoisting bags of wheat and drums of fuel onto the back of his truck. Eddy was sick of the railways, and wanted a big truck like Kasey's to drive. He asked me to con Kasey into finding him a truckie's job. That was fine by me. Maybe if Eddy was happy, I could get my hands on enough of his pay to actually buy our food. I hated going to the grocer's because he looked at me with narrow eyes as he wrote the amount in his credit book. We were hundreds in debt just for the bare essentials and Eddy's booze.

I did not belong in Spalding. I raged at the women in the main street who whispered behind their hands as I walked by. One morning, to defy them, I wore a mini skirt into the post office. 'It's disgusting,' snapped a lady at the counter and stormed out the door, nose in the air. Spalding was like the Deep South of the USA. There was a sense of suppressed hatred. If I walked down a street, wives grabbed their husband's hands and dragged them over to the other side.

The elite of this tiny country town, for there is always a self-elected cliquey mob with money, loved me. They were the women whose husbands chucked their car keys in a heap and the wives shut their eyes to pull out the key for the night: raffles in the pub, wife lotteries in the lounge-rooms. In 1967, the Swinging Sixties had come to Spalding.

Eddy left the railways and drove a he-man truck. We moved out of town to an old house with ten rooms and a passage a cricket pitch long. I loved it. We were three miles away from the stares, the cars driving slowly past the front of our cottage, the self-righteous disapproval. The old house was haunted by the ghost of Mrs O'Dowd, who had died alone, her body not discovered until a week later. But I didn't mind her occasional visits to peer at us and rattle about in the kitchen.

Many a morning Eddy nearly joined her in the great beyond. It took him one and a half hours to eat breakfast. He cut each slice of hot toast into exact squares. He put them in the exact middle of the plate, a little nudge this way, a touch that way. He buttered each square, exactly to the edge of the crust. Then he buttered the crust, slowly rotating the toast to make sure every bit of the crust was smeared with butter. He turned it over and methodically covered every crumb of the other side. I sat on my hands whenever I had to be there. After toast, he drank his tea. An exactly level spoon of sugar. Scrape the teeny bump smooth with a finger, wipe those three grains back into the dish. Ready? Tip it in. Stir three times, no more, no less, always three perfect circles from the handle back to the handle, then 'ting, ting' the spoon on the lip of the cup, and slowly lift the cup. Pause for one breath. Sluuuurrrp. To watch somebody eat is to know why you hate them.

Sometimes Eddy could move fast. He resented little Ryan raiding the fridge at night, so he would sit on top of the kitchen door and wait until there was the creaking of the floorboards in the dark. Jump! Scream! Gotcha!

The truck gave Eddy more chances to escape. He'd disappear for weeks on end, and not send money. Once more my life began to fall to pieces. I went to Kasey for money. He was the only person I really knew in the town. It was Kasey who took me to hospital when it was time for Michelle to be born.

Jeff, my first husband phoned, and said, 'I'm in trouble for pulling a bit of a shonky. Can I move in with you for a while. I'm having a bit of a rough trot.'

Some days after Jeff had moved in, he sent for his wife and their kids. I came home early from taking Michelle to the hospital and found my husband and Jeff's wife, hard at it on the lounge. That was a good lounge that I had paid for from my own work as a nurse's aid at Clare. We had words. Eddy told me to shove my rotten kids up my arse. I remember breaking the coffee table.

In the heat of battle I decided to get my own back, not just on Eddy, but on all men. It was a cool, rational decision. All those years I've thrown away on men, I thought, as I chased Eddy into the kitchen. The toaster smashed to bits on the wall just above Eddy's head. Slowly I backed him up against the sink, the heavy glass butter dish in my hand, another bloody wedding present. Eddy made a break for the door.

I stormed out of Spalding, car crammed with six kids, suitcases, teddy bears and nappies. Kasey followed me. He walked, hitched rides, headed for the city where he knew I would go.

# Kids

*I moved into a Housing Trust double-unit in Elizabeth, a satellite* city built on the hot plains north of Adelaide. Elizabeth was full of Poms, single mums, reffos with large families, chemist shops that made a fortune selling Valium, dusty gum trees, Holden factories, thousands of school kids, pubs with English names like 'The Rose and the Crown', and a feeling of up-yours to Adelaide, which looked down on Elizabeth as a slum on the edge of the civilised world.

I was a new arrival. Like a New Australian, I was dispossessed, trying to make a go of a changed life. I felt like an alien in my own country; worse, I felt like a failure. Other migrants could look back and imagine their previous good life, even if they came from countries smashed by war. There was no way I could see my life through rose-coloured glasses. I had lost them years ago.

To make a sense of home and family, I built rituals with my children. I wanted to give them what I had missed out on. For Christmas, I got a tree from Woolie, and a heap of decorations. The kids went ape, and when we tried to decorate it they all fought for the coloured balls and strings of tinsel. I had to wade in and smack bottoms to stop the brawl. Bloody kids. After all that, there was a world war over who'd put the star on the top.

Then it was time to wrap the presents. I sat in the top bedroom and called them one by one. Jack was supposed to be first. I heard a lot of whispering, then Cassie appeared. I don't know how she did it, but somehow she always seemed to get first turn. She tore in the door and stood gaping at the bed. There were seven pairs of identical pyjamas lined up, and a pile of little nick-nacks so they could each have something individual. Cassie chose the pyjamas that fitted her, and took ages turning over the pile of little presents, until she at last chose a pencil sharpener shaped like a racing car. Together we wrapped them up, and I labelled hers with a texta pen.

'Now off you go, and send Jack up.'

Cassie ran down the passage, yelling, 'I know what you've got.'

The place was humming on Christmas Eve. The kids were like sparrows fluttering about in their rooms. Then Cassie ran out and asked, 'How does Father Christmas get in? We haven't got a chimney.'

'Through the front door, of course,' I said.

More farting about in the bedrooms, and then I heard one of them say, 'You ask her.' 'No you ask her.' Then Cassie ran into the lounge-room. 'How do we know he's been?'

'I'll leave the front door open, and he'll see the little meal on the floor by the tree. Okay?'

'What little meal?'

I had to put a piece of cake, a sandwich and a bottle of beer on the floor, which was a good excuse for all the kids to run out and see what was going on.

By ten o'clock I was going mental with the noise. At this rate they'd be over-tired for tomorrow and fight and howl all day.

I charged up and roared, 'Right. If you don't keep quiet and go to sleep, he's not coming. I'm going down right now to shut the front door. You hear me? Just one peep out of any one of you by the time I get to the front door, and that's it. No Father Christmas.'

Ten minutes of silence, then whisper, whisper, giggle.

When at last they had fallen asleep, Kasey, who had found me and now lived with us, had to take a bite out of the warm sandwich, leave a few cake crumbs on the plate, and drink the beer, the only bit he really enjoyed. The other five bottles were kept for Christmas dinner, when Kasey would share them with our guest. Each Christmas I arranged with the Salvos to send some lonely bloke to our place for lunch.

As well as Christmas, I set up rituals for every day. At night, after tea, I'd say, 'Bathy Time,' and watch the kids' eyes light up at the thought of the fights to see who went in first after Mum.

I'd lie in the deep, hot bath, and listen to them going hammer and tongs. I knew Cassie would win. She always did. My dear little thin Cassie, who I called Skinny Minnie. She hated that. 'Just call me Skin.' My fragile little Skin, with her blue eyes, who had been so sick as a youngster with migraines, just like mine. I spent some fearful nights and days sitting and stroking her poor little arms, listening to her quick and shallow breathing. I was terrified of my children being sick.

Cassie always won the battle of the bath because she let the others fight in the lounge-room while she hung around the bathroom door and listened for the splashing as I climbed out. As soon as she heard the slap of my foot on the floor, she banged the door. 'Me first. Cassie.'

We stuffed a tissue in the key hole because Ryan and Pepe, seven and six, were peeping Toms. Cassie tipped some more Radox in the bath, stirred it around, and climbed in behind me. While she washed my back she chattered away. 'Mum. Why don't you ever put your face in the water?'

'What a funny question. I don't know. I'm scared of not being able to breathe. Maybe somebody pushed me under water when I was too young to remember.'

Cassie stood up in the bath to tip a jug of hot water over my shoulders. 'What else are you scared of, Mum.'

'Heights.'

'Heights?' Cassie couldn't believe it.

I loved to talk with her. 'Yes. I must've been about four, maybe six, I don't know, but Aunty Jean took me to the circus. I'd longed to go to a real circus and see the man on the trapeze, the lion tamer, clowns, the lady riding two horses at once . . .'

'Can we go to a circus?'

'One day. Now soap my back again. That's right. Well, Aunty Jean and a man took me in a car. I saw the lights of the circus under a big bridge, near the railway station. I nearly peed myself. All those coloured lights and a huge tent. We parked the car and set off across the bridge. I looked over the side and saw these cars way down below. I yelled and fell down on all fours like a dog, my hands grabbing at the footpath.

'I could feel the bridge moving. Aunty Jean dragged me up by one arm, and pulled me along, belting my arse all the way. I screamed and screamed in case she didn't see a hole in the darkness. I never saw any of the circus. I just sat staring at the sawdust under my seat, knowing we had to go back across that bridge way up in the sky.'

Cassie's hands had stopped moving. 'Wow. Hope I'm never scared of heights.'

There was a scratching at the door, and ssh-ing sounds. Bit by bit the tissue was coming out of the key hole, pushed by something from the other side. Then it fell out. I was out of the bath, turning the key. The little brats squealed and ran back to the lounge-room.

Time to teach them a lesson. Usually when the bath was finished I'd lie in my dressing gown on the lounge floor while Cassie brushed my hair, and I'd fall into a swoon. But not tonight. I dried myself quickly, put on my gown and called all the children into the kitchen. Jack, the oldest, was twelve and wore his long hair in a Beatles hair cut, even though it was against the school rules. He sighed, and put his elbows on the table, giving me the What is it now? look. Blondie, eleven, was still chubby. She'd weighed ten and a quarter pounds at birth. Cassie, nine, and pink from the bath, sat at the head of the table.

The two little peeping Toms sat side by side, eyes scared. They knew they were in for it, but they didn't know what. Michelle, four, I sat on my lap. Chris, my seventh and last, was Kasey's child. He sat in his high chair and grinned at all the world.

'Right. Eyes here.' That was my sergeant-major voice. I stared around the table right down the barrel into their brains, waiting for them all to submit.

'Now, Ryan and Pepe' – two little boys tried to shrink and disappear – 'time for you all to know a few facts of life. And I don't mean the stupid birds and bees stuff.'

Jack groaned, and Blondie gave me the look that said, Oh no,

Mum, not me too? With boys here. Cassie gave a huge mischievous grin.

'Okay. You older ones can go, if you want to. But the rest of you are staying. What I'm about to tell you is important, and it'll teach you to stay away from strangers. Kasey. Come here.'

Kasey came in from the lounge where he had been watching tele, and stood by me. I gave Ryan and Pepe my Earth Mother look. 'I know you two have been playing with each others' doodles in the bath.' They jumped with surprise. 'I know, because I've watched you through the keyhole.' Jaws dropped all round the table, except for Cassie's, because when we'd heard the boys' dirty snickers we'd both had a good perve through the keyhole.

'When I was a child, nobody told me anything about sex. That was bad. I don't want you to suffer the way I did, from not knowing.'

Jack and Anne had already guessed where all this was leading, and left the table.

I turned to Kasey, my faithful Kasey, whom I couldn't have done without, and whose name I had taken by deed poll, because I refused to marry him.

'Kasey. Drop your dacks.'

Out flopped his doodle. Shrieks. Crashes of chairs. 'Mum. You treat us like poo!'

I reached across the table and held the two boys in their chairs. 'Sit. You will not move a muscle until this lesson is finished.'

# *The grave*

*On Mother's Day, as I did every year, I went to the Enfield cemetery.* I walked from the bustle of the world into the quiet city of the dead. Figures moved silently across the lawns. Family groups, heads bowed, quietly sought the right headstone. Others walked on the curved paths. The cemetery was a huge park, the wide lawns pitted methodically with small depressions where, set down into the grass, there were rows of small headstones. I saw three mounds of earth beside open graves. A solitary woman, all in black, her head covered in a lace veil, lay curled up like a baby on the grass, the cold May wind ruffling her veil. I knew her pain.

Nan's grave was in the Catholic area. As I drew close, I saw the bunch of roses, now dead and brown, which I bought on her birthday. I replaced them with chrysanthemums, teasing out the soft blossoms until they made a pretty arrangement. I took a small cloth from my handbag and leaned down to clean the headstone, where the black words had already turned grey. Mary Robbins.

The ground hurt my knees, so I sat beside Nan and began to pluck weeds out of the grass. This was a precious time to sit and think. I gave a quick glance around, to make sure nobody was close and, as usual, began to talk to Nan. 'Ten years since you died, Nan. And I still can't say goodbye.' I pulled savagely at a thistle. Its stem snapped and the white milk oozed out. If only I had gone to her house that night.

'There are so many things I don't understand, Nan. Why did

your family wait until three in the afternoon to tell me you had died? I was just around the corner. Did they hate me that much?'

I asked Nan, as I always did when I visited her grave, 'Why did you just sit by the window and wait for death?' As always, there was no answer. 'I saw you that morning in Reverend Mary Ariola's church, I saw you start to lift your hand to say the rose was yours. You always wanted to be the girl skating.'

A yappy Pekinese dog ran past, his lead trailing on the ground. An old lady hobbled past in hot pursuit. 'Come back. This instant. You naughty boy. Come back.' The dog turned, tongue hanging out, and waited until she almost grabbed the end of the lead, then took off again. Little bugger. He wouldn't have dared get up to those tricks with my Nan.

As though I was back in 37 Pickering Street, I saw Nan lifting her walking stick to crack me on the bones. Now I smiled. Silly old troll. Tried to stop me buying the green coat. Strange. That day I hated her. Now, I felt sorry for her.

I remembered the night I woke up and Nan's bed was empty. I had heard her whispering to somebody, and then the front door opened very quietly and I heard the footsteps leaving from the house. I had leapt out of bed in a panic, thinking that Nan was running away. I must have been only about five or six at the time. When I got to the front door I looked down the street. Underneath a street light, Nan was getting into a taxi. There was Aunty Doll with her. I let out a huge scream. Nan started up, looked all around, then came stomping furiously back to me.

'Stop that horrible racket, you little monster.' She was furious, and lashed out at me with her stick, but I stepped back inside and Nan missed. She turned and called up to Doll, 'You go. I'll wait here.'

Nan was as mad as ever I had seen her. I hid under my bed, right over against the wall. When Aunty Doll returned, I found out that Nan and she had planned to sneak off to the Old Spot hotel, which sold booze after hours.

Now I looked down where she lay. 'You poor old thing. Having to look after me really stuffed your life up. I always thought I was the prisoner.'

Only since Nan's death could I pour my heart out to her. I

sighed. My knees hurt from being doubled under me. I stood, and stretched them to ease the pain.

I walked to the foot of the grave, and sat again looking for weeds. I thought about the year I had learned from Aunty Jean that I was not an only child. My father had a son, called Peter, born illegitimate to one of the girlfriends. She tried to abort it, but the abortion failed and the baby was born with some deformity of the head and brain damage.

All those Sunday afternoons I had to make my duty visits to my father, I never knew my brother was in the children's wing of that same hospital. I think the worst thing the adults did to me, even more damaging than the sexual abuse, was deliberately keeping me in ignorance, never trying to explain why.

A gust of cold wind blew across the cemetery. I looked up. There were dark clouds racing overhead, but they were too thin for rain. 'Jack's a real little man, now. Pity Pepe's not more like him. I don't know what will become of Pepe. He steals money from my purse, he runs out to the playground without permission. I've got my hands full with him.

'Ryan's started whingeing because he's had his seventh birthday and I've stopped hugging him. I told him, just like I told the others, "Once you're seven I stop hugging. With seven kids I just haven't got time for it. You get all the cuddles you want until seven, then the next ones have their turn. It's my rule. I have to make the rules, or go bananas."'

Here I was, gossiping with a ghost. I was approaching the dreaded big three-o, and what did I have to show for it? Seven kids, two failed marriages, one brutal de facto, another de facto, too many abortions. Married at fifteen.

'It's no good Nan. Nothing seems to have worked. Not marriage, or de factos, or going it alone, or living with a friend. I'm nearly as old as you were when you moved into Pickering Street. Will I look so old in a few years? I haven't lived yet, and I'm really scared my life will be over before it's begun. And I'm so short of money, Kasey or no Kasey. How can I enjoy life if I'm always battling to keep the wolf from the door? I want to live my own life, while I've still got a chance, even if it's just a new illusion.'

I sat quietly a moment and wondered what I'd lost of myself in all those years, and what was left. 'Look, Nan, I've met a lovely man called Gordon. Weak as piss, a real mummy's boy, but he's crazy about me. Takes me and the kids to the zoo and rides on Popeye. He buys the kids clothes and things. Takes me out to dinner at the best restaurants. And you know what? I love it. I love the attention, the adoration, the fun. Sure, I pay with my body. I'm sorry if that offends you. But what've I got except my body? That's all I've got left, and it'll soon be carted off to the wreckers.'

I patted Nan's grave. I stood up and walked away from her. What I hadn't told Nan, was too scared to tell her, was that, after thirty years of feeling hopeless, the last fifteen of them thrown away on useless men, I had found a way to break out. Who cared if it made me miserable? At least it would be my life, not the life somebody else decided for me. For too long I had relied on men.

*Madam*

# Freelance
# working girl

*If only Nan could've seen me. Spiked heels, evening dress scooped at the* breast, my arms bare, around my neck the silver chain with a crucifix, and my crowning glory, my hair, which took all afternoon to prepare at Nilia's hair salon. Blonde, Zha-Zha curl on my forehead, and at the back, the hairpiece of do-do curls, with a million hair clips holding it in place. If the Sims scrap metal truck had driven past with its big magnet, I would've been carted off, stuck to the magnet by a ton of hairclips.

I went out to discover the world and have the best time of my life. Gert the nympho and I hit town like a couple of loonies. Nan had said, 'Keep away from Hindley Street and those fucking New Australians.' Yet here I was, dolled up and queening it along Hindley Street. I could go berserk, knowing the kids were safe at home with Kasey.

We'd made a few pick-ups in the Elizabeth pubs, but we wanted the big time and, from my nights at the Latin Quarter, I knew where to find it. I was a thirty-year-old adolescent, starved for the excesses of the teenage years I had only briefly tasted. It was 1970 and, if I didn't act fast, the frenzy of the sixties would be history. The dowdy housewife caterpillar was about to emerge.

At home in Elizabeth, Gert and I were frazzled mums. In Hindley Street, joined by Sonya, we became the Three Muske-teers. Believe me, we hoisted a few jolly rogers.

Gert and I went two nights a week. She had to. If she didn't get a screw, she couldn't sleep. If a bloke was not up to it, Gert would have to trash the room. I did it because I needed the money to buy my freedom, but also, as the money began to roll in, because I enjoyed the power it gave me over men. Unlike in the past, I could pick or choose the men I wanted, if I wanted them, and make them beg for more. Each one of my regulars needed me. I didn't need them. It was not for love – the earth shaking and bells – and not for the glitter, but because I was boss of my life for the first time.

We swanned our way past Miller Andersons, the windows full of fuddy-duddy store dummies standing like they had a swarm of bees up their bums. Then we passed the hotel where the farmers stayed for their once-a-year shopping spree: a new car for Dad, a fridge and new outfit for Mum, a night out at Wests pictures for the kids, and a sly sideways glance at the working girls.

Gert and I went down the stairs into an Italian coffee lounge: mozzarella; cappuccino, olives, garlic, fake wood panelling on the walls, heavy silver plates hanging on the wall, pot plants, red table cloths, laughter, old friends, and Rosa's shining smile.

The men were there for us. The Italian wore a black short-sleeved shirt to show off a flying eagle tattoo on his hairy arm. He always had a bottle of Kaiser Stuhl Cold Duck open and ready. The German had a moustache, sideburns that leaked down to his jaw, and thin hair combed forward over his bald patch. If I had a dog that ugly I'd shave its arse and teach it to walk backwards. But business was business.

The Yugoslav's shirt was decorated with a design of a farm scene with big orange butterflies flitting about. The Greek was into photographs of me to carry next to his heart. He snapped his fingers at the photographer, sat close to me, his champagne glass raised in a toast, one meaty hand draped around my shoulder, and smirked into the new-fangled Polaroid self-developing camera. It was a great invention because, as the advert said, 'You didn't have to wait for *this* picture!' You just counted to ten and there you were, with a wide chemical splotch up one arm, and no negatives for his wife to find at home.

Gert and I sat on the lounge and waited for the men to make the moves. Beside me was my packet of Alpine menthols and slim cigarette lighter. I never gave men the come-on, but

Gert's left eye must've got sore from winking. A man would glide over, totally suave, not like the Australians who hung about upstairs on Hindley Street and said, 'Do you fuck?' and got a smack in the mouth. The men in Rosa's tried to impress me with bottles of Cold Duck and lots of fawning. As often as possible I'd tip my glass into the pot plant or in the bucket old Antonio hid beside the end of the lounge. I had Cold Duck running out of my ears. My test to see if I'd had too much was to go to the toilet and, if I couldn't pull my knickers up, it was time to call it a day.

We got beautiful Italian food, the men got drunk, and Rosa kept conning fifty dollars out of them for cheap plonk, so there was hardly enough money left for us to earn back in the motel.

We got a buzz from working as a team. We'd crack up laughing at each other's performances. Gert was so hot she'd do it swinging from chandeliers. If the bloke couldn't keep it up, she'd get furious and reach for the Coke bottle from the motel fridge. If she saw anything that looked like a penis, whammo.

Gert and I also worked as a team for safety's sake, unless a man insisted on just one of us. One night we took an Italian guy with us. Not the one who tried to impress us by leapfrogging the fire hydrant and collecting his nuts on the way over. I never knew why men made such a fuss. He screwed up his face, bent right over, tenderly cuddled his family jewels, and threw up. Really, it's just a couple of things hanging between their legs. No, this Italian was rich, beautifully clean and as randy as a busload of nuns on Spanish Fly. In the motel room, Gert and I tossed to see who'd go first. I won. Ho hum. She sat and watched while I tried to hurry him along and get it over with. Then Gert had her go.

He was well endowed, and Gert was in her glory. To help him raise it again she opened her legs so wide you could just about see her tonsils. He hopped on and Gert moaned. I reckon the more she moaned the more she enjoyed it. And she really enjoyed it. After a while, I got bored. No tele, no books except the Gideon Bible, nothing to do but check my nail polish and listen to Gert going 'Oh, oh, oh.' So I scooped out the little bottles of spirits in the fridge and put them in my handbag.

Then I looked in the drawer by the bed. I couldn't put my eyes back in. Packets and packets of opals. I wasn't leaving without one of them. Surely he wouldn't miss one or two.

Next day, my lover Gordon rang up. I could hardly understand him.

'Phwat uh phwuck you uffto?' he mumbled.

'What do you mean?'

'You took phthat floke's opaphls.'

'How do you know?'

'Because I'm phringing up from phucking hofsphital.'

Poor Gordon. They thought he'd set it up. Plaster on one arm, head bashed in, lips like bananas, all he remembered was opening the door and there were two big blokes. Poor bastard. Gordon was only a boy, just over twenty, and I was his first love. He had ulcers over me, and now a thumping. It was cruel the way I had him by the balls. I'd tell him he was a pain in the arse, that he gave me the shits, and he'd beg for more. Hands shaking, he'd finish a cigarette in one eye-bulging drag, and fling his arms around me.

I had to give the opals back, or one of us would be dead. I told Gordon, 'Get the bloke to meet me in the Elizabeth Hotel car park tonight at seven-thirty. But tell him he's going to pay for them.'

I rocked up to the car park. A car cruised past, pulled up, and a big bloke got out. He was a gorilla, but as he got close I saw his eyes were all right. Not like the man who everybody reckoned was the Mafia boss, whose eyes were the coldest, deadliest, most terrifying eyes I'd seen. The gorilla said, 'You don't know what you've done. You're lucky to still be walking. They have your name and address. They know all about you. They could take your kids, do anything.'

'If you want the opals back, it'll cost you.' On the way out of my lounge-room to come here my eye had caught the phone bill. $350. A small fortune for me. Chicken feed for them.

The gorilla just stared at me. Then he reached into his pocket and took out a roll of money. 'I've never heard of anyone asking for money to give back something they stole.' What about the taxman? I thought. He counted out the notes. I kicked myself for not asking for more. He shook his head as he handed the money to me. 'Lady, you should be pushing up daisies.' I had a good laugh. I'd got double pay with a bonus for one screw.

Then there was the night Gert and I were locked in the YMCA. Holy moly. We met this guy at Rosa's. We were all dolled up like the pox doctor's clerks. He came into Rosa's loaded, and, like so many, left empty. I had to chat Rosa. 'Fair's fair. Leave us our wages. We bring the blokes here for you.'

Gert, the bloke, and I sneaked in the front door of the YMCA hostel. Full of men, it was Gert's idea of heaven. 'More pricks than a dartboard in here,' she gloated. It was not the place for me because there'd be no big spenders in a hostel. All the way up the creaky stairs, the guy kept whispering, 'Ssh, shush, stop giggling.' Along the squeaky lino floor of the corridor and past room after room with thin partition walls, the bloke tried to keep us quiet. There was snoring coming from everywhere. He got to his bed and I sat on the end of it. Thankfully I didn't have to screw him, but I took the money first, to play safe.

Then Gert stripped, jumped him and went to town, moaning and thrashing around. What a laugh. The walls began to shake as men pounded on them. Agonised voices cried out in the dark. 'Shut her up, for Christ's sake. Oh shit. I can't stand it. Stop the moaning.' That encouraged Gert, who threw in a few long screams for luck. Gert was good at her job. She'd have no trouble getting references. In fact she later became president of a national Welfare group. After about an hour non-stop the YMCA was full of groaning, shouting men hitting the partitions, and thumping the floor.

Gert's bloke was hopelessly wiped out, begging for mercy. He couldn't sit up to get the money out of his pants for the extra time. Gert and I went to the men's showers, laughing ourselves stupid. Because we were a team I got half the money just for watching.

When we tried to leave, at three o'clock, the doors were locked. I cracked. We couldn't get out until six. I had to be home when the kids woke up.

# *The raid*

---

*The life of a freelance girl was not enough.* Not enough money, not enough freedom, almost no power, and certainly no future. I had delusions of going straight. It would be great to be a secretary, or something respectable. A secretary. Now that would impress my mother. I saw an ad in the paper for a receptionist at a massage parlour. So what if I didn't have thirty words to the minute and couldn't draw the Pitman curls and hooks? I knew the hooker game and this was my big break. Bugger the application rigmarole. I dolled up and marched up to the door. Receptionist? Ha. I'd seen enough films of girls filing their nails, answering the phone and making a monkey out of the boss.

The manager opened the door. He was a mean looking ferret with red eyes and thin lips. 'G'day. You don't need to know who I am. Call me Barry.' He put a finger in his ear, jiggled it around and brought out a lump of yellow on a fingertip that he examined triumphantly, as though he had captured some Viet Cong after months of guerrilla warfare.

'I'm here for the job.' Please wipe your finger or I'll stick it in the pencil sharpener and do the job for you, I thought.

He gave me the once over, gave me the job, and smeared his finger under the edge of the tabletop.

'There's your phone. You answer by saying, "Touch of Class."'

Touch of arse, more like it, I reckoned, and I'll disinfect that phone in case you've touched it, I thought.

I reported next morning all in a tizz. I sat at the desk like Lady Clavor of Clavor Castle, opened the drawer, tidied the pencils,

186

put the answer pad at just the right angle and sucked the last thin sliver of Butter Menthol.

It was a push-over. I zapped the clients with my sultry voice tuned up to melt their zips over the phone. It was as good a use as any for the elocution lessons.

Barry weaseled his way back into the office. 'The compere can't show. You gotter do it.'

Blank stare.

'Tonight's show, I mean.'

'What? I've never done that.'

'Who gives a shit. Do it or there's the door.' He took a swig of beer from his can. He loved being a boss.

'How much?' Actually, I rather fancied myself holding a microphone.

'Fifty.'

Done. Not a bad bonus on top of my wages. 'What do I do?'

'Take a mattress down to the factory. The drivers will help. And don't forget a clean sheet.'

I sat in the back of the car with Kinky and Gopher. Kinky was five foot nothing and a total moll. She gazed out the window, bored out of her brain. Gopher was a nice young man who was Barry's assistant. Not a bad looker, blond hair, but a brick short of a load. He gnawed at loose bits of skin around his finger-nails. I tried to imagine their performance. In the car behind us were two girls sent along in case any men in the audience got too excited. Barry had sold two hundred tickets in the pubs, at fifteen dollars a pop. Not a bad price in 1970.

'No, problems,' Barry had said. 'Just introduce the act, and make sure the blokes pay you for the girls before they have them.'

We drove through the factory gates and bumped across a rough yard to the sliding galvanised-iron doors on a huge shed. The place was an old dump, with rusting iron walls and high windows made of green perspex. Inside was a circle of long plank seats around a hollow centre where we dumped the old mattress and covered it with a white sheet. Along one wall were trestle tables. There were plates of Saos and cheese, dinky little fairy cakes, sandwiches by the dozen and paper plates covered in celery and chicken pieces. Two trestles had beer schooners lined up on them. There was a loud hiss as a man pierced a keg, then filled beer jugs with froth.

A driver unrolled a long extension cord from a wall socket, and handed me the microphone. 'One, two, three, testing, testing.' My voice boomed off the metal walls. I remembered myself as a tiny tot up on stage for the Radio 5AD Kangaroos on Parade. I had started to sing 'Slow Boat to China', and my voice echoed off the back wall of the auditorium. I stopped dumbfounded. The pianist harrumphed at me and we started again.

Now I was worried about my name. I needed a stage name for the show. I checked out my costume. Black spiked heels, black fish-net stockings, suspenders and garter, bright green tight dress, and Humphrey Bear, my fur coat, hanging open at the front. A regal trollop. But what name? The green dress sent the word 'opal' into my mind. Opal would do. After all, I was a colourful woman.

Beside me stood the two girls. One of them, Celeste, was only seventeen, and it was her first night on the job. What a bastard Barry was to make this her first night. Celeste tugged my sleeve, pointed to the mattress and said, 'I don't have to do it there?'

The poor kid was twisting her fingers into knots. 'No way, dear. That's just for Kinky.'

The long doors were dragged open and out of the night a pack of men raced and fought for the front seats. Suddenly I was scared. What was I doing here with trestles of fairy cakes and soggy Saos and this mattress? It wasn't stage fright. I just wondered how the girl from Pickering Street had ended up here.

Two hundred men crowded around, sloshed down booze, went for refills, and sat leering at us. Celeste began to cringe against my side, and her fear let me hide mine, by looking after her.

When the audience was well charged, Kinky and Gopher, like prize fighters, stepped into the ring. The audience cheered, whistled and yelled, 'Arrgh, go for it. Good on yer, lad. If you need a hand, har har har.'

'Good evening, welcome to Barry's.' There were shouts, thumps of shoes on the floor, a glass smashed. 'My name is Opal . . .'

'Show us your tits, Opal.'

'And for tonight's entertainment, let me introduce Kinky and Gopher.' Roars and catcalls.

Kinky stripped, lay down on her back and opened her legs. The audience went off its tree. I was in the company of true blue, ridgy-didge, scum.

Gopher went whiter than the sheet. His fingers fumbled at his belt. 'Carn, get into it boy.' Kinky played with herself, writhing and moaning on the mattress. 'Ergh,' somebody yelled, 'put you right off oysters.' Another hurricane of guffaws.

At last Gopher stood naked, five foot two, skinny legs and little knees locked together. He looked down at Kinky who licked her lips and thrashed around for a bit of effect. Then she held her arms out to him. Poor Gopher. His doodle hung as limp as last month's celery. The audience exploded. Guys wept with laughter, held on to each other, screamed at Gopher to crack a fat. But no fat was to be cracked. In fact, his doodle began to slowly shrink back into his groin. He looked at me in absolute despair. I mimed for him to get down. Gopher knelt beside Kinky and she did her best. She licked and grunted and carried on, but his dick just kept disappearing until only a weeny little knob poked out from his pubes. Kinky, desperate, pulled him down on her and wrapped her arms and legs around him. At last he got going. Or did he?

Four men stepped up to the mattress, each grabbed a corner of Gopher, as though he was a sheet of masonite, and prised him off Kinky. They lifted him high and peered underneath. Then they dropped him. Shrieks of laughter, but also some nasty cries of, 'We want our money back.'

A man sprang from the audience, stood beside Kinky and tore off his clothes. At last Kinky got into real action. The audience forgot about going home. They applauded wildly. The windows smashed in, green perspex showering down. The doors were forced open. Men smashed through the windows lilke paratroppers. Pandemonium. A voice yelled, 'Raid,' but my brain couldn't cope. 'We're busted. Run for it.' Whistles blew. Men flailed their way out of the seats. The air was filled with shouts and whistles. Running fights broke out all over. Kinky and the

Stud just kept on minding their own business.

The picture of a jail cell flashed into my mind. I grabbed Celeste's arm. 'Let's scram.'

I saw a closed door at the end of the shed and we ran there, dodging among the brawls. Praise God, it wasn't locked. We slammed the door behind us and stood in a small room. A body crashed against the door. Any second now and the cops would break in and grab us.

There was a little window. I pushed Celeste through and then tried to climb out, but Humphrey Bear got caught on a nail, and I had to rip the collar in fear of the hand that at any moment would grip my shoulder.

Teetering on our spiked heels, our ankles buckling this way and that, we hobbled through the dark yard, around a corner. Coming towards us was a line of police dogs. We'd be eaten alive. For a moment I didn't know whether to stop, shit or run. I dragged Celeste back into the dark and we cut across to a house fence, hoicked up our skirts and tumbled over into a row of tomato plants.

'We're gonners if we stay here,' I whispered.

'I can't go on,' Celeste wailed.

'Shut up or I'll bash you. Just think of a fake name, any name, and we'll make a break for it.'

Not long afterwards I was in my dressing gown, darning socks by tele, my innocent kids around me, practising their line, 'Mum's been here all night.'

Barry was chucked in the clink for the night. The Stud and Kinky had coitus nastily interruptus. Gopher disappeared, and was still running at the state border. For a week the police kept prowling around for a woman I'd never heard of called Opal. Somebody else I never saw again was Celeste.

# The
# 'B and D' job

*'Just get in the room and do it.'*

'But I'm your receptionist. I'm not here to do that.' I was terrified, and furious at Barry for even asking. To him, the word 'receptionist' was as elastic as a Madam's garter. I had heard of 'B and D', but never done it.

'You either go in there and do it, or no job.'

What a bastard. What right had he to expect me to do a kinky sex job. I was furious that he was taking advantage, but I had those unpaid bills.

'I've no idea what to do.' I felt sick.

Screwing goes with being born, but this bondage and discipline stuff was sick. What about the weirdo who managed the construction company? He had to be bound up in barbed wire until he bled. Did I have to tie up the man waiting for me in that room? Maybe I should tie him anyway, to give myself time to escape if he went crazy.

Barry leant his freckled hands on the desk and breathed his foul breath in my face. 'Listen, can you see any other girls here this morning? Hey? Do you understand English?' My lips squeezed tightly together. I looked aside and nodded. I was so near to smashing his ugly face and running. He smirked. 'Well, go into the room and do it. Now.'

I loathed being held to ransom. Even more, I hated begging. One day I would run my life the way I wanted. One day Patti would make the rules. But how? All I was good at was lying on my back and opening my legs for the next customer. This job as receptionist was meant to be my big break. Big deal.

'You can do it, Patti,' Barry said. 'Just make it up as you go. As long as you beat the shit out of him, he'll be happy. Just don't leave any visible marks.'

My stomach was in a knot, and both my fists were tightly clenched. Real specialists loved the work. They fought like alley cats to get the 'B and D' jobs because they were a chance to take revenge on men, for double the pay.

The man waiting for me was a real toff. When he had spoken to me on the phone to make his appointment, he had a real plum in his mouth. I squirmed. Why was it that the higher up the social scale, the more respectable their place in society, the more kinky the men became?

I stood up and straightened the top of my blue pants-suit. I was really very frightened. Somehow I managed to force a smile. Suddenly I thought of those 'uncles' at Pickering Street with their lips open and their pushing, hurting fingers. I felt sick at the memory, not violent, and just wanted to crawl away.

As I touched the door handle I felt like the victim, about to be sacrificed. If the creep tried to touch me, just once, I'd slam him against the wall.

He was standing in the middle of the room. He was a skeletal man, with long bony fingers, and fish eyes. His suit was immaculate, and he wore gold cuff-links. His shoes, maybe size four, glistened. He was almost bald, had grown his hair long on one side and plastered it in long, lanky streaks across his head.

From his briefcase he took a short cane. He held it out, saying, 'It's willow. It won't snap.'

At the touch of the cool willow, a sweat broke out on my forehead. I stood there and stared at the switch. He made a soft coughing sound. I looked up and he was glaring at me.

I murmured, 'I'm sorry. I don't know what to do.'

He was horrified, then furious. In a spoilt brat voice, almost crying he whined, 'You're not allowed to say sorry. You're supposed to be in control.' He turned his face aside and paced distractedly around the room, waving his arms. Then he stopped, stamped his foot and burst out in a tantrum. 'I'm the naughty boy. You must be the angry mother and smack my botty.'

He began to wrestle with his belt and the zip of his fly. He pulled his trousers and white underpants down, exposing his bony little bum, and bent over the table. 'Now, count three and spank me.'

I looked at the switch, took up my position a bit to one side of him, and counted to three in my head. I had belted my kids' arses, but that was in a temper. This was in cold blood. I gave him a hesitant tap on the bum.

'No. Not like that. Count out loud and hit me hard.'

One, two, three, whip. It left a thin red line. I closed my eyes. One, two, three, whip.

'Harder, harder,' he demanded.

One, two, three, the willow whistled as he cried out, 'Harder, More, More.' My voice got louder and louder until we were screaming together, 'One, two, three, hit!' Then he started to rave, 'Mummy, no, you mustn't, Mummy.' I opened my eyes and there were welts all over. 'Don't stop. Keep yelling, hit, hit.' He was masturbating in time to the whips. I shut my eyes again, and kept on whipping. He gave a shriek and screamed, 'Stop!' There was blood on his backside, and he was drooped over the table, cleaning himself in front with a white handkerchief.

Time to get out of here.

# *Life begins for Patti*

*Seventeen hours a day, seven days a week, I slaved away as a 'recep-tionist'.* It was crazy. Here I was killing myself for the sake of the good life and to feed my kids, and I had no time to live or be with the children. Or if I did see them, I was so tired and irri-table I seemed to do nothing but yell at them, and shut myself in my bedroom.

All this for a measly two hundred dollars a week. I could have made twice as much on the streets, and I began to wonder if a regular office job meant security for me, or a safe way for the boss to use me up. I started to understand the meaning of the 'rat-race' which our clients whinged about to the girls.

We'd just made the change from being a massage parlour to calling ourselves an escort agency. This got around the law about girls screwing on the property. What with one thing and another – hassles with the police, extra paper work, more work organising pick-ups and returns – I was starting to feel like a zombie. In early September I had my youngest, Chris, down with the chicken pox. Pepe was in strife at school for selling lawn clippings rolled in newspaper as marijuana joints. The silly kids believed him, took a puff and staggered around going 'Wow, man, what a hit.' My salary only just paid the bills; and I won-dered what had happened to the Patti who was supposed to be boss of her own life.

Bit by bit I'd let my hard-won independence slip through my fingers. I was back to being somebody else's drudge. In the early days with Barry I was so scared of losing my job, I did anything he asked, even the 'B and D'. Now I reckoned he needed me as much as I needed his money.

I caught Barry as he oozed through my office. 'How about a weekend off?'

He stopped, gave his stupid weak grin and, as always when talking, looked at a spot somewhere beside my left shoulder, 'A weekend? Our busiest time.'

'So? Get in Melanie or one of the other girls. They know the ropes by now.'

'No way.' He licked his narrow lips, and for a second looked just like a goanna. 'You're the only one with all the know-how.' He squinted. I knew what he was thinking. If I took time off, he stood to lose money. He didn't give a stuff about me, or the girls. He was no better than his customers.

I felt my temper rising. 'Look. You pay me as a receptionist, but who really manages this dump? Everybody gets a holiday, except me. You and the girls get days off, but not good-old-reliable Patti. Well, now it's my turn. It's been solid work, without a break. Either give me some time off, or I'll take it.'

How they hate it when the worm turns. He turned on me, feet astride, and said with a snarl, 'Then take it, but don't bother to show your face here again. I can do without you.' With a glimmer of inspiration, he went on, 'Yeah, Melanie could have your job. What makes you think you're indispensable?'

That word, again: 'indispensable'. My fist closed over the tele-dex. I pushed my chair back. Sleaze Bag saw the look and held his hands up to protect his face. He wasn't worth the effort. I opened the desk drawer, took out the petty-cash tin, and counted out the dollars for my week's work. In a tired, quiet voice I told him where to shove his job.

I walked out into the sunlight, which felt good on my face. Now what? Back to Hindley Street? As I strode down the foot-path, carefully stepping over every crack, my mind played the comforting, reassuring ritual fantasy. Patti was not the frumpy street-girl, stumping her way down a shabby suburban footpath back to the old caged mouse wheel in the pet-shop window. No. I was Patti, the Madam, standing in my green velvet dress at the base of the grand stairway in my bordello, the greatest whorehouse in New Orleans. I was queen of all I surveyed. The bar was gleaming mahogany, the longest in the land. Against it leant Kit Carson, his holster on his thigh. My girls wore finest satins and had feathers in their hair. The men were southern gentlemen, gambling away their lives. The room was full of laughter, the swing doors opened wide, and in walked my Rett Butler . . .

I sighed. Better pick up another bottle of Calomine lotion for Chris's itchies. He was scratching the chicken pox in his sleep, and I didn't want him marked for life.

On Monday morning, there was a knocking at my gate. Melanie and Angela stood there. Melanie screwed up her face, and said, 'We've quit too. Can we come in?'

Over a cup of tea, Melanie said, 'Why don't you start your own agency, Patti?'

My heart began to pound. These two girls thought I could do it. Was it possible? How would I start? Without much further thought I put my cup down and said, 'Fuck it. If a man can do it, so can I.' Melanie gave me a huge grin.

I put an ad in Tuesday's *Advertiser*, in the Health section, and we started work. The first few weeks we made maybe only a hundred dollars clear. But Melanie and Angela were excellent girls, and the word soon got around. Customers and more girls came to us, and suddenly I needed a proper office.

If I said 'Jump!' to Gordon, he didn't answer back, just asked how high. He had given me diamond rings, paid my bills, and idolised me. Now I needed a special favour.

Gordon came with me when the land agent took me on a tour of houses for sale. The first house was in Churchill Road, Number 165. It had a scabby front lawn, cement verandah with an iron roof, walls of stone blocks and, inside, lots of bedrooms for the kids. Out the back there was more than enough room to swing a cat. I had one look through and said, 'I want it.'

The land agent was flustered. 'Yes, but, we haven't made a proper inspection. And there are much better properties I can show you.' I had seen that 165 had two toilets. One for me, and one for everyone else. I loathed using a toilet if a man had been there. 'I don't care. I want it.' Gordon took out his cheque book and paid the deposit. You Beauty!

On the Labour Day holiday, October 1972, we moved into Number 165. Seven kids, two dogs, twenty budgies, Kasey and Ralph. The two men would share my bedroom for years. Kasey slept in the single bed, with his camera. Long, tall, string bean Ralph, was to be my good friend for twenty years, and slept with me, unless I brought home a special client.

The day we shifted into Churchill Road, was the biggest step of my life. I went from being a number in a government file in the Relief Office, to being my own person.

# A day
# in the agency

*Kasey poked his head around the sitting-room door. 'The new girl's here.'*

'Tell her I'll be a minute,' I said, but kept my eyes on Trixie, who squirmed in her seat. 'Look, Trixie, I've had more fights than hot dinners over this. The clinic says you have chlamydia, and that's that. You're off work for ten days, starting from now.'

'And what if the clinic is wrong?'

'Don't try to bullshit me. I've got my contacts, and they have never been wrong yet. You just pack your gear, collect the pills and bring me your clinic clearance in ten days.'

'That's all right for you to say, but I'll starve.'

Trixie flinched as she saw my eyes narrow. I clenched my fist. You've got to win every battle or the girls'll tread you down. Watching us were Melanie filing a split fingernail, and Rachel, her tapestry in her lap.

'I've had just about enough of this. Do you imagine I don't know you get the dole under your real name? Do you think I don't know you screwed Craig last Saturday and I should sack the both of you and put you back on the street?' I wasn't going to let Trixie know I showed a blind eye because she was one of the best and earned top dollars. 'Do you think I don't know all the tricks? Well?' I moved forward, as though to stand up, and that was enough for Trixie. She had seen me smash Crazy Carlie through the security door. Trixie cringed, glanced to one side like a naughty schoolgirl caught smoking by the headmistress, and then whispered, 'No, Patti. I mean, Yes, Patti.'

At times I felt like Mother Superior at a school of imbeciles.

In the three years since I moved into 165 Churchill Road, I'd expanded my business fast, learnt quickly, and now ran so many agencies there wasn't much I hadn't heard before.

'Good. Just don't forget it,' I told Trixie. 'And don't try to freelance. You go dancing at any club, and I'll know what clothes you wore, the colour of your mascara, and what drinks you ordered. You try picking up at the Gateway, and I'll know who it was, which room you were in, and the length of his dick, before you get home. I'm not having you stuff up my reputation. It's taken me years to build up this place into the top business. I'm not about to let you, or anyone, take it away from me. Any trouble and you lose your bond. There are plenty of other girls out there.'

I paused and she waited, eyes down. 'Just go home, Trixie. Have a holiday. You won't lose any of your clients. They can't live without you. You're a total screw-happy. Make them miss you, suffer a bit for a change. Do the bastards good.'

I rose to my feet. 'And before we forget. Who's your client with the infection? I'll get Kasey to phone him.'

Trixie gave just the hint of a flounce as she walked out the door. She was always highly strung. One of my best girls. Her mum was in jail for killing her own husband, who had bashed her and molested Trixie. After years of horrors and despair, one night the poor mother snapped. The law, made by men for the benefit of men, called her a murderer.

I went to interview the new girl. The youngster scrambled to her feet, face flushed, and hitched her handbag strap higher on her bony shoulder. I caught my breath. She had dark rings under her eyes, and her nervous fingers flicked back the fringe from her face. Her lips were pressed tightly together, and she had an awkward lopsided stance. The white dress with lace across the bust could only be her wedding dress cut down. This poor galoop was me a few years ago. Young enough to be my daughter. But genuine. No cop could fake her look of desperation and fear.

'Sit down, Debbie.' I waved at the lounge suite. Debbie sat with the grace of a camel, all knobbly knees and elbows. This one will take a bit of training, I reflected. By now I knew all I wanted to know about her. I sat in the armchair and peered at her long enough to let her know I was boss, now and for as long as I chose.

From the corner of my eye I noticed Kasey at the reception table giving her the once over. With his right hand he was stroking Chou, the Siamese cat, who lay right in front of him, among the pens and clutter of the table.

'And your full name?' I asked Debbie. 'You've remembered to bring your birth certificate?'

She blinked rapidly and opened her handbag, searching for the certificate among her tissues, cigarettes – Marlboro Reds – and make-up. 'Here it is.'

Nineteen. At her age I already had two babies and a stomach ulcer. That was the year Nan died. I looked at Debbie, and felt a pang of sorrow. Did I look so pathetically young at that age?

The phone rang, and Kasey reached for it. '45 9321. Good afternoon. This is Patti's Escort Agency. Can I help you? Yes, sir. I'm sorry we don't have Miss Australia or Brigette Bardot on our books. But we do have many beautiful girls here. What did you have in mind? I see. Blonde. Tall. Thin.'

While Kasey took the order I watched Debbie, who was getting more and more skittish and ready to bolt for the door. I was certain she wasn't a freelancer here to steal clients' phone numbers from our Day Book. No need even to ask for Debbie's card from her previous agency. She was new, all right.

Kasey finished writing the details in the Day Book. 'Now, sir, I'm sure you'll be happy when Melanie arrives at the door. But we do ask you for ten dollars in case of cancellation to cover the cost of the car and petrol. Your name, sir? Thank you. And will you be paying by credit card? Very good. The driver has all that is needed in his briefcase. Thank you, sir. Have a nice day.' Kasey hung up, and immediately dialled on the phone. 'Craig. In forty minutes. Airport Motel. Melanie.' Then he hoisted himself out of the chair and wandered into the sitting-room. 'Melanie. A new one.'

The new girl's eyes were swimming. In a soft voice I asked, 'Does he beat you, Debbie?'

She jumped as though with an electric shock. Biting her

bottom lip, she nodded.

'Kids?'

Debbie smiled crookedly. 'Twins.'

I remembered my twins. 'Tell me about him.'

Debbie sucked in a deep breath, tried to speak, and then asked, 'Can I smoke?' I nodded. She took out the cigarette, flicked the lighter once, twice, and again, her eyes starting to flash with embarrassment and annoyance. At last she lit the cigarette, took a deep breath, held it, and slowly blew out the smoke. 'He's hopeless. Sits around all day getting drunk or goes over to Mike's place fooling around with old cars. Two years ago he did his back in at work and got put off. Now he's given up trying to find a job and blows the dole on booze and parts for Mike's stupid cars.' She looked straight at me, eyes glittering. 'I can't keep borrowing from Mum. I already owe her heaps. Yesterday I had to pawn my engagement ring to buy some food for the kids.'

'Where do you live, Debbie?'

'Blair Athol.'

'I need the street name and number for an emergency, in case the driver must pick you up.'

Her eyes widened, she paused, and then whispered the address.

'Don't worry. Your husband and neighbours won't know. The driver will pick you up at a safe place nearby.' I thought for a minute. 'If I decide to take you on, I'll give you a room in my agency in North Adelaide. That'll be on your bus route. You know the Piccadilly Theatre? Opposite that. I've got ten waiting-rooms there. You will be with some good girls who can teach you the ropes and look after you.'

Debbie looked aside and absentmindedly reached out to touch the statue of the leopard sitting beside her. 'If I decide to take you on.' Debbie froze, and then drew her hand back into her lap.

'There are some things I must be satisfied about before I decide. First. No babysitter, no job. Who is your baby-sitter?'

'My friend, Marlene, next door. We always look after each other's kids.'

'And what will you tell your husband?'

Debbie blushed. 'A nurse's aid. If I can get a uniform.'

I smiled. 'About a third of my girls are nurses.' Debbie looked shocked. 'Oh yes. This is another part-time job for many professional people. Lots of nurses work for me. And teachers. You'd be surprised. One girl is well on the way to buying her own town house. Another is after a thirty foot yacht.' Then to test her reactions, I added, 'Some of my top earners are lesbians.' Debbie looked startled, and blushed. I went on, 'They are wild, manic, with men.' Debbie blinked. 'And quite a few girls have been sexually abused as children.' Debbie did not flinch. So far so good.

The phone rang, and I waited for Kasey to answer it. When he came back into the office, I saw he had pulled in his stomach – as much as he could these days. He had rolled his sleeves up high to show his biceps. He gave the usual patter on the phone, but then went white and his mouth fell open like a fish. He put his hand over the mouthpiece of the phone and whispered at me, 'It's some woman, from Singapore. Wants a bloke.'

I moved fast. 'Give me the phone. Good afternoon, madam. Yes, this is Patti speaking. From Singapore. A beautiful city. Certainly, we can help you. I'll have a gentleman there in thirty minutes. I hope your stay in Adelaide is very pleasant.'

I hung up. What a break. But who did I have? All the drivers were out. I broke my brain trying to think of a man. Not Kasey, he was past it, and I needed him in the office. Who could I send who was young and clean? The duty drivers that day, except for Craig, were as ugly as monkeys; and all out on jobs. There was Russell out the back in the swimming pool. Oh, no. He was about as handsome as a lump of goat poo. But at least he had a dick, and I suppose he knew what to to do with it, if we were to believe his boasting.

'Excuse me a minute,' I said to Debbie. Then I said to Kasey, 'Get Russell in here on the double. Move.' I hurried into the girl's sitting-room. Russell slouched in looking like a drowned rat and stared at me with his vacant eyes. Why am I surrounded by halfwits?

'Russell, get dressed. I've got an urgent job for you.' He stood, dripping, long hairy arms hanging down to his knees. 'A rich bird from Singapore has just flown in and wants one.' The girls shrieked. Slowly, so slowly, Russell's jaw went slack.

'Go on. Move your arse. Suit, tie, the works. You've only got a few minutes.' His feet refused to work, and so I spun him round and pushed him out the door.

Claudette fell sideways along the lounge, face down, and her body shook. Rachel had her hand over her mouth and stared at me with wide eyes. I sat and reached for my packet of Alpine menthol. My brain was going a hundred miles an hour: the jet-set market; time to get male escorts on my books; could I set up an office in Singapore? If we can hook this Singapore lady . . .

Russell snuck back in the room and stood there with all the irresistible charm of the complete wacker. Rachel looked up and snorted.

I went very close to Russell and looked straight into his eyes. 'Now get this, Russell. This is a classy lady. She flies her own private jet. She is a millionaire, with lots of millionaire friends. She won't want your idea of foreplay – grunt, hey, wanna screw? This sort of client may want conversation. So. What do you have to remember?'

Silence. A tortured frown of thought.

'Talk. Smooth talk her. Flatter her ego. She has to be the most intelligent, beautiful woman in the world, and if it comes to it, the best root you've ever had, and you'll tell her so.'

'Go for it,' said Rachel. She flung herself back on the lounge and stretched out her body. 'Russell, oh, Russell. You hunk, take me, take me.' Claudette went to Russell, and caressed his shoulders. 'You big whitey buck. How will you do it to me?'

'Aw, piss off.'

'You've got twenty minutes. Go.'

I returned to Debbie. She hadn't run away. I pointed to the plaque on the wall – Patti's Ten Commandments. 'Read them please. Aloud.'

Debbie blushed and screwed up her eyes. Experienced girls hated this, but I didn't give a pinch of cocky's. Work for me, obey my rules. And this test showed me which girls were illiterate.

'No condom, no job. No clinic, no job. No babysitter, no job. No fraternising with drivers . . .'

'What does fraternise mean, Debbie.?'

She rolled her eyes like a little kid trying to remember her three times tables. So I told her. 'It means you don't screw your driver. Sometimes girls fall in love with their drivers, even marry them. But when you are on your shift, every minute of your time is mine. If you try it, I'll know, and you both face the sack. If he asks you for a screw, how will you know whether he's for real, or checking you out to report back to me? Same as my trusted clients who will ask for you to go with them out of your work time. How can you tell if they've fallen for you, or doing it for me, in exchange for a freebie?' Debbie looked at me and opened her mouth to speak but suddenly shut it tightly. 'Think about it, Debbie. Every screw out of hours is one less job for another girl, and we all lose money. Do you understand?' Debbie blinked her eyes and nodded.

There was a knock at the front door and Kasey went to see who it was. He returned carrying a carton of Seaview champagne wrapped in red cellophane paper. On the top was a red rose tied in a pink ribbon. Kasey dumped the carton on the floor and examined the little envelope stuck by the ribbon. 'Sonya.' He sneered, 'It's from that silly old bugger.' Then Kasey hurried into the girls' sitting-room. 'Hey. You'll never guess . . .' Debbie looked the question at me.

'It's from Horrible Harry, the Greek. He's twenty stone, is as ugly as sin, and has droopy lips. He's gone troppo over Sonya. Pays her an extra five hundred dollars to be seen in public with her or have dinner with him or sit in the Greek cafes and drink coffee.' For the first time I saw Debbie give a little smile, more of a grimace, but she could scrub up into a real beauty. 'It's almost sad. Sonya is cleaning him out. Horrible Harry has gone through all his money and now he's selling off his furniture. Men. Huh! Keep their brains in their doodles.' This time Debbie gave a real grin.

'You'll have guys going crazy over you. Shower you with expensive presents.' Debbie glanced at the diamond rings on my hands. 'There's no stopping them. Some will steal for you. Not that my jewellery is stolen.' I smiled at Debbie and sang the old line, 'Diamonds are a girl's best friend.'

I glanced at my watch. 'Well?'

Debbie swallowed, and nodded.

'Good.' Maybe she'll become a top earner, I thought.

I leant forward and stubbed out my cigarette. 'Do you know how to put a condom on?' She nodded. 'Well, Debbie, you just make sure you do it. Some clients will put the hard word on you for sex without a condom at double the price. That's why I'll check up on you. You will have regular medicals at the clinic, and I'll have you taken there and back by one of the drivers. Okay. You got some questions to ask me?'

'What name will I use? Can I have Brigette?'

'Taken.'

Her shoulders slumped. She ran through the usual favourites, all used, until I suggested Monique, which she loved instantly. 'Yes. I just adore French names. Monique. Sounds great. Monique. I once heard a man speak in French and, oh, I went all gooshy. He could have done anything to me.'

As she gradually relaxed I began to see flashes of the real girl hidden by the years of hurt.

'How much do I earn?'

'Sixty dollars a half-hour; eighty for an hour.'

'How much a week?'

'Depends on how much you want to earn. Most of my housewives do three nights a week. Say seven clients a night. They make a good dollar.'

Debbie's lips moved as she did the sums in her head. I watched her eyes suddenly open wide.

'That's right. Even taking it easy, you rake in over a thousand for your part-time job. You're sitting on a gold-mine.'

Debbie sat up straight, eyes sparkling.

'Hold on,' I said. 'Don't get too excited. I take my expenses before you get your cheque on Friday.' She waited. 'Fifty, fifty.' Debbie blinked and leant forward, frowning. 'If you don't like it, you can try paying for your own advertising. My advertising bill is nine thousand dollars a month. The phone is at least two thousand dollars a month. Then there's the fleet of cars, the drivers who get ten dollars for each delivery and pick-up, rent on all my rooms, and taxes. That's right. We're illegal, but we have to pay our taxes or go to jail. Why do you think you are paid by cheque?'

Debbie continued to frown, and I felt my face getting hot. 'You can leave right now.'

Her face went white and she looked quickly at the door, and then at me. She lowered her eyes. 'Sorry, Patti.'

'Good. Don't ever try to cross me, or you'll be out on the bones of your arse quicker than you can bat an eyelid.'

I went to the filing cabinet and took out a handful of money. 'You need some decent clothes if you're to become Monique.' She kept her eyes fixed on the money as I peeled off note after note. 'Here's three hundred dollars. Get yourself spiked heels, good stockings. We might be tramps but we don't have to dress like we are. Elegant long frock, after-five. Saturday morning you will go to my salon and we'll fix that mop of hair. I have a strict dress code. We have the best clients all with hard-as-concrete double standards: celebrities, television personalities, politicians, sports champions, bank executives, doctors, interstate business-men, entertainers, as well as the guys off the street who just want a poke. Our clients expect top quality girls. If you don't pass muster on a clothes inspection, another girl gets the job. That would be stupid if you were booked by a talker who doesn't even want sex, or our bank manager who just sits in the ward-robe for half an hour while you watch television then collect the money.'

I loved to teach the girls how to dress and put on make-up properly. Working girls are felines. Many came to me scraggy, like moggies from the back streets. They left like Persians, sleek and elegant.

I may have mothered them, but they also educated me. They opened my eyes. Working girls like Melanie and Angela, who first worked for me, taught me lots about the profession. Those girls helped to make me. Others, such as the university graduates, taught me about the world. When we talked I soaked up the knowledge although, as I soon learned, the highly educated girls thought in the same way I did. I felt a victim of my mind, which went round on the same unanswerable questions. When I listened to them talk, I was surprised that their minds were on a hurdy-gurdy too. They used bigger words, and were very clever, so smart that I was ashamed of my lack of education, but their thoughts went round and round, like bees in a bottle. Like me, many of these girls had been sexually abused when children. All the knowledge in the world couldn't set them free.

Others, like Debbie, had come from homes where book learning didn't count for much. I handed Debbie her money. She turned it over and over in her hands, started to count it, glanced up at me nervously, and quickly shoved it in her hand-bag. She wrapped the strap tightly around the bag and held it in her lap with both hands on top of it.

'You might even have a dollar left over to treat yourself. Of course, this is an advance to come off your first pay. In a minute I'll take you in to meet the girls. But before that . . .'

Loud cries and crashes came from the kitchen. Cassie stormed in, with a face like thunder, a red mark on her cheek, and tears in her eyes. 'Mum. Pepe won't peel the potatoes. I tried to make him.' She saw the palm of my hand rise.

'Can't you see I'm busy now. How many times have I told you not to interrupt me during a business meeting?'

I kept a strict divide between family and work. The girls had their own lounge with their own coffee machine and fridge. They were good to the kids, but little Chris was scared of the girls and burst into tears if one came near. It was against my rules for the girls to wander into the living area unless a client had refused them a shower; and it was against the rules for my kids to cross the boundary.

'Yes. But it's not fair. I've done the carrots.'

'Don't you answer me back.'

I turned to Debbie and raised my hands to the heavens. 'Kids. Not home from school for half an hour and there's fights.'

Then I took Cassie by the shoulders and gave her a little shake. 'You're my daughter. You can cope. Go back in there and sort it out yourselves. If I hear any fighting, I'll be down on you both like a ton of bricks.'

Cassie scooted off to the kitchen. When I looked at Debbie she gave me the grin of one mother to another.

'Now, where were we? That's right. Can you start Saturday night? Good. This is what happens. You be here by 6.30 so I can check you out before your shift starts at seven. I'll set you up with a regular client for your first job. So it'll be easy, and you'll have a good time. I'll pay for him. No, not another advance; this one's on the house.' I saw her hand move as though she was about to raise it in school. 'What is it?'

'What do I do?'

I laughed, 'Well, if you don't know by now . . .' But I could see her nervousness, and remembered my own stage fright with the first client. Funny how I've never forgotten his name – Malcolm.

'Don't worry. He's a bit of an old dear, but straight, well, as straight as an accountant can be, and he's done this for lots of my girls. He'll tell you what he wants. Play your cards right and he'll slip you into the old-boy network of the private schools. Then you're laughing all the way to the bank.'

Out of the blue Debbie blurted out the question she had been dying to ask, but wasn't game. 'How do you know if a man's got – you know?'

'Squeeze his penis and the stuff comes out. You'll know that something is wrong. Then you say, "Excuse me, sir" – always be courteous and tactful – "you seem to have a problem, and I'm sorry but I can't help you tonight. I think you should see your doctor or go to the clinic."'

'I can say no?'

'Of course. We are escorts. We don't have to have sex if we think something's wrong. And that reminds me. If a man gets violent, or you are frightened, we have a red alert code. You say to him, "Sir, I can see you are upset. Perhaps I can get you a drink." Whatever you do, keep talking and persuade him to let you use the phone. Say something like, "I understand that you are very unhappy, but I have a little baby at home and I think I left the iron on. I'm really worried that it will burn through the ironing board and start a fire. I'll just ring home and make sure everything's all right." You phone me and say, "I think I've left the iron on." Then all hell breaks loose. We get all our heavies to you, they smash in the doors and take care of things.'

Debbie's eyes were round with astonishment. 'Have you ever had to kill anyone?'

'Well, not actually. But don't worry. It's the poor street girls who get beaten up and knifed. The clients know about our drivers, and the things they can break. You'll have Craig, one of my best. He picks you up from the waiting-room, checks your clothing and hair are okay, and drives you to the client. He walks you to the door and greets the client. "Good evening Mr whoever, I'm Craig from Patti's Escort Agency. This is Monique. Do you mind if I come in to complete the business transaction?" That gives the driver a chance to check the place for other men and so on while he fixes the credit card. Craig will have the little machine for credit cards in his black brief-case, with a few other necessaries. If he suspects anything, other men in the bathroom or in the wardrobe, he'll say, "May I please have a quick look around?" Craig is a real heavy, and has a way of asking so politely that it's hard to refuse. If he finds a bloke in the bath, he says, still tactful, "Sorry, sir, I can't leave Monique with you. Something is not quite right." When every-thing is hunky-dory, he checks his watch in front of the client and says, "It is 8.20. I'll be back at 8.50. If Monique is not at the door, I may have to break it in, you understand sir?"'

I stood up and stretched my arms. 'Well, that's enough for you to remember now. Come along and meet some of the girls.'

At that instant the phone rang on the table beside me and I picked it up. 'Hello. 45 9321. Patti's Escort Agency. Can I help you?'

I knew the voice, the Singapore lady, and she was as mad as hell. With venomous sweetness she said, 'What is this Port Adelaide Football team? I have an idiot in my room who has talked non-stop about goals, and screamers, and out of bounds, and I don't know what he is talking about, and I don't want to know. In fact I never want to hear again the name Port Adelaide Football team . . . and no, I don't want another of your male escorts . . . not even free . . . just refund my money to the American Express number, goodnight Patti's Escort Agency.'

At eleven o'clock the next Saturday night, Kasey came into the sitting-room. He looked frightened. 'It's whatsername, Monique. She's left the iron on!' The girls froze. Kasey stared at me with blank eyes.

I roared to my feet. 'Well, move, you bloody idiot. Get the drivers on the phone.' I crashed past Kasey who dithered in the doorway and rushed to the reception desk. Monique. Monique. I ran my finger down the night's list. There. Shit. The surgeon. What if he's flipped? He knows how to cut. Kasey was at the phone, dialling madly.

'There's the address,' I told him, and shoved the Day Book around for him to read. 'You stay here by the phone.'

I grabbed my car keys and ran out to the white Lincoln. Fuck the speed limits. What was that man already doing to Monique? I was past the city and on Greenhill Road in six minutes flat. Turn right, mash the accelerator and there was the place; two of my cars outside, and neighbours beginning to drift out onto the road. I blasted the horn to scatter the people and screamed to a halt.

I was on the front lawn, looking up at the first floor balcony. My heavies bashed at the front door. Craig was already climbing up the creeper. Monique was his girl, and I was sure he'd got his gun on him.

I cupped my hands around my mouth and yelled, at the top of my lungs, 'Monique! Are you all right?'

A light came on in the bedroom. Craig was already reaching over to get a grip on the wrought-iron fence of the balcony. Two figures appeared on the balcony: Monique, wrapped in a towel, and a portly man holding a sheet in front of him.

'What has the bastard done to you?'

There was the sound of splitting wood as the front door gave. Craig hauled himself up on the balcony rail. The man yelled with fright. Lights went on up and down the street.

Monique, in a thin little voice, said, 'Nothing Patti. Nothing.'

'But you said you left the iron on.'

Craig took out his gun and rested his wrist on the rail for a steady shot. Monique began to cry. 'But I thought that was the signal to say everything was all right.'

Craig turned to stone. My heavies stepped back from kicking the front door and stared at the balcony. Neighbours stood in the driveway, and a quavering voice called, 'I say, is everything all right here?'

What could I do but call up at the client, 'Sorry. Would you like a freebie hour?' But I guessed he was right off his jollies by this time. He just looked at Craig's gun, at the weeping girl beside him, at the crowd standing silently in his driveway. Then he gave a strange little cry and rushed back into his bedroom.

'Monique!' I called. 'Get your arse back to my place. I am the iron, and I'm going to flatten you.'

# Spare
# the rod

A *bloke up the road from 165 Churchill Road committed suicide more* often than a street full of heroin addicts. The circus act began, usually, during a huge fight with his wife. After a lot of smashing and crashing, he rushed outside yelling, 'I'm going to kill myself.' His method always drew a mob of onlookers. One night in September he seemed extra het up; the breaking of crockery went on longer than usual. When his front door slammed we all ran out to watch.

He climbed onto the roof of his Holden and looked down at the crowd of his own kids and neighbours surrounding him. His face filled with terror. He screamed, 'I'll jump, I'll jump.'

'Jump, you silly bugger'

'All right, I will. You wait and see. I can't take it any more. Tonight I'm really going to do it.'

'Stand back you kids. Give him room.'

He clenched his fists, stiffened his arms, rocked his body back and forwards and stared down at the ground far beneath. Like a kid on the edge of a swimming pool, he gathered his courage, took a deep breath, leant forward, hesitated, took another breath, shut his eyes and at last took the fatal plunge.

He fell with a great cry, crumpled onto his hands and knees, knelt there for a while like a Moslem at prayer, his forehead touching the bitumen, then rose unsteadily to his feet. With tragic dignity he limped back inside, accompanied by his kids, who held his hands and patted his back, which was turned against the street with its sounds of cheers, wolf-whistles and raspberries.

The show over, I hurried back into Number 165. Never a dull moment. The girls were in their lounge, getting ready for that night's shift. I looked in on Rachael, who was all teary, and maybe not quite up to it that night. Her husband had found out she was a working girl, given her a hiding and shifted out, taking all the furniture. I sat beside her and took her hand, holding it in my lap. Rachael leant against me. She looked down at a soggy tissue she was shredding between nervous fingers. 'What'll I do, Patti? All he left me was one broken light bulb and the toilet brush.'

'You're better off without him. Make a fresh start. There are plenty more fish in the sea.'

'But he'll have told all the world. My mum. Nobody'll speak to me again, ever.' She gave a huge sniff, turned the soggy tissue over and over looking for a a dry patch and wiped her top lip with the wet little ball.

'Maybe. Maybe not. Now's the time to see who your real friends are.'

Rachael gave a loud sob and hung her head. I stroked the back of her hand, and said, 'One thing's for sure. You're good for neither man nor beast tonight. Look, Rachael, why don't you take the night off. Stay here with us, if you like, for a bit of company. See how you feel in the morning. Maybe you could phone your mum, see how the land lies. Who knows, she might hate your husband, and blame *him*. Take a fortnight off, sort things out, even treat yourself to a holiday up on the Gold Coast or somewhere.'

Rachael burst into another flood of tears and buried her head in my shoulder. I looked across the room at the other girls. Josephine, who'd been through all this, gave me a wink, and went on shaping a fingernail with an emery board.

I was needed in the kitchen. Tonight I was throwing a party for Big Nick, the gorgeous Russian, the love of my life. So much to do. So much could go wrong. I felt sixty-five nervous breakdowns coming on. I kept checking through the window for clouds. If it rained, we'd never all fit inside the house. I had agonies of anxiety that the entertainer's plane would be held up at Sydney airport because of unexpected fog. I couldn't trust the sound system people. What if Johnny Mac or Big Pretzel started their act and the microphone howled. Worse still, had I written down ten dozen or twenty dozen party pies for the caterer? I'd have to phone and check, or go mad.

When I'd worked myself to a nervous exhaustion, and at the very moment the first guests arrived, my two eldest kids began world war three in the bedroom. I left the guests by the swimming pool, ran in to check the oven, hurried outside to make sure I spoke to everyone and that they were having a good time, then checked the level of the ice covering the drinks in the laundry troughs, calmed down Cindy, the guard dog at my toilet door, then went to fix the kids.

Gordon, poor love, got plastered. Jealous of Big Nick, he knocked back scotches until his blood turned to alcohol. Gordon adored me. I was the Galloping Gourmet with him. We'd dine at the best places. All that good food and booze gave me a weight problem, but if a girl's got to eat, why not make it the best? After wining and dining me, Gordon took me back to his mother's motel. The best part of that was the spa. I hated the sex bit with him. He needed so much warming up. If I wore black and red underwear, then teased him, that helped him raise it. But then he'd take one and a half years on the job. I'd get sick of it and punch him and throw him around the room.

While people splashed about in the pool, or danced to the music, Gordon dragged me around the side of the house to the aviary. He grabbed me and held me in a tight embrace. 'Patti, Patti, I love you. I'm crazy about you.'

I peeled him off and held him at arm's length. 'Gordon. I keep telling you. I'm no good for you. Give it up.' I put my hands on his cheeks and made him look me in the eye. 'Gordon. You've been so good to me.' He nodded like a six-year-old, and I smiled tenderly as I went on. 'Where would I be without you? I can always depend on you. We've been an item for years and years.' I took one hand away from his cheek and waved at the house. 'Remember the day you put the deposit on this place? You helped me to become somebody. I'll never forget that, but neither will I let it rule my life. You knew what you were doing. You knew who I was, and still am. I must've told you this a hundred times, but you never seem to believe me. You're wasting your time on me. You're just in love with love.' Gordon glowered and sulked, his face as grumpy as the Magic Pudding. 'You know I've got to have at least four men at once. It's not for the sex. You give me the best nights out in the best restaurants. With Big Nick, it's his kindness. He really understands me. He's the only man in all the world who treats me like an equal.'

Gordon flinched and drew away. I added hastily, 'You're the sweetest kindest love in all the world. I've still got your beautiful diamond engagement ring in my drawer.' He looked down at my hand. I replied, 'Of course I wear it, sometimes. But tonight I'm wearing Big Nick's ring because it's his special night.'

I paused, and thought, This time I've got to get it into his head. So I kept going. 'And you know I can't do without Kasey managing the business. He's given twenty-four hours a day since we moved in. He's married to it and I'm as good as married to him, even have his name. How do you think he feels? At least I don't make you pay. But Kasey has to pay the going rate. But I don't charge him when I let him take photos of me in action with Ralph.'

I looked carefully at Gordon. He was weaving like a punch-drunk boxer. His eyes were glazed with grog and shock. So I finished it. 'You know me. I run my life the way I want it. I'm just being me. You men are a necessary evil, and you've got to learn to cope. Now give us a kiss and let's get back to the party.'

I went back to Big Nick, and Gordon went back to his bottle of scotch. I predicted almost to the minute the time Gordon snapped, jumped in his car and roared up and down Churchill Road, drunk as a skunk, trying to hit stobie poles. I called the cops to come and arrest him before he hurt himself or somebody else.

The best part of any party was when everybody had gone home or fallen asleep and I had the backyard to myself to sit by the pool, pour myself a brandy and dry, light a cigarette, relax for the first time in days and say to myself, What the fuck was that all about?

This night turned out differently. There was a knocking at

the front door. It wasn't the Johnny Hoppers, but a kid from up the road, eyes wide, dressed in his Ernie and Bert pyjamas. 'Please. My dad's dying.'

I ran along Churchill Road, aware that Cassie was right behind me. The bloke sat in a pool of blood on his kitchen floor. His kids stood around and stared at him. His wife, drunk and distraught, stood with her feet in the pool of blood and stared down stupidly. The poor man held his throat. Beside him was a rusty old pocket knife. When he saw me, he let go of his throat and blood spurted out. I knelt down and pinched his throat to stop the bleeding. The bastard was ruining my dress.

He whispered, 'Let me die.' It was the suicide freak.

I snarled, 'Another time. Another place. But not while I'm around.' I looked up at the woman. 'Have you rung the ambulance?' She nodded.

The bloke's eyes started to roll. I was furious at his stupidity and at the stains on my dress. 'I'll tell you what. You've done some dumb things in your time. But this takes the cake. You could've used a sharp knife.'

He'd lost a lot of blood and began to slip into unconsciousness. As he went, he gave me a weak grin. I took the hint and said, 'You want me to do you a favour? Let go of the artery?' He got a frantic look in his eyes and raised one hand to hold mine against his throat. So he passed out and I sat there and held his throat, thinking of the fountains of blood when Jessie slashed her wrists, thinking of the car smash outside 165 Churchill Road when the man's leg bone burst through his skin, went up through the steering wheel and impaled him in the throat. Just like then, I squeezed with all my strength to hold life in until the ambulance men arrived.

When I got home, I hurried into the bathroom, flung my dress in the bath and turned on the cold water. From the backyard came the noise of music and laughter, a great splash and yell as somebody fell into the swimming pool. I stood at the handbasin, washed my forearms, the backs of my hands and then scrubbed my nails to get out the caked blood. I kept wiping out the handbasin to swill the red water down the drain. My face, white, without expression, stared at me from the mirror door of the cabinet above the hand basin.

When I was sure all the blood was gone, I wrapped a towel around myself, unlocked the bathroom door and made a dash for my bedroom. As I ran past the boys' bedroom, I saw Jack throwing clothes into a suitcase. My heart sank. What now? I flung on a dressing gown, went back to his room and closed the door to give us some privacy. Jack kept his back to me and pushed the lid down on the suitcase.

Just what I needed. 'What is going on here?'

Jack stood up, would not turn to look at me, but I heard his words clearly enough. 'I'm going and you can't stop me.' His voice was all choked.

I felt a rush of dizziness. The bitterness in Jack's voice stirred up the dread of my children abandoning me. What if they rejected me, all went their own ways, and I was left alone? That was too horrible to think about, and I pushed it to the back of my mind. I wasn't going to let them just drift away. Not without a fight. 'Well, perhaps you could have a bit of consideration and let your mother know what it's all about.'

Silence. His head was bowed. Then he spun around, eyes flashing with tears. 'You hardly know I exist. And when you do it's just to find fault.'

I waded into the attack, hearing my voice, wishing I'd shut up and deal with this some other way. Who was I kidding? I knew no other way. 'Don't lay that one on me, kid. All that "you're not the mother I wanted" crap.'

'Well, you're not.'

This was my child. Fifteen years old, but still my kid. He stood defiantly, afraid, eyes glittering. 'How do you think it feels when other kids at school pay me out? "Your mum's a prostitute." My mates aren't allowed to come here. All my life I've not been able to bring friends home. What sort of a mother is that?'

I heard my voice getting louder, knew I shouldn't over-react, and cursed my quick temper even as I shouted, 'What sort of a child is it who can't see past the end of his nose? So, I'm a bitch, but I'm here with you. You're mine whether you like it or not. You've got far more than I ever did. A roof over your head, plenty of good food, education, new clothes, not hand-me-downs. Don't come at me with any "poor me" bull-shit. You've got no idea. When I was a kid I had sweet FA.'

I'll give him credit. He was a tough fighter. He stood to fight me toe to toe. 'Oh, sure, sure. Poor old Mum. Nobody ever had it as bad as Mum.' Jack took a deep breath. 'And how long will this place be my home? Let's face it, I've had more roofs over my head than birthdays. And more fathers.'

Behind him, on his cupboard, was a photo of Jack on his first day at school, a little case in his hand, a big smile on his face. Why do sweet kids grow up to be such arseholes? I bunched my fist. Jack backed off, but was trapped against his bed. This was the kid I'd taken all Sid's beatings for. If it wasn't me, it would've been them. I had put my body so often between Jack and the world. And this was all the thanks I got.

I should've smacked him across the face right there, but for a moment all the sting went out of me. My first child was taller than me, his face had lost its child's softness, and the eyes that glared at me made me flinch with guilt at the things I'd got wrong as a mother. 'Grow up, Jack. There's no magic wand to make life the way you want it. Life's a Colosseum, and we're the ones who get thrown in to fight to the death.'

He suddenly sat back on the suitcase, awkward, embarrassed, out of puff. Head down, he said, 'Well, I'm sick of all the fights. For years I've cleaned the house, whichever one we were in that year' – his chin rose, rebellious again – 'done the washing, cooked, changed shitty nappies, had to share a room with little punks, all with a different father, who whinge all the time. I tell you, I've had to be my own father, and I'm sick of it. Why do you think I've stood on the railway station selling news-papers? To get enough money to escape from here.'

He blinked at me, tear-drops on his eyelashes, his eyes furious and vulnerable. When he batted those long black eyelashes, I was gone for all the world. I felt the hot rush of love for him in my belly. I remembered how he fought to be born. He was breach. Three long days to come out, with blood on his head, both of us exhausted by the struggle. I sucked in my breath. What he had just said was true. For years Jack had been the little man of the house. Now, for this precious moment we were really talking, even if it was another fight. Not knowing what to say, I said the first thing that came to my mind, trying to get him to see me, his mother, as a woman, as a person.

'I don't know normal. I learn as I go. I know I make lots of mistakes, but I'm doing my best. Perhaps I'm a bit strict, but I was taught if you spare the rod you spoil the child.'

Jack scoffed. 'Perhaps? You've handed out more beltings than hot dinners. You make the stupid rules and then belt us if we disobey.' He held up his hand. 'No. You listen to me for a change.' His voice got back the harshness it had lost for a minute. 'Who made up the stupid rule about not hugging her kids after they turned seven? Who took us on picnics to St Kilda beach then sat in the car all day, yelling at us to run away and play? What sort of a mother is it who's always so busy looking after her prostitutes that she can't even listen to her own kids? When have you ever just talked to us like a real mother, maybe just for once believed us, not belted and then interrogated us?'

'What about all those years of changing your nappy, taking you to doctors when you were sick, cutting your school lunch, reading you stories at night? Isn't that love?' My blood began to boil again at the thought of this upstart's ingratitude.

Jack swallowed and looked about, as though trying to find another argument. 'Any mother would do that. I mean the real things that mattered to us. You're always running around as though the world would stop turning if you didn't keep it going.' Then he threw me a really black look. 'Like. Where were you for the two years I was state junior champion? You never came to see me run. All the other kids had parents there cheering for them, patting them on the back if they lost. Everyone. Not me. I might as well have been an orphan, for all you cared.'

I snarled at him, 'How dare you. You know damn well what I was doing. Driving all the others to their soccer or whatever. I've not been a mother, just a bloody chauffeur for selfish kids.' Oh, how his words had hurt. Of all people, I knew exactly how it felt to have nobody there to watch me. And I had done to Jack what had been done to me. 'I came to see you that time at Urrbrae, when you won. I nearly cried to see my boy so fast and strong, doing that.'

Jack gave me a long, slow, sneer. 'Once. Once you came to see me in how many years?' When he got that sneer on his face he looked just like his father. All my hatred and anger at the father rose up against his son. I knew it was unfair, but it was instinctive, beyond my control.

He went on, 'I know what you were doing all those years. Do you think we kids couldn't hear you in your room, didn't know what was going on?' He curled his lip and turned his face away in disgust. 'Those noises. My mum and all those men. And don't forget Melanie. I don't care what you say. You're not the mum I want.'

'I wish you were a real son,' I shouted, all the time wanting to scream far worse at him.

We both stood, without moving, our words echoing in our heads. Neither of us could take the words back. It was too late. We couldn't look at each other. After a while Jack reached down and deliberately clicked shut both the locks on the suitcase. He lifted the case off the bed and stood it on the floor. 'I'll never get married.'

'Where will you go?'

'Nana Shirley's.'

'You'll be back.'

# *Night on the town*

*With Jack gone, the house felt strange. There was an emptiness, despite* the normal chaos and confusion. At night the little ones whispered in their rooms, and if I heard a sob, I'd sneak in and sit where such a short while ago Jack had been. How short is the time we have with our children. Even worse, how sad it is that the sins of the parents are visited on their children. No. We children imitate those sins.

Here I was in my mid thirties, a battler who'd fought to get what I wanted. Just as I should have begun to feel safe, I was afraid it would all run through my fingers like dust. The flight of my first-born child frightened me. The years as Madam, which brought freedom and triumph over my past, also put me under tremendous strains. I was so busy I had no time to wee. Things like the party for Big Nick left me exhausted. I was afraid my body and brain would give out, just when they should have enjoyed their rewards. There was so much in every day: the family, the business, a thousand problems demanding to be solved. I had to be so many people. If there was a cat fight among the girls, I'd drag myself out of a chair, and force myself to act the part needed: Patti the Tyrant. If I was to stay sane, and not entirely lose the enjoyment of everyday things, I must have some escapes.

I owed Cassie a night out on the town. To do it properly she had to have her hair done first. I took her into town, to Hindley Street. 'Hello, Patti,' called out men from the Greek Club. 'Who's the little Patti?' The old guys around the outside tables saluted

221

us by raising their weeny cups of Turkish coffee. Ted Mills stood at the door of his electrical shop, watching the world go by. His window display, as ever, was a complete jumble, more like a handyman's shed than a shop. 'Goodday, Patti. And who's the little lady?' I introduced Cassie, and Ted gave her a good inspection and added her to his memory of names, relatives, occupations.

In Hindley Street, everybody was there for everybody – camaraderie. If a shop owner broke a leg at one end of the street, the news spread like a bushfire. Within ten minutes, somebody would be there from another shop, to keep an eye on it. Others would do what they could to help the family.

Hindley Street was an outing, not just a place to shop. Cassie and I stopped outside the Olympic Photo Studio and watched two teenage girls line up in the queue, go inside the booth to pose for the camera, then burst out the door to squeal and die with embarrassment at the photos.

As we got near to Nilia's, a voice called, 'Hey, Patti.' It was Terry the gambler. He travelled the world, paying his way with what he won on board ship. He bet compulsively on anything, on two flies crawling up the wall, if that was all that was going. Terry was about twenty stone and loved his food and wine. 'A rule of life,' he would say, 'never worry about eating good food, or what you drink. Enjoy.' Terry knew every horse, every racecourse crook and the crooked cops. He knew things about people they'd forgotten themselves.

This day he greeted me as an old friend, as though we had just shared a meal, even though we hadn't seen each other for months. 'Patti. You are looking beautiful. My brother says you are Lana Turner. And who is this one with you?'

Terry tested the name. 'Cassie That's nice. Tell you what, little Cassie, your mother is crazy in the head.'

Cassie was startled by this, and looked up at me sharply. I grinned. I knew what was coming. The same old lecture.

Terry leant down and said to Cassie, 'Your mother should be at Monte Carlo, not here in Adelaide. She's bloody stupid to stay in this bloody town. She's got everything. Why does she waste it?' He gave Cassie's cheek a pinch and said, 'You tell her,

222

Cassie. Patti never listens to me, because she knows I am right.' Terry gave me a wink, turned and walked off, filling half the footpath, waving his arms. I faintly heard his voice, 'Bloody woman. You tell her.'

Cassie and I went to Nilia Puccini's Hair Salon at 114 Hindley Street. I should say 'Beauty Salon' because Nilia, the best in the city, wasn't qualified as a hairdresser. Her father was, in his barber shop downstairs, but not Nilia. Anyway, her father had just about gone broke during the hippy years when all the blokes had beards and long hair. Things had picked up a bit during the craze for skinheads, pierced noses, ears and nipples, but the days of the shilling shave and the short back and sides had gone, except for the few oldies.

It was worth taking Cassie to Nilia's just to watch Cassie's face when we squeezed up the narrow stairs into the salon. The stairway was crammed with people. Everybody held their paper ticket with a number, and chatted away like mad.

'Hi, Patti.' It was Rosemary, the stripper. And there were showbiz people – you'd bump into Tony Monopoly the crooner, or California Brown – and restaurant managers. Society dames from the eastern suburbs rubbed shoulders with working girls in short skirts and high boots. At the top of the stairs, in his floral dress and blonde wig, sat Kerri the transvestite, all bones and teeth, like a barracuda in drag.

The salon buzzed. Customers gossipped. Hairdryers hummed away. The air smelt of ammonia from the perm lotions and, as I looked along the row of chairs, I saw heads of hair coloured black, pink, blonde; a rainbow of rinses. Reflected in the long mirrors were lines of Liz Taylors and Grace Kellys – and old Mrs Tucker, eighty-seven not out and fast asleep under the dryer, her hands draped over the arms of her wheelchair. She'd outlasted two husbands and a batch of kids. She came to Nilia's for the glamour, the comfort of familiar faces and the pleasure of having some young girl fiddle with her hair.

Nilia had a staff of seven girls, dressed in green mini skirts, with platform shoes, pale pink lipstick and pink nails. They wore heavy eyeliner, gold chains with crosses and, dangling each side of the cross, the two curved horns to keep away evil.

Nilia stood behind the counter, her hands full of hair-pieces she tissied up. This day she wore a Rege deep auburn hair piece. When she caught sight of Cassie and me she gave her wide smile, dropped the hair pieces on the counter and came forward to greet us. The beautiful Nilia was friend, psychologist and Mother Confessor to half of Adelaide's women. She knew whose marriage was breaking up, whose husband was having an affair with his secretary, whose kids had run off. She could tell just by the feel of the hair if a woman was stressed, pregnant or grieving.

Nilia put her finger under Cassie's chin and tilted it up. 'So this is your Skinny Minnie?' Cassie squirmed. Nilia smiled. 'Yes, she is a pretty girl, but we must do something to keep her hair from covering her face.' She frowned and brushed Cassie's hair this way and that with her fingertips. 'Hey. We want to see those lovely eyes. Why be a sheepdog?' Cassie gave her a shy smile. 'That's better. Don't be afraid, I won't cut it all off, just give it the proper shape.'

Cassie shot me a glance which meant, You told her. Well, I had freaked that day when I saw the nits in her hair. I attacked her head with kero and petrol, but they were buried in the skin. Ralph cracked out his razors and cut the lot off. Shaved her bald. Cassie had a total nervous breakdown. She screamed, 'I look like Kung Fu's cousin!' She tore to shreds the good wig I got from John Martins. She jammed a black and white beanie on her head and refused to go to school. She hid in the wardrobe until it was way past school time. As time went by we all loved to stroke her stubble. It felt nice sticking up through the beanie. Her brother, Pepe, brought friends home and charged them their pocket money to sneak a look at Cassie. She went ape, beat them up, and yelled, 'If you're male, I hate you!'

Cassie and I got our numbered tickets and went back to the stairs and found a place to sit, knees under our chins. We talked to Marlene about babies, weddings and her rat of a husband. One day Marlene had been absentmindedly leafing through Nilia's photo album of customers and styles when she came upon the photo of the woman her husband called his secretary. In the photo she was certainly not dressed like a respectable secretary.

When at last we got to the top of the stairs we idled away the time watching women who called in to try on their wigs or hair-pieces. Cassie stared at a young woman not much older than her, and whose hair was cropped to the skull. The kid struggled past us and went to Nilia to collect a gorgeous blonde wig. 'Working girl,' I told Cassie. 'Look at her hands when she comes back past us. See, she's got short nails too. Three guesses where she's been for a few months. Not the Gold Coast, that's for sure.'

'Make way,' somebody called up the stairs. It was Nilia's mum, carefully balancing a tray of cappuccinos and toasted cheese sandwiches for the customers who'd ordered them. Nilia's father followed, went straight to a trolley, picked up a comb and slicked his hair each side, above the ears. 'Dad, we were just going to use that comb,' said Nilia. She took it from him, spanked the back of his hand with it, and threw it in a sink. As always, he held up his hands. 'Sorry, Sorry. Old habit.'

When it was Cassie's turn, she climbed into the chair, gaped around at me for reassurance, and stared at her reflection while Nilia experimented with her hair. 'We'll keep it simple. Something to highlight your eyes. Something you can manage at home.' Then Nilia gave instructions to the girl and went to give the next customer her attention.

I sat in the chair next to Cassie and closed my eyes. Before long I heard her chatting away with the girl doing her hair. 'Mum made a goobar out of me when I was just thirteen. It was the Friday night school dance. I had no bust. My nipples were too frightened to grow.'

I opened one eye, Cassie gave me a nervous grin, and kept talking. I smiled at her funny way of saying things, but it was a grim smile. I knew why she was scared of growing. My heart froze at the memory of the morning she cringed away from a man who was in our house. No questions asked, I smashed him and threw him out.

Cassie kept burbling on to the hairdresser. 'Mum felt sorry for me, so she tried to help. I'd rather she didn't.' Cassie lifted a hand to itch her nose. 'Well, she gave me one of her bras that changed me from a zip into a 44 double "D" in no time. She stuffed socks and tissues down inside those huge cups. Anything that wasn't nailed down went in. When I went into the dance there were chuckles all round from the girls who knew me. So I sit by the wall. Up struggles this new guy. Leans one arm against the wall so he can bend over me to give me the chat and have a good look down my bra. He says, real masculine, "I like you. Your boobs are so big." He leans right down, gives my left one a poke and all the stuffing slips, and when I stand up this orange falls out from under my dress and goes thump on the floor.'

The hairdressing girl had stopped work, just stood watching Cassie in the mirror. 'What did you do?'

'What do you think? I ran out and wouldn't go back to school for a week. Anyway, I'm exempted from school now. Mum's bought a hairdressing salon up the road and I'm allowed to be an apprentice. It's great. I can razz up and down Churchill Road in all the wigs.'

After we had finished at Nilia's, Cassie and I went home to tart ourselves up for the night. Cassie finished her make-up, looked at herself in the mirror and purred, 'Veeeeery posho.' The other kids scowled and hated Cassie, but as she so nicely said to them as we sailed out the front door, 'You can stop pointing those fingers at me and stick them up your bum.' She bounced out the gate to the long white Lincoln limousine. 'I love our car, Mum. You need a bloody torch to find your way around inside.'

We drove to Hindley Street and parked behind the Overway Hotel. First I took Cassie to Rosa's where men fell over each other to greet us. A Russian took Cassie's hand and, dribbling with charm, said, 'Why have I not met you before? Run away with me, marry me.' I was proud of Cassie's cool. She politely permitted him to kiss the back of her hand and said, 'Join the queue.' The man laughed, ordered a huge bunch of flowers from the flower lady, and put them on our table. As soon as we sat, Cassie wiped the back of her hand on the tablecloth and whispered to me, 'Want a drink? Want a kiss? Want me to die for you, Patti?' She sat beside me like Queen B. We were lavished with flowers until we were almost out of sight. Cassie giggled. 'Mum, you've got flowers until they're coming out your backside. Well, I suppose enough men live up there.'

She was almost as much like me as Jack. I felt the pang of five month's separation from him. All was not lost, however. Gordon had put the deposit on a block of land at Spalding and that would give Jack another choice of a place to live. It also meant that we had a holiday house near Kasey's mum. Nanna loved to have my tribe visit, and I longed for the kids to have a grandmother who spoilt them and, more important, accepted us. Poor Gordon. 'Who is it who keeps writing cheques? Then the other blokes get the lot, and I'm lucky if I get a handshake.' Dear Gordon. Finding his manhood was proving very painful.

I drove all gloomy thoughts away and said to Cassie, 'Don't you just love to see a room full of men fawning all over you?' Cassie nodded and sipped at her pint glass of lemonade and raspberry.

When the Cold Duck had reached my eyeballs we left Rosa's and went to the Paprika. It was a good feeling to be greeted by the hostess in the place where I had worked ten years before. I had a table booked, not up on the mezzanine where guests looked down on others, but right by the dance floor in the middle of the action. Cassie watched the dancers. Her eyes shone and her fingers tapped the table in time to the music.

'Come on,' I said, 'let's show them how to do it.' I dragged Cassie onto the floor and we began to jive. Cassie watched me with surprise. 'Where did you learn to do that?' I swung and twirled, one foot with a spiked heel flying out level with my ear. 'Listen kid, I was doing this in the real days of rock 'n roll, when you were only a gleam in your father's eye.' Cassie matched me move for move and we flung ourselves into it, trying more outrageous steps. A circle of people stood around and clapped in time. Harder and harder we danced, the band giving it all they'd got. Then a tramp named Betty moved onto the floor with her drunk pick-up and tried to compete with us. Talk about a pie dressed up as a pasty. She had a blonde wig coming loose, and her bulges appeared where they shouldn't be. She danced like the missing link, while her bloke cavorted around like a hippy orang-utan. All they were threatening was the foundations. It wasn't a competition, it was a wipeout. I swung Cassie through the air and she squealed but never missed a beat when her feet hit the floor.

When the band had thumped out the last notes, Cassie and I stood panting. She grinned like the cat who'd got the cream. Sweat trickled down our backs and the people clapped and whistled. Then we fell into our chairs and reached for a drink. Cassie's face shone, her flat chest heaved. She reached over the table and touched my hand. 'I've never seen you this happy, Mum.' Straight away my eyes filled with tears. 'This is when I'm me,' I said, then, checking the pins on my curls, 'this is Patti.'

Some time around midnight we left. A mob of my men insisted on keeping us company down Hindley Street. As we came near the Overway Hotel, I caught sight of Liz, my beloved Hairylegs, from all those years ago at Carrington Street and Tea Tree Gully. She was walking along arm-in-arm with her second husband, the ballroom dancer. Liz saw me, stumbled, looked at my hair, at the men around me, and put her face down. She tugged at the arm of her husband to pull him across the road. I watched her back as she hurried across Hindley Street, and I sensed I'd never see her again. I took a deep breath to stop myself crying out. Is this what Patti did to people? Or was it something in them, not me?

I remembered Liz's face at my door. 'Patti, Patti, come quickly.' We ran back to her place where her baby lay in the cot. I had helped Liz tuck him in only an hour before. He was dead. Yet there had been nothing wrong with him, no signs at all. He just went to sleep while Liz cooked tea, but he didn't wake up. That was the Liz who'd been my sister, my other half. Even after she brought Sid to the caravan park our friendship kept going. She was afraid of nothing, except her own mother and father's disapproval. She scuttled away across Hindley Street and disappeared into the crowd.

'Who was that, Mum?' Cassie looked right into my face, reading the signs. She never missed a trick.

'Just somebody I knew a long time ago. Damn these new spiders,' I said, and fiddled with my false eyelashes.

We partied on at the Overway, and watched my friend Pat,

whose stage name was Big Pretzel, glide into the spotlight, stretch out those gorgeous long legs, swirl about in thirteen miles of see-through Arabian costume, then strip it off until she was down to next to nothing. A Go-Go dancer, Big Pretzel rotated the tassles on her boobs in different directions at the same time. Amazing. I could never work out how she did it. Pretzel really made those tassles swing.

Later, I saw Cassie's eyelids begin to droop. She looked like she did as a baby, struggling to keep awake. Her eyes glazed, the lids slowly closed, then jerked open again. 'Time to go, Skin.' She tried to protest, but it's best to leave when you're having fun.

The blokes clamoured around, and walked us to the Lincoln convertible. As I nosed the limo out onto Hindley Street, some silly tart with a death wish drove across the end of the driveway and parked so nobody could get in or out. I gave her a blast of the horn but she just gave me the finger. I heard Cassie say, 'Oh, no, watch out lady.' I got out of the Lincoln, went to the other car and looked in the driver's window. I asked her in a sweet voice, 'Would you please move your car? I can't get out.' Cassie was right at my heels. She wasn't going to miss out on the fun.

'You can get stuffed,' the driver replied.

I looked over at the passenger. 'Would you tell your friend to move her fucking car before I punch her lights out.'

The driver forced her door open and stood up to me. 'Look over there,' I said, all very blasé, pointing to the ground on the other side of the car. 'That's where you'll land when I hit you.'

'Ha, ha, ha.'

Pow. She went over the bonnet and crashed out of sight onto the driveway. The passenger slid over behind the wheel, speaking in a high squeaky voice like the Chipmunks, 'I'll shift it, I'll shift it.'

We drove home, over Morphett Street Bridge, up past the golf course and along Jeffcott Street to Wellington Square, past the place where the girl's home had been, and we did laps of the square, our tyres squealing, while we hung out the windows yelling, 'Yippee!' and seeing how many fast corners we could do without spewing.

# The clients

*Fantasy, self-delusion, glamour; these make the world go round.* One of my academic clients told me that the word 'glamour' means to cast a spell over someone, to have them in your power. Glamour was not beauty but oppression. The professor could talk. That's about all he could do. He used words like a junkie used heroin. And it was no wonder he hated glamour. He was gross, smelly, lived in a pig-sty, and had to get drunk on words and VSOP before he could raise it. He despised sex, in fact was slightly nauseated by it. Words were his glamour. They gave him power over his students. He could write 'Fail' on a piece of paper. He was a kind of crooked cop, but students, not working girls, were his victims. His fantasy was to write a book that would make him famous. 'Publish or perish,' he grumbled to me while he fished about in his kitchen sink, looking for a clean glass among the greasy pots and pans. I shuddered at the thought of those hands on me. His house was full of books – thousands of them in bookcases that went from the floor to the ceiling. Hundreds lay scattered about on tables and the floor. I thought about him a lot. All that knowledge, but as a human being, where had it got him?

I learnt a lot about fantasies and self-delusion, nausea and obsession. Glamour, the casting of spells, was my speciality.

French maids were popular with clients and the girls. The girls loved dressing up in the costume of black spiked heels, net stockings, suspenders and the little white hat. In a way, the girls had to have their fantasies too, or go round the bend. They loved the French names I gave them more than the names given by their mothers.

Clients loved the costumes because it let them act out their fantasies. For those into schoolgirls we had a wardrobe of uniforms for the elite girls' schools. Tartans, pleated skirts, sports tunics, socks, and the ribbons to tie up the pigtails. I did a survey around the agencies, so that I could buy what my clients needed. The men mostly asked for twelve to thirteen-year-old girls. They would phone in an order for, say, a Grade Seven St Jerome's girl, red hair. My working girl got out the right gear and went to the man. He sat her on his lap. 'Let's play a little game.' He'd do what he wanted, and whisper his fantasy. 'This is what I want to do, Amanda, my nine-year-old niece.' What worried me was that there were more sadistic attacks on the schoolgirls than on the French maids. I often wondered how many little girls were saved from rape because the fathers and uncles came to me.

Lots of Catholic men wanted nuns. We had our wardrobe of habits. The men loved it. They really believed they were screwing a nun. They were supermen because they could do the impossible. They were getting back at the church, at their education, the strict upbringing. Their revenge was a worry. Sometimes they hurt my girls. I suppose my girls and, when I come to think about it, all women, are both the craving and the enemy. As Nan taught me, love and hurt go together.

The priests and ministers loved to suffer the hell fire of guilt. The greater the guilt, the bigger the thrill. They were a bit like the sadists: the worse the pain, the quicker the orgasm. Of course, the men of the cloth were never any bother about payment. To pay the girl meant no responsibility, no hassles, no relationship. The girl was a piece of meat. After all, God was a man. Maybe that's why men are rotten.

Sometimes a priest, like other men, got so frenzied he lashed out and smashed the girl. But it was the habitual sadists who worried us more. They used the girls as paid rape victims. I wonder if it isn't something genetic in men, some chemical in the brain, a hormone. Their cruelty is more than just the way they're brought up. For sure, society, schools, films all teach men that it's great to hurt and kill and step on the face of all those you've defeated. But the violence in men is more than the violent world does to them. I don't believe all that victim of circumstance crap. Nor do I believe the sadists should get away with it. We made our own black list, refused to service those men, let the other agencies know their names, and when the cops needed help in tracking down somebody who'd raped a kid, or bashed them senseless, we were glad to help. I reckon a lot of my girls would have voted for capital punishment.

Other male fantasies were bizarre, but pretty harmless. There was the man who loved crabs, the sort that hide under rocks at the beach. He'd make the girl arch over backwards, belly up, balanced on hands and feet. Then he'd get her to scuttle around sideways while he tried to get it in. While he was prodding away, the girl had a hell of a job trying not to laugh. These girls needed a sense of humour to survive and one of them told me she'd think all sorts of stupid things, like, 'Hey, how many people realise they're related to a man who's really into seafood?'

There was the sad case of the man whose fiancé was a celebrity. You could bet your bottom dollar that a few hours after she was on tele, or on the front page of a paper, he'd phone in and ask for Helga. He dressed in his fiancé's underwear and Helga gave him 'B and D'. 'Crawl over here, you bastard.' Then she kicked him in the face for crawling.

Other men were just stupid. The phone would ring. 'Got any girls with huge tits?' It was The Blob. He was twenty-four stone and loved the Greek way, anal. French is a head job. Spanish means between the boobs. Oz is ten seconds.

There were always the weirdos who wanted nursing mothers. The phone. 'Any of your girls feeding a baby?' He had a real toffy voice. 'I want mother's milk.'

I tried setting up Fantasy Phone Calls for the wankers. Trouble was, how to get the mongrels to pay?

We came across all sorts of nut cases. There was Screwball, who would only take a girl at the end of her shift, after at least six other men had her first.

And there was Rin Tin Tin. He'd phone in. 'I'll have the usual.'

'What?'

'Claire knows. Ask her.'

So the one who drew the short straw had to go outside with a paper bag and a trowel and fill the bag with dog turds. Rin Tin Tin paid his money to sit on the floor and get the girl to watch him eat it.

One fat old fellow loved lesbian scenes. Actually, I've never met a man who wasn't turned on by watching girls do it. This old bloke told the girls what to do, and away they went in a sixty-niner, faking huge orgasms. But he was a smart old prick. He got real close and yelled, 'I'm paying. You do it properly. Get your head down in there.' He pushed Cleo's face right into Angela. Cleo was sick, and they left. When they returned to Churchill Road, Cleo raced to the bathroom and stuffed her mouth full of toothpaste. While she brushed away like mad, Angela told the rest of us the story. Cleo must've heard the laughter because she was livid when she came back in. Angela just laughed at her. 'You've been in my fanny.' Cleo wouldn't speak to Angela for a week, even though they shared a flat.

For the Golden Shower, some men lay beneath a glass table, going their hardest while the girl peed over the table. Other men preferred no table.

The girls needed twenty-four hours' notice for the Brown Shower. When the message came through the girls went into hiding. The one chosen for the Brown Shower threw things about, made a big drama. They hated it and regarded it as the most degrading thing they did. It meant loads more money, but all the money in the world would never have persuaded me to do it. You'd have to cut off all thoughts of yourself as a human being. But some girls found it hard to resist the money, and after a bit of hysteria went out to buy the Laxettes.

There were as many fantasies as kinds of clients. We had politicians, civic leaders, lawyers, police, welfare officers. These people wouldn't say shit for sugar in public; but with our girls . . . Adelaide is all beautiful on the outside. Inside it is full of maggots.

Of course we had many of the media celebrities. The sports commentators thought they were big heroes. The girls moaned, 'Oh, you're so big. Be careful with me.' The silly wankers believed it. The girls knew which customers to tell, 'Oh, you're the best I've ever had, swear to God.'

Interstate and overseas celebrities got their managers to phone in two days before to get the right girls lined up. International sports teams on tour took a bit of organising. Pop groups sent for all my best girls to fill their hotel suite with glamour for the media sessions. When they came back from giving a concert, it would look like a room full of fabulously beautiful groupies. The girls had a wow of a time. All that free food and drink, and doing nothing for it except crowding in front of a camera. Every job deserves it perks.

Other nights were fun. Celebrations at the end of season footy and cricket were always good money-spinners. Bucks' nights were a laugh, especially the Italian ones. There was the traditional raffle for the prostitute, and it was always rigged so the groom won. It was great to see him squirm. Will I, or won't I?

Girls preferred Caucasians. The Japanese and Chinese made the girls open their legs wide and they'd finger them, peering in for signs of infection or crabs. The girls thought it was disgusting, but the money was good, and none of the Asian men lasted ten seconds. When the girls got back to Churchill Road they'd sit around and have a bitch and a laugh about it. They had to let off steam or go mad. The Arabs would take a girl to the Oberoi for two or three days. The money was excellent, but the Arabs used their fingers to clean themselves after the toilet and then came back to bed without washing their hands.

One thing I didn't realise was the money to be made in the male homosexual trade. Adelaide had thousands of homosexual men, but they were secretive. They had to be, because of the organised poofter-bashing. They met in the gay bars and seemed to have their own systems of pick-ups. But in those early days, before it was fashionable to come out, there were many miserable frustrated homosexual guys out there. Some of them preferred male transvestites. It was hard to organise my transvestites and keep them on call. They wouldn't sit in a room and wait, like my girls did. They'd go off to the banks of the Torrens. At least they stuck to their regular territories, marked out by toilets, so my drivers had a chance to find them. The homosexual men on my books were so fiery, jealous, temperamental. You had to be very sure of yourself to enter the gay scene even well into the seventies.

Lots of our straight clients were the recently separated, the lonely, the talkers. Some fell in love with the girl, and a few married them. This gave the girls a chance to go respectable. I was never sure about this 'Rescue the Girl' fantasy. Those magic words 'I love you' that fool so many usually mean, 'Please tell me that you love me.' When someone wants to 'rescue you', or says, 'Let me do this for you,' they are just putting their weaknesses on you.

The girls didn't mind the normal blokes. There was one poor fellow who took ages to get it up and going. Angela was a marvel at pacing him. Just on the end of the half hour he'd start going hammer and tongs, and be about to have his jollies. Angela would look at her watch, push him off and say, 'Time's up. That's it. Or pay for another half hour.'

We all adored Old Tom. He had the palsy with old age. The girls knew he'd only last a couple of seconds, but they'd give him the works, and a few kind words to reassure him, then send him on his way.

If Old Tom set the record for the oldest, I reckon the youngest was a boy of no more than ten. Cassie looked at him. 'You're not quite eighteen.'

'Yes I am. I'm just short for my age.'

Maybe, at a pinch, he was twelve. Cassie sat on the bed and said, 'Well, let's see the colour of your money.'

The boy took the cork out of the frog money box bottom and tipped a mound of coins on the bedspread. 'This is all my pocket money. I've been saving for yonks. I want to do it.'

Cassie spread some coins in the palm of her hand. 'Is this enough for half an hour? You'd better count it and make sure you've got eighty dollars. I won't do it for a cent less.'

'Eighty?' he said, and looked sick.

The boy began to count. He kept making mistakes with the one and two cent coins. His piles of five cent pieces, each making a dollar, fell over and got mixed up. He shifted the lot to the floor and started again. By the time he'd got to seventy-three dollars and thirteen cents he'd run out of money and time.

Cassie sat on the floor beside him, just like his big sister, and helped him pour the money back into the frog. Then she gently took his face and said, 'It's no good throwing eggs against a wall and hoping they won't break. Look for me again when you're really eighteen. I reckon you'll be a real hunk.'

As Madam, I reserved some men for myself, as my favourites. For a while I was fond of Matt, a lad of twenty. Because he was a favourite, he didn't have to pay or use a condom. I cared for Matt, but he gave me thrush because he wasn't circumcised. So I made him go off and have it done. Poor lad. When he came out of hospital he wasn't game to try it for months. By then I had taken other favourites and didn't have the time for him. He never had me again.

Old Kurt was my pet for a couple of months. He was a gentleman. There was no pressure to get into bed and stand on your head, or run round the room barking. He loved dinner and long conversations. When he left, he gave me an American hundred dollar note, framed, to hang on the wall. 'Keep it for a rainy day, Patti. You never know.'

For some of my favourites I was more mistress and friend. The relationship, as with Ken, often lasted for many years.

One day, Ken greeted me at the motel door. 'Patti, come in.' He gave me a hug and a kiss on the cheek to show he had missed me, and then quickly checked the courtyard and closed the door behind us. Once we were in private, he gave me a proper hug, sighed, patted me on the back and said, 'Patti, dear Patti, it's good to see you again.'

On the table was a bottle of wine, Spumante, which I loved but which he said tasted like lizard's piss. We poured the wine and drank our ritual toast, Ken trying not to pull a face as he took the obligatory sip. He phoned through for the dinner to be sent to the room. Lobster Thermidor, to please me, and warm crisp bread rolls with curls of butter, side plates of salad, and strawberry pavlova for dessert.

The kitchen knew our routine and the meal was sent immediately. With it was a bottle of Grange Hermitage 1965, which Ken held up to the light and sighed as though he had died and woken up in heaven.

'How's work?' I asked.

He glanced over at the bed that was littered with papers. 'I don't know how long I can keep up the pace, Patti. New York next week, but it's Rhonda's graduation ceremony. She's already given me the ticket. What will she think of me if I put work first again?'

'Ken you'll be pushing up daisies if you try to keep up this pace. You've got to begin looking after yourself. Don't go to New York.'

He looked down at his glass. He pushed his food this way and that with his fork. 'Who else can I trust to send in my place? I'm talking about multi-millions. Besides, nobody else but me has the power to make decisions on the spot.'

Quietly I said, 'If Rhonda really loves you, she will understand. Besides, isn't it about time your children showed you a bit of consideration? You've worked your fingers to the bone for them.'

Ken had the twitch back in his left eyelid. With a weak smile he said, 'I'm afraid I'm not handling things as well as I should. Margaret wants me to have counselling, even see a psychiatrist.'

I laughed. 'Why pay for somebody else's skiing holiday in Switzerland?'

That gave me an idea. 'Why don't you stay over a week in New York? Fly Rhonda over and have a holiday together. That would cost less than a shrink and do you a bloody lot more good.'

For an instant I felt Ken take the bait. Then he shook his head. 'It's not that easy, Patti.' His face was screwed up with tension. 'The follow-up work on this trip is – ' He waved his hand as though brushing away flies.

'Don't tell me. The boys. How could you take Rhonda and not her brothers? Families.' I thought of my children and poured my glass full. Families are where we learn to hate.

For a while, as old friends can do, we sat in silence, each lost in our own thoughts. Then I asked, 'And how is Margaret?'

Ken put both hands behind his head and leant back in the chair. 'Menopause, menopause. It's been how many years since Margaret and I, you know, lost contact? But her bonsai classes are coming on fine.'

I knew that gesture. When Ken looked most relaxed he was seething with tension. 'Come on, Ken, you're a real worry. Off with your things and up on the bed.'

Methodically he sorted all his papers and packed them back in his briefcase. Then he undressed, carefully draping his trousers and shirt over the backs of chairs. Always think ahead, was his motto. Mustn't be any funny creases, or fluff from the carpet. Ken was so busy calculating the futures that never happened that he had no present, well none that was much fun. Still in his Y-fronts, he climbed onto the bed and lay on his stomach.

This was the part I enjoyed best. I was no Einstein, but I loved the conversations we had while I massaged his neck, back and legs. I think this was time Ken was at his happiest. As usual, he instructed me that I was wasting my money, should invest it and then retire from the game. 'Even ten per cent of your $250,000 a year should roll over into a tidy sum, bla bla bla.' I wasn't really looking forward to the time when Ken would roll over and we'd have to do the sex stuff, but for now it was great fun for us both to let our minds wander. After he'd finished being Patti's financial consultant, we switched to politics, religion, the meaning of life. He was the only client who really listened to me, and didn't despise my lack of education. The excitement of a new idea was more fun for me than an orgasm.

Then we would do it, both of us thankful when it was over. Ken would hold me close and said, 'Patti, you are the only woman in my life. Apart from my wife. A true friend. I will always be faithful to you.'

That spoilt it. I had never met a man who in a crisis was not a liar or a coward. One day Ken would be the same. I would need the money, or someone to talk to, and he would not know me.

I had one fantasy that had never been fulfilled. I'd seen doodles in all shapes and sizes and colours. But I'd never had a big black one. I think every woman has the fantasy of a wild night with a big black buck. I got mine at an auction.

I planned a show for a north-east suburbs footy team, because my youngest, Chris, played in the juniors. News got around that it would be a hot show, including some sort of auction, and the club sold buckets of tickets. Somebody got excited and painted, 'Patti for Pope' on a wall of the local shopping centre.

My drivers set up the music and sound in the club rooms. I had taught two of my girls a strip routine the night before. The club rooms filled to overflowing, and we were all ready to roll. When the bump and grind music was about to start I grabbed the mike and said, 'You move while my girls are doing the show and it'll all be stopped.' The mob yelled, 'Yeah. No worries, Patti.'

Stephanie began as Teacher's Pet: lollipop, cane, spiked heels, school uniform torn in all the right places. She showed bits of tits and a flash of fanny. What a laugh. Good money, and no hassles.

Then came a complete surprise. A gorgeous black man prowled onto the stage. He was a panther, and all the women wanted to get in his pants. They went berserk, and the guys gaped. He wore leather tights, a leather jacket and leather cap with studs. He flicked a whip against his thigh. He was stunning, beautiful. I wanted him for lunch. What a doodle. If I'd seen it in the jungle I'd have hit it on the head with a hammer.

I went crazy for Stud. When he flexed that muscle I leapt on stage, shirt-fronted him and he went down with me on top. There was uproar, and hands tore me off him. A voice said, 'Fair go, Patti. You'll have to wait for the auction.' I had planned to auction a girl. Cancel that.

It was a cert that Stud was mine. In my mind Stud was up on stage like a slave in chains – to be bought. As the auction began, none of the women wanted any of the white guys up there in line with Stud. The bidding went up and so did my temperature. Some society dame wanted him and started to give bids that wiped out all the opposition but me. Up yours Miss Hoity-toity, I thought, and came in all guns blazing.

I got him. Panic. Where could I go? What would I do with him first, and second, and thirtieth? And I had kidded myself that sex wasn't all that exciting for me.

I took him away in my big white Lincoln convertible. Everyone thought I'd dragged him straight off to bed. I took him to dinner, first, at the Buckingham Arms, where the homosexual men hung out. Eat your hearts out boys. Then I took him home to meet the kids. Their eyes popped out and their jaws hit the floor.

Then I took him to bed. Not at home, but in my flat above my Glenelg fashion shop. All my birthdays came at once. He definitely had no hangups. What a stayer.

I lost track of time not just that day but for the next few weeks. It was easier for Stud to move in, but I kept him hidden at Glenelg. All my women friends kept phoning. 'Where is he?' Throaty growls and heavy breathing. 'Can we come round and have a cup of coffee?' No way. They'd pack rape him. My friends were more randy than the entire haberdashery department at David Jones. Then came another call. 'We've formed a syndicate and have enough money to hire him from you.' It was a lovely feeling to hear the anguish in their voices. 'Tough titties, girls.'

Then Stud pulled a couple of moves on me. He was screwing a hotel manager. So I broke a record over his head and threw him out. He gave me a heap of soul music as a farewell present. Whenever I hear soul, I think of that beautiful bastard. I wonder if there's a place women can mail-order them.

# *A rifle*
## *on my lap*

It didn't matter how much I tried as a mother, nothing seemed to work. If I took the kids under my wing like a mother chook, the little darlings shit on my shoes. When I tried fear and threats, they sneaked off and lit a fire behind the outside toilet. If I acted all hurt so they'd feel rotten guilty, they bowed their heads, said, 'Sorry, Mummy,' then went outside and let down somebody's bike tyres. It was no good separating them and sending them to their rooms. None of them had a room to themselves. If I shut one in, and said, 'Stay,' they got stuck into somebody else's pencil case and broke all the points, or drew on the wall. Belt them, and they plotted revenge. Ignore them and they half killed each other. If I gave them chores to keep them out of mischief, they'd complain like mad. 'He's only got six carrots to peel, but I've got seven potatoes. It's not fair.' It was hopeless to use reason in their disputes. Up went the temperatures and voices until Krakatoa erupted and there were beltings in all directions.

So I ran the place like an army camp, or like a jail. I was boss, I made the rules, and they obeyed or took the consequences. That didn't stop the fights. There were more rivalries in my place than blowies in a country dunny. Kasey, the only father living with us, got Chris a Yamaha mini-bike with a helmet. All the other kids raged. 'I never get a special bike.' Chris was only four, but he was up the gum tree like a goanna, and stayed out of sight for hours.

Later my special love, Big Nick the Russian, gave Chris a

pocket knife for his birthday. What did Chris do but waltz up to Pepe, point the blade at him and say, 'I'm gonna stab you.'

'Oh, yeah?' Peter was nine.

'Yeah.' Chris was five.

'You wouldn't have the guts, you little punk.'

'Yes I have.'

'Go on then, I dare you.'

'Yeah?'

'Yeah. Shithead.'

'I will. I'm not scared of you.'

'Go on then.'

Stab.

Pepe came screaming in from the backyard, blood dripping from his head. Chris shot through. Later when I'd brought Pepe home from casualty, I belted both of them, and give Big Nick a flea in the ear.

To settle the endless arguments between the kids, I bought a pair of boxing gloves. On Saturday afternoon we marked out a ring in the backyard, and the kids could punch the shit out of each other, with Big Nick or me as referee so that the little one, Chris, would live to see another sunrise.

Some Saturdays, I locked myself in my room and listened to the races. If anybody dared to come near me I yelled, 'Get out, get out, you'll bring bad luck on my horse. If it loses, I'll belt the living daylights out of you.'

We had some good times, I think, at the zoo, or going mush-rooming in Spalding Creek, or giving Kasey's mum a surprise party at Spalding. She was a darling, and I got so much pleasure from seeing her face when I walked in with the birthday cake, all the candles burning. The kids also liked going out to flash joints on Hindley Street. But I never could tell if I was doing the right thing. Sure as eggs, if we went mushrooming, at least one would whinge, 'I'm bored.' One thing I did know for certain, I loved them and did my best. That didn't stop them trying to make me feel guilty for being in the wrong. If they were five minutes late home, I went troppo with fear. Then they blamed me for causing a fight. When I was a kid I could never please the grown-ups. Now I was an adult, the kids gave me heaps.

I missed Jack, who'd been gone for a year. For a long time I fell into a sadness. During this time I had repetitive headaches. For years I'd had migraines, but now they became regular. I was so ill I'd lie motionless on my bed, the light out, the blind down, my head splitting into two halves which swelled like balloons until they were so tight they felt like they would burst. Even to turn over made me dry retch. These migraines began in childhood but became more severe after the Polish man put me in a coma. In the Finsbury Hotel one night he bad mouthed me, and I flattened him with a haymaker to the jaw. Weeks later, he sneaked up behind me in the Paprika and smashed me over the head with a bottle. I was unconscious for three days. The doctors said I was lucky to be alive. I went to the police, but nothing was done. They said there had been no report of any evidence. I wondered how much the bastard had paid them off.

Pepe, at ten years old, had just stolen his first car, a blue VW parked up the street. He was too small to reach the brake pedal and pranged it into a stobie pole.

It was my eldest daughter, however, who became the main worry. Blondie, whom I called Bucky Beaver, because of her front teeth, would swear the moon was made of green cheese and work herself up until she really believed her own nonsense. Sometimes she invented such a convincing lie that I fell for it and, in rage, lined the kids up in the passage, their pants down, and threatened to work my way along and belt their arses until I'd discovered the 'culprit'. And I'd do it, until we were all in tears. Later, when I put all their stories together, the penny would drop. Blondie had set it up.

One night, Blondie didn't come home. They all knew my rule. There was five-minutes' latitude, then they copped it. From ten to half-past I got into a temper. Then I began to worry. Before long I was sick with fear. When she got home I gave her a hiding.

After Blondie became pregnant, I got her boyfriend to move in with us. It was safer to know where she was, even if they did share a bed. It was a strange feeling seeing my child in bed with her lover, but I suppose I could hardly complain.

I had a phobia about weddings. I wanted Blondie to have a dream wedding. I planned everything to the last detail. It was going to be a beautiful day. A few days before Blondie's wedding I sent Cassie into their room to wake them.

'Come on, you lazy slob,' I said to Henry, 'why don't you get out and at least pretend to look for a job. Or maybe I'll abort the baby.'

They dragged on their clothes and wandered off up the street. When they had been gone a while, I got a horrible feeling. I sensed something was wrong. I jumped in my car and went look- ing. Nowhere. I came home, frantic, and tried phoning around. Nobody knew where they were. I phoned the minister and cried, 'Don't marry them today.' I was half an hour too late. Blondie had been married in her scraggy dress she wore every day. Henry was in his daggy shirt and dirty jeans.

Steam started coming out of my ears. I sat on the back door- step with a rifle on my lap.

At three-thirty, they came home in a convoy. Henry's father drove them in his car. A police car followed.

I remember how scared I'd been when I'd had to ask my father's permission to marry. Jeff had waited down at the corner while I went to my father's house and called him from outside on the footpath. I stood a few steps away from the gate. 'Now, Dad, promise you won't leap over the fence and belt me when you hear what I've got to say. Okay?' I stepped back a pace or two. 'I'm getting married.' He lunged forward. 'I know, I'm under age. But we're expecting a baby.'

As the cars arrived, I put the rifle down at my feet and folded my arms across my chest. Cassie came out to stand beside me. They all got out, formed up in a single file, and came in the gate. First a policeman, then Henry's dad, a tough guy, then the kids, and at the end of the queue, another policeman. I waited until they were within range. Henry's dad flexed his muscles, rounded his shoulders, and came on all masculine.

I bounded out, straight through the first copper and got Henry's father by the throat, knocking him flat on his back. Blondie screamed, and ran back to shut herself in the car. Henry stood, not knowing what to do. I was strangling away like mad and the two cops were trying to peel me off. I screamed blue murder into the face beneath me. 'You knew all the time, you bastard.' I bashed his head up and down to make sure he got the message. The thought of the wedding invites and the reception gave me strength.

The cops got me off and held me, while Henry's father struggled to his feet, all groggy and gagging like a tommy ruff. Henry was in the car with Blondie, hammering down all the door locks. Thinking it was over, the cops slackened their grip. I pounced and grabbed Henry's father by the throat again. He went down with a look in his eyes of, Oh no, here we go again. Then began a long tug of war. I wanted to kill the bastard, he wanted to live and the cops were at his back trying to pull us all out onto the footpath. I preferred to kill in my yard, where it could only be labelled a domestic. Out on the footpath it was called assault and creating a nuisance.

While they dragged me inch by inch towards the gate, my hands locked around his throat, I yelled to Cassie, 'Get the bridal stuff.'

She didn't move. Poor kid. I can imagine how she felt at the thought of what I was about to do. 'Move!' and she ran inside like a scared rabbit.

When she came out, arms full of Blondie's wedding clothes, they had got me a few yards nearer the gate. 'Throw it in the dirt!' I screamed.

'No, Mum, no,' Cassie whimpered. My Skinny Minnie, full of romantic dreams.

'Throw it in the fucking dirt.'

I heard Blondie howl from inside the car.

'Now,' I growled at Cassie. 'Step on it.'

Poor little Skin. She shut her eyes and put one foot on the wedding dress. Then I let go of the throat or nose or chest or whatever I was twisting at the time, and leapt onto the clothes. When they were a total wreck I picked them up, ran out to the car and threw the clothes all over it. The father staggered into his car, the cops took a breather, and I watched Blondie's car zoom off, wedding clothes flying off onto the road.

Then I sat Cassie down on the front step by me and gave her a twelve-course lecture that if she ever turned out like her sister . . .

As it turned out, Blondie's marriage lasted less than a year. Just like me, she married young, and regretted it. Cassie also made the same stupid mistake. That first marriage of hers was so hopeless. Violence, drugs, poverty. What else was there for Cassie to do? Cassie moved into the game after that. Like mother, like daughter.

# *Transvestites*

*Les Girls came to town. I was intrigued by men who dressed as*
women. Why did they do it? Who were they putting down?
I already knew Katherine from Nilia's Beauty Salon. Katherine
was beautiful and dressed elegantly in evening gowns and spiked
heels. But there was something sad about the way he'd sneak
up to Nilia's counter and slip hairsprays into his handbag. Of
course Nilia knew, and when she wasn't feeling soft-hearted
she made Katherine put them back.

The advert in the paper for Les Girls, however, showed a
line up of gorgeous men who were having a wow of a time. I
had to know how they did it. How did they get that cleavage?
Was it drugs, or falsies, or did they push their chest into a shape
and use sticky tape? What did they do with the family jewels
to look so smooth in their costumes? How did they survive
when all the world seemed full of poofter bashers?

Maybe my interest was warped. Back in the late seventies,
despite the gay revolution, feminism, and equal rights for Abori-
gines, transvestites were still seen as freaks. I knew, though, that
I had something in common with them. Maybe we all do. They
dress up to be the person they want to be. It must be a terrible
thing to look in the mirror and hate the body you are in.
Believe me, I know all about that. So much of my life was an
escape from the person I longed to be. It is an unbearable strain
to live a lie, day after day.

The show was in the Castle Hotel-Motel on South Road. The
audience sat around tables, cabaret style. There were old ducks

247

with so much make-up their faces wouldn't crack in an earthquake. There were lots of businessmen with women, some couples, and small groups of women, there for the perv, glancing about anxiously. And, of course, the footy blokes.

Drums rolled, and into the spotlight stepped a monster. On his head was a huge wig, as big as a sheep, with pretty bows tied here and there. He wore a ghastly house frock, had long hairy legs, footy socks and boots. He didn't have to say anything to have us in stitches. He just stood there, inspected us through Edna Everage glasses, and scratched his balls while he waited for us to stop falling about. The noise of whistles and yells was deafening.

Rusty Rae was the compere and comedian. He won me. He came back on as Shirley Temple, carrying a lollipop as big as an umbrella. His dress had an elastic top which he pulled down to reveal not boobs but a big, red heart stuck to his hairy chest. Then he changed to Humpty Dumpty. Later he was a Salvation Army girl in full uniform. He bashed a tambourine and sang dirty ditties. Another time he pranced on with huge plastic knockers sticking out, and sang like Tina Turner. I laughed until I cried. Through my tears Rusty Rae was a rainbow of wild colours. I laughed so hard my eyelashes fell down on my nose, and I jumped because I thought a spider had dropped on me.

The women in the audience laughed themselves silly. They adored Rusty because he was a fantasy of outrageousness. Rusty Rae was just what these housewives and businesswomen wanted to be: all colour and fearlessness. He could say and do whatever he liked, be adored for it, and we paid him to take the piss out of us.

Men tried to put him down with stupid macho drunken heckling, but Rusty was so sharp, so quick, he put the dickheads in their place.

'And what star sign is yours, darling?'

'A Pisces,' yelled his wife.

'Pisces. Well, well. That explains it. You screw small animals and pick your nose when driving. But people don't mind you. They think you're bisexual.'

The crowd hooted and pointed at the victim, and his wife

laughed the loudest. After a few of these, the dickheads lost their nerve.

The show was full of energy, power, beauty, dazzling costumes, fantastic singing and dancing. These men flaunted their difference. Near the end, Rusty sang the Frank Sinatra song 'I Did It My Way'. He stood there in drag, strong, dignified, a human being, and suddenly the audience was quiet. He sang about being born different. He sang of the sorrows of being a woman living in a man's body. I caught my breath. At the end of his act, he sang about courage to be yourself. There was no cringing in Rusty's light voice, somewhere between a man and a woman's, only defiance. Rusty wasn't singing just about himself. He was putting himself on the line for freedom.

After the show Rusty came back in front of the stage. He stood and peered into the crowd as though looking for someone. He had changed into a red evening gown with a huge white rose pinned high on the collar, almost brushing his left ear. On his head was a blonde wig, teased into flamboyant waves, with a fringe down to his eyebrows. He called a waiter over and spoke to him. The waiter turned and pointed to my table. As Rusty walked towards me, I slipped the big dress ring off my finger, and clutched it in my fist. What would Rusty think of me, the Madam?

Rusty sat, and looked straight into my eyes. He wore enormous false eyelashes, white eyeliner, blusher – but not like the clown's rouge of his act. His teeth were beautiful, and I wondered if they were his own. His lips were carmine red. He had a full bottom lip, and just below it was a beauty spot. I was surprised to see how plump his double chin was. On stage he seemed skinnier. And younger.

'Hello, Patti. I've heard all about you.' He flashed me a devastating smile.

I handed him the dress ring. I tried to be my most regal self, but my voice was nervous. 'For you to wear whenever you like, to remember me.'

Rusty took the ring, slipped it on his little finger and held it up to the light to examine the blue stone. 'It's beautiful, Patti. You know how to dress. Isn't it fun to make a woman's head turn twice when she sees us. I imagine she goes home, has a tantrum, and throws out half her wardrobe.'

'My Nan always said the way you dress is a statement. I like to dress so people think, She's this and she's that, but she's something else as well. I like to turn heads because I look different, more dazzling.' Then I said, 'When I walk down Hindley Street, it's like the parting of the waves. I'm moving against the tide. It makes me feel I'm not just dressed up as Patti. I really am Patti.'

'I relate to that,' Rusty said, and looked at my hair. 'Who's your hairdresser?' We settled into an easy conversation about hair styles, costumes, make-up, and shoes – as though we had known each other for years. I was thrilled that Rusty took me seriously, treated me with natural respect, liked me. That feeling was so rare. If only more men were like this, actually able to communicate with a woman and be nice to her, I thought.

'You know, Patti, we're alike in some ways.'

I laughed, to cover my confusion, and blurted out, 'You're a rainbow, always changing, always unexpected.'

Rusty sat very still, and then said, almost to himself, 'Music to the ears of this gay, old queen.' I could see his age creeping up on him; the slight sag of the cheek near the jaw line, the crows feet that the wig did not quite cover, the old skin of his ear lobes from which hung long silver danglies. Rusty blinked quickly, then reached out and held my hand.

How were we alike? Did women fantasise about me, want to be like me? Or was it just that we both told society to get stuffed?

We were interrupted by three stunningly beautiful young men from the chorus line who hurried to the table. They gathered around Rusty like chickens around a mother hen. They adored him. They fell over each other to explain a spat behind stage. They called each other cats and bitches, but laughed and preened, aware that eyes were on them. It struck me that Rusty was as much a mother to his troupe as I was to my girls.

They kept glancing to the back of the room, where a mob of men waited to pick them up. There were at least five blokes for every performer. Many of the hopefuls were gorgeous hunks, and I thought, Gee whizz, what a waste. One of Rusty's men simpered, 'Oh, look at the behind on that one.'

Rusty caught my eye. 'I've got to watch out for some of my little pets. Shameless hussies. I'm too old to flirt. It's a waste of time, and just between you and me, my dear, I'm terrified of rejection.'

Rusty turned to his men. They all had distinct breasts, and I wondered which of them had had the op. 'All right. Off you go. But I expect to see you at breakfast.' His men sailed away to their courtiers at the back of the room.

As they left, Rusty said to me, 'Adelaide. The most liberated state in the country, just about in the world, since your Donny D. But sinister. So many wowsers, so many creeps. I still have to do that awful footy socks and boots routine here, or the men in the audience get really nasty.'

'Adelaide is a big cake covered in icing,' I said. 'Every time a kid goes missing or another homosexual is murdered, they just slap another layer of icing over the lot. But inside it's rotten.'

Rusty shivered. 'They are so frightened of us. The poor little loves need so much reassurance that they're real men.' Then his face lit up as a young man approached him, carrying a huge sheaf of flowers. 'Looks like I'm in luck,' Rusty said to me. 'Nothing like playing uninterested to get them going.'

Rusty accepted the flowers graciously, then looked at me fondly. '"All the world's a stage. In our time we all play many parts."' Rusty stood, came around to me, leant down and kissed me gently on the lips. Then he straightened, and said deliberately, '"Most friendship is feigning, most loving mere folly".'

His young man touched Rusty's sleeve. Rusty's face was alight. He cradled the flowers like a baby. 'Remember, Patti, keep on laughing.'

# *Arrest*

---

*By 1978 Patti was riding high. The little girl from Pickering Street* who clomped off to school in second-hand high heeled shoes now owned two hundred pairs of shoes, and five wardrobes of outfits. As a child I lived in a dark house that shut out colours. Number 165 Churchill Road was full of light and colours, with huge windows opening onto the swimming pool. There was a poker machine in the lounge, lots of music, and bright green walls in the kitchen, the same colour as the coat I had fought Nan to buy all those years ago. The child not allowed to bring friends home threw parties for crowds of people I loved. The prisoner-child now wandered the city at will, not as an unknown street kid, but as Queen of Hindley Street. The four-year-old, sexually abused, was approaching the age of forty, but no longer cringed in fear and horror from the men who hid in shadows. Now the men waited in the wings. The only child had grown to a woman with a house full of her own kids and, in their lounge-room, the working girls who called me Mum. I had defied the fate meant to be mine. I was not another Nan, who sat by a window to watch life go past, and wait for death. I no longer had to create fantasies to keep the secret Patti alive in my mind. That Patti was out there kicking up her heels.

I knew Patti was doing well because of the threats to blow up the white Lincoln convertible, or to abduct the kids. Whether the threats came from my competitors or from some dingo in the Vice Squad, I could never be sure, but I sent a car driven by one of my trusted men to collect the kids straight after school and asked the teachers to watch my kids until they were in the car.

Through all these years I still made the occasional pick-up, because I couldn't resist the tease, the drooling adoration, and the laughs. As the years went by, however, I wanted it less and less. I still had Kasey in his single bed in my room. Ralph had stuck by me and was allowed to sleep with me sometimes. Big Nick the Russian, the love of my life, would always be with me. Gordon had gone by this time. He had run off overseas and so I replaced him in recent days with Greg, my gardener. There were also my special clients to whom I was mistress, friend, confidante for a decade or more. I was the alternative world that they craved. I was their escape from normality.

One evening I was dolling up for the night when Johnny Hopper came to the front door in street clothes, and asked for Fay. Kasey should've been wary straight away. Only strangers came to the front door. But Kasey took the money and sent Fay across Churchill Road to one of the flats I owned. Fay didn't know it was a copper. She just thought he was one of those who only wanted to talk. After ten minutes of sitting in the room, talking, he arrested her, dragged her terrified back to Number 165, and arrested Kasey.

At that time my son, Chris, and I were just going out the side gate to shop at the deli. As we shut the gate, two big blokes rushed towards us. I panicked, remembering the death threats. One grabbed me and the other flung little Chris against the galvanised-iron fence and pinned him there. They were so violent I knew we were done for. 'Don't shoot my little boy. Let him go.' The guy holding me, my arm twisted around my back, said, 'We're not going to shoot you. You're only under arrest.'

They were coppers, but I was still terrified, not knowing what was going to happen next. They dragged us through the yard. They saw Greg digging in the garden, and one asked, 'Who's that?' Greg looked scared. 'Just the gardener. He's nothing to do with us.'

Inside the house, they sat us down and went through the formalities of the arrest. The more they talked, the less terrified I was, and became angry. Normally the cops and I lived and let live. We'd say goodday in the street. There were cops with brains, respect for their jobs, and they were gentlemen. We played a cat and mouse game. If the mouse was caught, bad luck. If the mouse was quick enough to get away, it was okay. The cat would live to laugh another day. At times, some would call in for a coffee and chat to see if I could help track down some deviant molester.

We knew each other's games and accepted that whether we liked it or not, the city needed us both. The cops knew I ran my agencies clean. They understood that in my way I was doing the state a service. If the weirdos weren't putting their dicks in my girls, then how many kids would be hurt, or worse? I some-times had the bad luck to take on a girl who was stupid, and into drugs, and it would take a while to discover her and kick her out. I really freaked over drugs. They scared me. But the cops also had a few bad apples who were paid to close their eyes in Hindley Street. We knew some marijuana went from the streets into certain cops' pockets, from there to ex-cops who acted as fences, then back to the streets for another deal, another bust.

The cops I couldn't stomach were those one or two mongrels in the Vice Squad. For a while, in the seventies, until they were got rid of, there were a couple about the same age, on the take, more vicious than most of the criminals they were supposed to be chasing. They stood for the hypocrisy and rottenness in the heart of the city. There were plenty of guesses about the iden-tities of the crime bosses – those respectable men with their luxury offices, who bled the state dry. Why weren't they being arrested? Adelaide had a sickness.

So I asked this Johnny Hopper, 'What the hell are you doing in my house?'

He said, 'Patti, I am arresting you for employing prostitutes with sexually transmitted diseases.'

'Don't be such a bloody idiot. You know I run the cleanest business in town. If any of my girls pick up an infection it's me who puts them immediately off work. The clinic records prove that. And don't even think of trying to beat up a charge that I run a brothel. You know any magistrate will throw out the charge. No work is done on the premises. I am the manager of an escort agency, which is entirely legal. If I'm not legitimate, why does the Tax Department recognise me as a business? Why do I have to pay a small fortune in tax every year? My girls pay for your bloody salary.'

The pie face went on. 'And we are impounding your white Lincoln convertible.'

'What for? Consorting with a Kingswood?'

'Based on information we have received, we will inspect it for drugs.'

'Bullshit. You're just jealous. You've been dying to get your grubby little paws on her. It's only an excuse for you to have a joy ride, at my expense.'

But the bastard had all the right papers. I was not so fazed that I forgot to go to the bathroom and get my choppers from the glass. I ran a comb through my hair, just in case they were going to take photos. The formalities over, the cops began to search my home for drugs. They tore my bedroom to pieces. The kids huddled together, terrified. I thought, I'll never take that again.

My anger was on the slow boil as we drove to the police station, Johnny Fucking Hopper following in my car. They shoved us in cells out in the courtyard. Kasey in one, Fay and me in another. Young officers came out to look at us, as though we were monkeys in the zoo.

'Cheer up,' I told Fay, who was white with fear. 'Don't be frightened. That's what they want. They expect you to hide under the bed. No way.'

But I was frightened. I didn't know the rights of people who had been arrested. I had no idea how to get out on bail. I knew they were determined to fix this bird who was becoming too successful. The crime wasn't sex, it was the money, and I was making lots. If they'd got me on a real charge, and I was guilty, then I'd pay the penalty. But if I hadn't broken the law, why should I put up with their games? I'd had enough injustice in my life. The thought of those men prying about in my Lincoln was more than I could tolerate.

I made trouble. I complained about the room service. I hassled them about delaying us too long. I told Fay, 'Nobody's got the legal right, or any right, to tell you whether you can screw for money or not. You are just doing with men what respectable women do, except they're too stupid to ask for money. It's your body. You've got the right to do with it as you choose, especially if you're not doing any harm. So don't let these bastards get to you.'

I thought of another reason for the raid. I knew things. What if I opened my mouth and named a few names.

We were in there for two hours. Then, having had their bit of fun, they let us out. We were nothing to them, except as a part of their power games. I was furious. I reckon it was in those hours I decided I'd never give in to the system, even if it was a great tidal wave.

Next day I went to a lawyer who said to me, 'Look, Patti, it's all right. Let me take care of it. Like it or leave it, you do as I say. I'll guide you.'

Yeah, I thought, right into the shit. 'And just to keep the record straight, why don't you warn Johnny Hopper that I'm thinking of laying a charge against him for consorting. He didn't tell us he was a cop. He asked for the girl, he paid the money, and he was alone with her for ten minutes. I reckon I've got him on toast. If we're criminals, then he's paid money to consort with us.'

The lawyer went off for a confab. I don't know about lawyers. They say, 'Do this and it'll get you out. Do this and it'll get you in.' I reckon all they're really interested in is your money. In this world it's not what you know, but who you know that you can pay. Sometimes I felt that lawyers just played with peoples' lives. A bit like the bent cops: if they didn't like the colour of your hair, then you never knew what deal was being worked out. Whether you're locked up or let off, they'll go to the pub and have a good laugh about it.

In the end a deal was worked out. Next day we'd all rock up to the court, then it would all get adjourned. They would drop some charges, but I had to agree to sign that I ran a brothel. Stupid. I was so sick with a migraine that I could hardly see. I signed. I carried that with me for the rest of my life.

# Madam
## and mum

*As the frantic seventies roared towards the eighties, my business boomed.*
I opened more and more agencies, and many girls worked
seventy to a hundred clients a week. Money rolled in so fast I
hardly knew what to do with it. So did the paper work and the
strains of managing a big business. The pressures never let up,
and the girl with no education had to learn how to keep control
of one of the state's large industries. There were days when I felt
like a juggler with nine clubs, a couple of oranges, a carving
knife and a flaming torch all in the air at once, and the phone
was ringing.

It was a risky, exciting, exhilarating time of my life. And the
most anxious. Out there was always the father who crashed into
the birthday party and smashed the cake to pieces.

Often, when I was on my way home at four in the morning, I looked up at the bright Milky Way. I loved to find and
name the Saucepan, the Seven Sisters, the Southern Cross. My
eye was drawn to the brightest stars, which glowed red or
glinted with brilliant flashes of blue and green, like diamonds.

I'd stand and think about my life. My Nan had seven kids;
so had I. Nan had been cut off from her mother; so had I. My
mother sometimes came close to me. There was the time she
borrowed some of my clothes to take on a cruise. For a moment,
standing there by the wardrobes, checking on the evening gowns,
we were like girlfriends. Then she took out a raunchy black
dress, her lips went tight, and the moment of mother-daughter
intimacy was lost.

In a way my mother was as much a prisoner of her religious upbringing as I had been a prisoner of Pickering Street. She was the victim of adults who owned all truth, for whom God had created all the stars and our planet – all the seas and mountains, all history for the chosen ones. Their mob knew the absolute truth, and everybody else was wrong. In their own way they were as brutal and inhumane as my mad, alcoholic father, who was also terrified of life and went on the only kind of rampage he could think of.

I was almost thirty-eight years old. Life was slipping through my fingers like quicksilver. My family was fading away so fast from my life it frightened me.

Jack had gone, sometimes to return, only to go away again, hoping never to come back. Blondie had married her slob and went to live a few streets away, which may as well have been at the end of the earth. My darling shadow, Cassie, moved into a flat across the road, was married, and about to be divorced, at sixteen. Like mine, that marriage was dying as she walked down the aisle. All of them, like me, were desperate for the security of love and the comfort of kindness and affection. Despite my promises, and my good intentions, I had still inflicted my child-hood on my own kids. I could hardly bear to think about it.

The forces of separation were like an undertow. No matter how hard I swam on the surface, the strong rush of water dragged me from shore. One night I heard strange, terrifying screams out the front. It was Cassie, hanging onto the verandah post as though she was in a hundred mile an hour gale. She laughed and cried, then screamed at me, 'Look out Mum, your face is on fire.' Her stupid husband stood in the yard, watching. I pulled Cassie inside and looked at her. She was falling all over the place, mumbling, 'Why is the table on the wall?' In a blind panic that she was dying, I slapped her face to bring her to her senses. I yelled at her, 'What is it? What's wrong?' But she just made choking noises. I stuck my fingers down her throat, and she threw up. Mushrooms. I glared up at her husband who gave a stupid giggle and said, 'She took them.' Bullshit. Cassie was terrified of drugs. He would have conned her for a joke. He was six foot four and built like a brick wall, but I smashed him. I was afraid. I thought Cassie was dying. Cassie was off her trolley, laughing and stumbling about. I got her in a headlock and yelled, 'Stop it!' I dragged her down to the ground, screaming at her, 'Stop it!' Then I ran for the phone. I didn't care what trouble she got into with the law. My other daughter, Blondie, raced her off to hospital. It was all too much for me. While the doctor was checking her, Cassie kept trying to get off the couch and pick up her right arm which she said had fallen off. When the doctor pressed her stomach, Cassie went coy and giggly. 'You can't do that,' she said, 'because there's fingers sticking out of my belly button. See? Someone put them down me.'

Pepe became a street kid at the age of fourteen, just like me, except he didn't come home. I threw him out the day I found him with his head in a plastic bag, sniffing glue. I grabbed him by the shoulders and shook him until his eyeballs rattled. 'If you won't listen to me, if you want to kill yourself, then do it some-where else. Not in my house.' Pepe ran a couple of streets away to live in the adventure playground of Prospect Primary School. His roof at night was the tunnel little kids played in during the day. He drank himself stupid and got stoned on grass, living off money he got from drugs. I spent hours, hidden around the corner, watching him, my heart breaking. The postie kept an eye on him too and let me know each day how he was getting on. At last the strain became too much. I marched around to Pepe's playground, fronted him and told him to come home. He refused, so I rolled up my sleeves and we had it out. If I won, he came home. I flattened him. He slept at night in my car, or went over to Cassie's where he slept in her car or under her window. She would hear him scratching around and know he was safe. Pepe felt secure with Cassie, and she took custody of him; she was his real mum. She fed him, looked after him, and stood up for him in court as guarantor of his good behaviour.

The more things went wrong, the greater the pressure of business, the harder I tried to hold everything together by the power of my will and the force of my own physical strength. I was exhausted. At the very time I had the happiness I had slaved to earn, I was losing it. I endured blinding migraines, worked manic hours, and thought that if I could hold myself together, the rest would be all right. I lived on willpower, work that I didn't need to do. I was a zombie on tranquillisers. I kept going by habit, keeping up the appearance of control.

For my thirty-eighth birthday I made a deal to buy myself a nightclub – Silvers – in Hindley Street. The grand years of Hindley Street were passing away. Wests Theatre and the State Theatre had gone, and with them the trade that kept alive so many small businesses, like coffee shops and the Black and White Milk Bar. The Latin Quarter had been burnt down, as had the Paprika, leaving only the Baygenew and Silvers. Then organised crime moved in, and gangs of druggy kids took over. The night life declined, and people stopped coming into the street. The good times were disappearing. The sense of family had gone, which saddened me. So I bought Silvers Nightclub, partly out of nostalgia.

On the night of my birthday I had a wild party in the Overway Hotel. Nan would've died with her leg in the air. I was surrounded by friends from Greece, Italy, all over. Towards the end of the party I decided to leave and drove home to Churchill Road. Kasey would follow later, bringing Michelle and the girl who was being billeted with us from the Port Pirie school. As soon as I got home, I had a horrible intuition that something was wrong. An ambulance sped past, its siren wailing. I jumped in the car, grabbed my boyfriend Greg the gardener, and took a short cut back to the city.

It was not a car accident I saw, but the glow of a fire in Hindley Street. A crowd ran from Morphett Street into Hindley Street. I sat in the car at the Overway corner. The sky was full of flying sparks. Great balloons of flame rolled into the night sky. Silvers was a roaring inferno. Windows exploded. Huge sections of roof collapsed inwards with a thundering roar. Flames gushed out of windows, out of gaps in the wall. The fire brigade had given up and was trying to save the nearby buildings. I felt my heart collapse with every crash of bricks and timber.

I drove away from the fire, back over Morphett Street Bridge, and left the city through the parklands, following the River Torrens. Ahead I saw blue and red lights flashing. My stomach went cold. Where were Kasey and the girls? I couldn't make sense of the jumble of vehicles. A man stepped out from behind an ambulance and into my headlights, waving at me to slow down. It was Kasey.

I was out and running before the car stopped. I saw two big policemen and yelled at them, 'Where's my children?'

A policeman said, 'They're all right, they've just gone for a little trip in an ambulance.' I hauled back and aimed for the policeman but Greg got in the way and collected an upper cut. Then things became wild. Kasey was down on the ground writhing around holding his ribs. A copper came into view and got a smack in the kisser. Two men, maybe the drivers of the other car, hurdled the fence and ran off into the darkness of the golf course. When I'm mad I'm pretty strong.

# *The wheel keeps spinning*

*Money gave me power, privilege, and social conventions. It could never* cure my need for love. Time and again men came into my life then faded away. Women also loved me. One of my girls, a lesbian, courted me. One night Miranda kept flirting with me until I thought, Why not? I took her to my bed. That was the best night of love-making I ever knew. I was the bloke and not a bad performer. Afterwards I felt elated, peaceful. Nevertheless, my heart wasn't in it, and lesbianism remained for me a brief experiment.

Through all these troubled, glorious years as Madam, the man I needed most was Big Nick, the Russian. I met Nick in my early days. It was on a cool Friday evening, at the Brenner Hotel, Junction Road. I wore a long lime-green caftan dress with gold edging. Fashion had gone through long frocks, minis, maxis, and knee-length dresses. Now it was all Demis Roussos tents. I stood at the entrance and looked down into the huge room where everybody had their own table. There was a man on his own. As I walked past his table he stood politely and drew back a chair for me. He was about five foot ten, tall to me, and strongly built. He wore a blue suit. He had hazel eyes and his blond hair was receding. His face seemed vulnerable. There was a quiet dignity about him, and I sensed his kindness. More than that, he was relaxed, as though to say to me, You're not needed. I don't ever want to need. Let's just get along.

We chatted on about ordinary things, and I was startled at how relaxed I was. I talked as eagerly as if Nick was somebody

I'd known since we were kids. I was the Madam only with those I was wary of. With Nick, I let down my defences.

Nick told me about his work as a nurse at an old folks' home. He told me how he fed and washed the elderly people, and about those who cried because they had no visitors, those he took out for a walk to the shops, and those who died. I was touched by his gentleness and his love for the old patients. He was not ashamed to tell me he took bunches of flowers to old women. Yet he was a strong man. He had fought in Vietnam. The more he revealed of himself, the more I realised that he was a man I could rely on. I took Nick home to meet Kasey. If I introduced a man to Kasey that meant he would be around for some time.

As it happened, our relationship was not sexual. Nick was impotent, and so we had a friendship. A precious part of it was that, over the years, Nick played father to my children. Big Nick had never married or had children of his own. He never visited without presents for mine – chocolates, or a paper bag full of live frogs that all escaped, except Chris's, squeezed almost to death in his little fist. Nick loved Chris as the son he could never have. They hid out in the backyard and smoked Nick's thin cigars, which was against my rules, but, when I saw this big man and my little boy sit together yarning or practising smoke rings, my heart melted.

Nick took us for walks in the city, and one day a group of Hare Krishnas came towards us, bells jingling, orange cloaks swelling out in the breeze. Chris screamed and hid instinctively behind Nick, clinging to his legs. One weekend Nick paid for Chris and me to go to Melbourne. The other children tore their hair with jealousy, although the older ones were happier to stay home with me out of the way. We went to the Show where Nick and Chris slid down slippery dips on mats, chose the most scary rides on the Octopus or Wall of Death, and made pigs of themselves with hot dogs and waffles. I was glad they had that time together as father and son. But I didn't appreciate their chauvinism: they expected me to wait outside while they went into Time Zone and blasted shit out of fighter planes and jungle commandos. I had to stand outside with my handbag over my shoulder like a bloody hooker.

One day at Number 165, Nick got all the boys to play a Vietnam war game in the backyard. Chris was off his brain with excitement. Here he was playing with a real soldier. Nick gave the air rifle to Chris and said, 'When I tell you to cease fire, don't shoot.' Then Nick sneaked off and hid in the shed. Chris used the grapevines for an ambush. He held the air gun up and waited. All the yard was silent, then Big Nick jumped out and yelled, 'Cease Fire!'

Bang. The pellet shot Nick in the face. Blood poured out just below his eye. Nick screamed, Chris ran around yelling. I rushed Big Nick off to hospital. He was so angry I was afraid he'd never come back to us.

He returned a few days later, and I sat him out in the backyard in the sun, took off his shirt and washed his back. Big Nick had been in a helicopter in Vietnam when some dust they were dumping on trees had blown back on him. His back was covered in rotten sores full of pus. I sat behind Nick and squeezed the sores to clean them out. The smell was awful. The pus squirted out. Then I washed his back with scented soap, but the smell was still there. While I gently washed him we talked about his father who had disappeared during the second world war. We often talked about his missing father, and Nick believed he was still alive somewhere. I knew how he felt.

By a strange coincidence, his father's best mate, who was Nick's god-father, lived near me, but would never tell Big Nick what had happened to his father. It was something about his father being in the ss.

Nick was so serious about me that he took me and Chris to meet his mum. She was a dumpy little lady who kept looking from Chris to Nick, comparing their eyes, the shape of their foreheads, their mouths. Whatever she saw was in her imagination, because there was no doubt that Kasey was the father. Nick's mother didn't approve of me because I wasn't a virgin. Worse still, I'd had my tubes tied. She nagged at Big Nick that I was not a suitable woman. That woman had her own ten commandments and ruled her son with a rod of iron. Nick always showed her respect and I admired him for that. The poor man was caught between his mother and me. The Vietnam veteran found himself fighting another war he couldn't win and which wouldn't go away.

I loved Nick but would not marry him. Even his smallest kindness moved me almost to tears. One day he turned up in a new suit and said he bought it especially to wear for me. Even if he'd been standing there in his birthday suit I'd have loved him for saying that. Later that evening he proposed to me. I said no, because it would ruin our friendship.

One night I was at my make-up mirror, preparing to go out for the night with Greg the gardener. Big Nick was jealous of this other boyfriend. Nick stood behind me and said, 'You are not going out.'

'You can't order me about. I'm not a bloody Russian peasant woman like your mother.'

He swatted me like a fly. I swayed sideways. I thought I'd been hit by a semi-trailer. 'Get out!' I yelled at him, and Big Nick left.

He paid me out by staying away and taking another woman. To torment me, he sent me her photo. I snatched his suit out of my wardrobe and cut it to shreds with the scissors and sent it to him. But I was really afraid he would turn against me.

I spent hours in the garden, mourning for Nick. I'd run my fingers over the wooden plaque he'd made and hung on a trellis that held up the vines. I ran my fingertips over his name carved on the plaque. I remembered how we'd sat under the vines and talked for hours. One night he had brought a pizza as big as the out-door table for a birthday surprise for Chris. He'd had it specially made by a friend. I remembered how we laughed as we tried to hold the giant slices and eat them.

After three weeks I couldn't stand the agony of our separation. I was dying to pick up the phone but was too proud. Then he phoned me. We talked in strained voices about ordinary things – the kids, the weather – pretending that nothing had happened. Big Nick came back to me and proposed. But by then, full of rage and confusion, I was already engaged to Greg.

When I told Big Nick that I was going to marry Greg, his face went white and set as hard as rock. My head was spinning as I took Big Nick with me for a meal with Greg and some of my girls at Jules nightclub. When those two men met, you could have cut the air with a knife. Big Nick began to lay down the law about taking care of me, and Greg got angrier by the minute. Not as angry as me, however. Was I going to sit there being discussed like a piece of meat? I walked out on them and went up Hindley Street to the Overway.

Three-quarters of an hour later, Greg joined me. There was no sign of Big Nick. I didn't know I would never see him again.

I rejected Big Nick for Greg, who had spun me yarns about being in Vietnam, and showed me a wound on the back of his hand. 'We were sitting in the jungle eating food from cans,' he told me, 'then the shooting started. My mate died in my arms. I copped that bullet while I was holding him.' I cried at the tragedy of it, and at Greg's goodness in caring for his mate. I was such a sucker for kindness that I believed all he told me. When I talked one day to his mother about the mark on Greg's hand, she said it was a cigarette burn.

He had also boasted to me of his time as a Grenadier Guard. It was only by accident, later, when his mum was going through some old photos, that she showed me a snapshot of Greg, at fourteen, dressed up in a guard's costume. She said, 'That's the nearest Greg ever got to being a guardsman.'

That should have been enough. But I was smitten. My love for Greg was out of control. It wasn't love so much as infatuation. I got high on infatuation. It was my addiction. I felt so alive as each new man came into my life. I couldn't go on unless I had the thrills of the first meeting, the man's desperate phone calls, gifts, the tease of dinners and waiting for the next move. Falling in love was such a buzz, full of risks and obsessions. The slow winding down of the relationship, the feeling that the honeymoon was over, would come in their time. They always did. The certainty of the death of love, however, could never take away the power of the first emotions.

Knowing something's stupid doesn't stop you doing it. Like the gambling junkies, you give it one more shot, because you've heard of somebody who won the jackpot. In a way, my roulette wheel and my drug was romantic love.

The things I did for Greg. He pleaded for a gun, so I got

him one, and the moron flashed it about in the pub. I had to cop the charge for unlawful possession. He told his mother he was my bag man and needed the gun to fight off the Mafia. He lived in a fantasy world of Buck Jones and Roy Rogers. His mother had brought up three spastic kids, and Greg told me that he spent his afternoons giving spastic kids free rides in his taxi. I was so impressed by his kindness. I was so touched in the head I arranged for Kasey to drive him to work in my car each day. Every night, Greg came home in his taxi and was dropped off by his 'changeover driver'.

When I phoned United Taxis one day, they had never heard of him. I rang all the companies; same story. I saw red. I laid it on him really heavy and he confessed he had no job as a taxi driver. He spent his afternoons going to the pictures, or the zoo, or the races. He was so sorry for what he had done I took pity on him. Any man who stood up to me I could give a good belting. But if they were ashamed, or worse still, cried, I didn't have the heart to.

I wondered why I was drawn to weird men. Or maybe they were attracted to me, like bees to honey. Greg was never there for my sake, but because of the power and prestige he got by being with me. Being Patti's man was big deal in his mind. I knew all this. Other men were the same. But by some horrible distortion, the more rotten they were, the more attracted I was. I don't know. Whatever the reason, the more I was with Greg, the more ill I became. My head was spinning with tranquillisers, exhaustion, and the mad daily rush. When I took up Greg I knew I was losing control, but I let it happen, almost as if I wanted some kind of disaster.

Greg came into my life at a time I had worked myself right to the brink of a nervous breakdown. The loss of Big Nick almost finished me off. I just wanted to shut the world out. I lay for hours in my bed, my head full of blackness. For hour after hour I lay there re-living the worst times of my life. I exhausted myself with hatred, and bitterness. I had no energy. Even to hold up a cup of tea was an effort. I began to let my appearance go. I'd sit around in my dressing-gown, too feeble to take control of the day. Some instinct told me it was a buildup of all the long years of work as a Madam, and the longer years of brutality before that.

I felt this great wave rising up in me – all the pains and sufferings of nearly forty years were rising up, like a slow, heavy tidal wave far out to sea, not all that high, but stretching from horizon to horizon. It rushed through the night towards the shore where it would suddenly reach up, tower over the trees and houses, then smash everything as it swept into the land.

I should have guessed something was wrong when Greg went to hospital the week before we were to be married. A bad back, he said. We still hadn't received a copy of his *decree nisi* for the divorce from his wife in England. His parents believed he was divorced, but I wanted to see the papers. Greg had sent urgent messages, and the decree was supposed to arrive in plenty of time. With a week to go there was no sign of it, and Greg suddenly got a mysterious back pain.

No way was I going to call off the wedding with only a week to go. The Overway Hotel was booked for the Sunday. Two hundred people had received invitations, many of them interstate or in country towns. The designer gowns were finished. I had paid six hundred dollars in advance for photographs. My mother and relatives were invited. If ever there was a last chance to please my mother, this was it. The thought of Hairylegs gave me hope.

On Friday, Greg was ready to come out of hospital, but the afternoon postie brought no letter from England. I was frantic. I hauled myself out of bed and rushed to the post office. Nothing had been left there. Nothing. It was too late to contact many of the guests. They were already on the way. I sped to the hospital and ran to Greg. I said, 'What are we going to do? This is a big-time wedding.'

He gave a stupid grin and said, 'I'm still married in England.'

My mind fused like it had been struck by lightning. I saw a picture of me dropping Greg's body in the river. I didn't know what to do, but I thought, You're not going to bring me down. In a deadly voice I told him, 'We're going through with it.' He sat there and grinned and nodded like a lunatic.

I grabbed a telephone book and tried to find Actor's Equity. There must be an actor who would marry us. At last I found a man who had been given a licence to marry homosexuals. I drove Greg around to the man's place. 'Will you give us a ceremony if we don't sign the papers?' The priest promised, 'By all that's sacred I'll be there.' Greg sat and smiled, happy to play out the biggest fantasy of his life.

By the Sunday afternoon I was wiped out on doses of two Valium at a time. I had split away from my body, just as on the day Nan died. All the way to my wedding I kept hoping the groom had dropped dead. As we drove over Morphett Street Bridge I was in a panic that the priest wouldn't turn up. When the car arrived, I was so paralysed with terror I said to the driver, 'Please go inside and see if there's a priest.' He looked at me strangely, shrugged, and went into the Overway. He came out grinning and said, 'Yeah, there's a minister. Everybody's waiting for you.'

We went through with it. We even held our pens just above the register, as though we were signing. While I was going through this charade, Big Nick had a heart attack in the street on the way to work in Melbourne. His brother got a message to me next morning. That was the end of me. All the lights went out. I told Greg, 'Pack your bags and get out of my life.' He said, 'Give me some money.' Then he moved, or I would have killed him.

I stood on the tarmac at the airport and watched them take Nick's coffin out of the back of the plane. His mother stood beside me, weeping. I was incapable of anger or tears. As Nick's body was wheeled away, nothing in me was left alive, and I gave myself over to madness.

*Decline and Fall*

# *Trapped*

*I retreated to my bed where I lay curled up like a baby. I was too weak* to sit up and eat, too confused to know how many days or weeks passed. Fragments of the past flew past my face: Nan's face in the coffin, Sid crashing through the skylight, the glittering eyes of a man hiding in the shadows behind the toilet, the cat lady hanging on the wire of her cage in the madhouse, Jessie's upraised slashed wrists. A dark wind flung the bits and pieces into my face, round and round. I have no memory of the world outside that bed.

When I began to recover, I found the running of the household too much of a strain. I put an ad in the paper for a handyman-gardener. Kasey took the phone calls and I chose the list for interviews.

Next evening there was a knock on the door. The first applicant. I crawled out of bed and pulled on some black clothes. I was almost too ill to stand. There at the front door was a man in a red skivvy and blue, flared pants. He had long curly black hair. He was skinny and stood with a nervous swagger.

I led him to the kitchen, where he sat at the table. I was so agitated that I didn't care about the interview. He was here. That was good enough. He looked about with open curiosity. There was a familiarity about him, an impudence, as if he owned the place. That helped me come out of my daze, and begin to take notice. I saw the tattoos on every finger, but his fingernails were clean: a good sign.

He noticed my look and stared back defiantly. His eyes were

brown. 'Yeah. I've done time.'

'What else have you done?'

'I been working girls out of cars in Hindley Street. Ten to fifteen dollars a trick.'

He spoke my language. I said, 'That's sick. That's why I'm in business.'

Algie said, 'I've been thinking of starting my own agency.' His look was a challenge.

I thought, Not another one wanting to be a male Patti. You've got no class.

I took Algie on. He was quiet, efficient, and an excellent cook – more a caterer than a cook – a skill he had learnt in jail. He was proud of his work, and he took away from me all the worries of running the house. I withdrew gratefully further into my private world of grief, blinding headaches and Valium.

There was something wrong with Algie's eyes. Somewhere inside was shattered like a car windscreen. Sometimes I talked to him while he worked at the kitchen sink. If the knife slipped, or he dropped a bit of food, he flew into a furious rage. His eyes glazed over, and he swore in an endless stream of real filth. I'd never heard anyone swear with such viciousness over the tiniest thing. It was more than a bad temper. He looked demonic. I was fascinated.

If there was some deep evil in Algie, there was also a mischievous devilry. When I told him about the Polish man who had smashed the bottle over my head, Algie gave a strange laugh, almost a snarl, and said, 'I know that prick. Did time with him at Reformatory when we were kids. Let's shoot up his fucking place. You get guns.' Suddenly I saw Algie's face change, as though he had put on a savage mask: hooded eyes, cruel, thin lips, something Transylvanian. He grinned like a wolf. 'Revenge is everything, Trish.'

I was shocked at the violence in his face, and in the arrogance of using a pet name for me. But he made me feel alive. He was like a naughty kid whispering, 'Sneak outside and play.'

Laughing, Algie half drunk, and me still away with the fairies, we drove past the Polish man's factory, and Algie in some kind of fury blasted it with shotguns. He shot great holes through the walls and roof, yelling, 'Fucking Polack.' Then we screamed away, high on adrenalin; Bonnie and Clyde.

Algie became a diversion from the noise and jumble in my head. Nobody, however, could rescue me from the long nights of sleepless terrors. I was furious and alarmed that when I had established myself as Madam, and for the first time in my life had control over my life, my brain made me a victim of its ceaseless voices; the chatter, screams and obsessive repetitions could never be silenced. I could cut out the light just by shutting my eyes. But my mind had no switch to turn off the sounds of memory. Gradually I drifted into deep depression.

Then Algie's sister told me that he was screwing a de facto. I fronted him and he yelled, 'Mind your own fucking business.' My head felt as if it was three times its size.

If I was not soon to take my last breath, I must escape the noise and terror. My doctor, Jack Tillyard, got me to sign myself into hospital. I found myself at a reception desk, filling out a form, underlining heavily the words, 'Voluntary admission'. Ward 9B: Psychiatric. I was, after all, my father's daughter. I was so afraid they would make me bow down, cry, shamble along like him.

I had tried psychiatrists years before this, but did not feel they had been much help. My first one was dressed in a leaf-green suit and leapt about his office like a jolly great goblin, raving about his sexual problems and peering at me for a response. The more he waved his arms about, the more I felt my stomach start to wobble with laughter that just had to come out. I wasn't incurable: he was.

In hospital all I wanted to do was sleep. If Mahatma Ghandi visited, I couldn't have cared less. But the rules said Group Therapy. On the first morning I sat and listened. Then I got pissed off. This wasn't a rest-cure. This was being hit with other people's problems. The session was an agony.

There was a long silence after some bloke rambled on about how the neighbour was dropping dog shit, deliberately, over the fence into his vegetable garden. I thought that maybe madness is just being ground down by a thousand stupid, everyday things.

The doctor waited for somebody to speak. We all sat like

stuffed potatoes. 'Tell us how you're feeling,' he urged, like a school teacher waiting for the right answer, which of course none of us knew.

I got to my feet and said, 'We don't know. Nobody ever knows why rotten things keep happening. So watch the dose they put in you.' The doctor at the back stood up, his face angry, that is, frightened. I held my hands up, 'You can't stop me. You can't even keep me here. I'm voluntary and can go whenever I want.'

I married Algie in October, 1979, a few months after I'd 'married' Greg. Part of my problem was that Algie, apart from manic rages, was a wimp. That was my vulnerability. I wanted to be strong for him. Feeling superior boosted me, and lifted me out of my sadness and weakness.

The first time he raised the back of his hand to one of my children, I let him have more than he gave the factory walls with the shotgun. It was our first argument. Algie went to bed and sulked for two days. He refused to speak to me or anyone.

Algie was insanely jealous of Kasey, which was all right in small doses. He was also violently domineering. As soon as we were married, he tried to take over. In a way, this was good for me. By fighting Algie, I was also fighting my disease. I wanted to battle back to who I was, and not let the world close in on me and shut the lid.

For my birthday, a few weeks after we were married, I wanted my usual big party with crowds of guests. I prattled on to Algie about the invitation list. I was excited at going out for the first time in months as Patti, my old self. The birthday would celebrate my marriage and be a sign that I was no sucker for neurotic depression. The more guests I mentioned, especially male, the blacker grew Algie's face.

On the day of my birthday party, Algie came in to watch me get ready. I hated anybody, especially men, watching me do my make-up. My wrinkles and I had a private understanding. Absentmindedly I said, 'Piss off while I'm doing my make-up!'

He lunged forward, grabbed my hair in both hands and pushed my face into the mirror. 'There. Have a close look, you fucking moll.'

The cold mirror was squashed against my face. I was too shocked to react. Algie put his face close to mine and said, so close I felt his breath on my cheek, 'Do you think any man wants to look at something so ugly. You're finished, Patti. Clapped out. And I'm sick of living in this stinking brothel.'

He let me go and stood back. 'Get me my fucking suitcase.'

I lifted his suitcase down from the top of the wardrobe and put it on the bed. I lifted up a pair of his socks from a drawer, and dropped them in the case. As soon as the socks hit the bottom of the case, I felt him move. He belted me on the back of the head. 'You bitch. That proves you want me to go.'

I was so stunned by the unexpected beating that I didn't hit him back. But my party must go on. Somehow I sat through it, with Algie in a towering sulk beside me. The guests were uneasy. The party was spoilt. Not since the brutal days of Sid had my house been so filled with threat and ugliness. As soon as the party was over, Algie left on what he called 'R and R'.

While he was away for three months, he phoned me. 'Guess who I'm with? She's so much better in bed than you could ever be, Patti. She's young, wild, the best.'

When Algie returned, he stood on the back door step, his suitcase by his feet. His first words were, 'I love you, Trish.'

I was all fired up ready to throw him out. When I saw his crestfallen face and his hesitant stance, something crazy in me said rubbish like, He must love me, he's so jealous. He just needs time to adjust to living with me.

He shuffled his feet. 'Look, Trish, I'm not very good with words. Please try to understand.' His eyes were lowered. 'Sometimes I don't know how to show my feelings. The only way I've known how to show my feelings since I was a kid is to lash out. It's hit first or be beaten up. Same in jail. I'm sorry I was so rough on you at the party. It's just my way. Fact is, I love you. You're a beautiful woman. Why do you think I wanted to marry you so much?'

He looked up briefly into my eyes. 'That's why I go off my fucking brain when I think of you with other men.'

I stood, impassive. Part of me wanted to make him sweat it out, to see what he would say. The other part wanted to fling my arms around him and hold him.

Algie paused. Then he looked sideways at the house walls. 'I know this doesn't make sense, but I don't need all this – the house, I mean. I'd be happy if all we had was a park bench. As long as we were together.'

All the alarm bells went off in my head. My brain yelled at me, Don't believe this crap. Remember how Sid came grovelling back, fawning all over the place with false promises.

Algie reached out and touched my arm. 'What I'm trying to say is I love you, Trish, and I'm sorry for all the shit I gave you at your party.'

I knew then, as I had never realised, how insanely I needed love. I held out my arms to Algie.

Within a few months my youngest daughter, Michelle, ran off. Then Algie hit Pepe, and Pepe left home. Then Ryan left home. Of all my seven children, only Chris was still with me.

Desperate, I bought Algie toys to play with. A new car, five new cars in the year, a shop, whatever. I had the money, more than I needed. My agencies were flourishing, and I didn't care if I squandered thousands on Algie. The only thing I wanted was love; a happy marriage. No. As time went on, all I wanted was peace, sleep untroubled by nightmares of my childhood and of my father's violence. There was no need to be in a mental asylum. I was turning my life into a madhouse.

I searched for clues to control Algie. I watched him with his parents. His mother doted on him, gave him the choicest morsels at meals. One night at their place for dinner, I said, half in jest, 'Algie's no angel.'

His mother's face went as hard as nails. She pushed back her seat, hurried around the table and stood behind him. She kissed the top of his head where he was just starting to go bald. 'He's still my baby. He has come back to me, even though he is married.'

I thought to myself, Why is it, whenever a prodigal returns, some poor fatted calf gets slaughtered?

Algie's father was embarrassed by me. He was a severe, old-fashioned European, and I think was ashamed of his son, the criminal. He had left Australia and gone back home for some time, only returning after Algie's marriage to me. I saw the sneer he gave Algie as the mother kissed Algie's head. Algie saw it too and went rigid with resentment. My heart went out to my husband. Algie had told me that no matter what he did, however good or useful, he could never please his father, who was self-righteous and groped me, calling me princess. There were things Algie and I had in common. I could still build a marriage out of the mess we were in.

Algie's sister, The Witch, was another matter. She had dark circles under her eyes. 'I know what the cat is thinking,' she said, and looked at me. I felt that she had a sinister power over Algie. They shared secret looks. They were up to something and I was tied up in their plan.

That night Algie beat me again.

'Get rid of him,' Cassie told me. 'Or it'll be too late. Look what's happened since he moved in.'

I began to have fantasies of shooting my husband.

Life slipped into a daze. I was wacko in the head from living with Algie, from grief at the loss of my children, from the smash on the head with the bottle all those years ago, from a feeling of being worn out, with no reserves of energy. My business continued to grow, never had so much money poured in, but I felt like Atlas, holding the world on my shoulders. If I let go, everything would collapse. I needed to find Algie things to do other than to bash me.

He gave me the clue I needed one day when he said, in a sulk, 'You never listen to my ideas about the agencies. You listen to Kasey, to Cassie, to the girls, but never to me. I've got lots of good ideas for expanding the business. Why don't you give it a try, and let me run the show my way?'

So that was it. Give over to him all my hard-earned business. Let a cheap pimp who had only worked girls from cars take over the lot? I didn't need to answer. He saw my face, and went white with rage.

There was something else going on at the same time. I was conscious of my rapid ageing. I was putting on weight, and felt gross. I had passed forty. I had the horrible feeling that Algie was my last chance at marriage. Soon I would be too old for clients. Too old for any man. What would life be like when I was sixty? How can anyone wake up to an empty house, or worse still, come home to a lonely house? If I had been ten years younger, I would have thumped Algie and thrown him out. Suddenly, all that was changed.

So, if he wanted to be king dick, I would give him some power and importance. I sent him to the Northern Territory and Queensland to open agencies.

I went to the Territory to check on progress. Eight police raided the business and dragged the girls off to the morgue to force them to look at corpses. I was told, 'Get your girls out or they'll have no faces.' I went to the newspaper and gave the story to a reporter. The newspaper refused to run the story and all hell broke loose. Staff went on strike. The 'Truth' offered to pay for a solicitor to fight the suppression of the article. But I couldn't handle all the tension and went back to Adelaide.

When Algie returned from, or was thrown out of the Territory, he began to nag me to move out of 165 Churchill Road, and into a better place in North Adelaide. 'Let's make a new start,' he said. 'This place is full of bad memories for you. The kids are gone. Besides, why should we live in an old dump? You deserve the best. Time to go up-market.'

It is a sign of how weak I had become that I even listened to him. The thing he kept coming back to was his idea, 'We need a place which is just yours and mine. A new marriage needs its own place. How does anybody feel using the same bed, the same kitchen as other lovers? Why do you reckon I go off my tree in this place? It's full of ghosts.'

The best years of my life were at 165. I had been happy, built myself a life, made a home. But the children had gone. And it was an agony to sit by the pool and look around the yard where Big Nick had played war games with the kids, where we had sat and talked peacefully while I washed his poor back with lavender soap.

We moved. If I wasn't going to give Algie total control, I had to let him have some victories, or he would became unbearable. On the evening of the shift, when some furniture had been transferred to Wellington Square, North Adelaide, I called back to 165, to say goodbye to those good times. I stood in the yard and remembered the parties, the early years of struggling to set up the business. I wandered over to the row of young poplar trees I'd planted in memory of Big Nick and stood for a while under the grape vine trellis he had built. I put my fingertip on the nail hole where once he'd fixed a plaque with his name on a trellis post. 'To remember me.'

When I went inside the house I felt my blood run cold. It had been plundered. Furniture and fittings were gone. Even light shades had been stolen. Somebody had cleaned me out. I wandered in the ruins of my life. Why did I instantly suspect Algie?

I stood like a little child, covered my face with my hands and wept. When at last I caught my breath and dried my eyes, I looked about in fear. Was this my fate? Then I realised I was grinding my teeth. If I didn't win against Algie, then I would only be good for the Wingfield Dump. I would not let him, or anyone do that to me.

I knew it was madness to stay with Algie, but more dangerous to give up. Life was now a battle for my own survival, my own individual future. The easy, quick victory of throwing him out would win a battle, but lose the war. I dug in.

Kasey and Chris moved out. 'I can't take the fights every day,' said Chris. 'When you decided to go with Algie and leave 165, it was you running out on me. It's not me who's going.'

Algie's brother Crowbar was out of work. Algie decided to give him an all-night hamburger shop. He didn't ask, he just demanded, 'I want the fucking place. Get it for me.' It was an all-night joint called The Owl's Nest, on Port Road; open five to five.

I paid six thousand cash across the kitchen table.

There was a house behind the shop, so I rented that too and we moved in. For a little while things went well. Algie, to give him credit, was good at the catering trade, and the Owl's Nest did well. Just for once, my persistence paid off. I had a sense of vindication. I hadn't given up on Algie, and it was a good feeling to see him working so skillfully in the shop. If he was happy, so was I. Not all hope led to disillusion. Out of the wreckage of our marriage, we were making a new start.

Some of my kids, damaged by life out in the world, by crime

and bad marriages, drifted back. I can't say how good it was to see Cassie living in my house again. I phoned Chris every day.

When Algie slapped me about, Cassie fumed. 'Why don't you leave him, or just chuck him out, Mum? He's bad for you.'

What could I say? What can any woman say who keeps hoping that her rotten husband has enough good in him to change? It was worse because he held me under a terrible spell – one moment of his kindness, or thoughtfulness, or real laughter and affection, an unexpected bunch of flowers, the tiniest hope that he was coming good, kept me his victim.

The Owl's Nest gave me a chance to do other things, to try and break out of the fog that surrounded me. Kasey was running the agencies. He worked twenty hours a day, seven days a week, and he held the business together.

On Thursday nights I went to Channel 9 to do an ad for the Owl's Nest. My commercials went on 'The Midnight to Dawn' show, along with the usual mob – a new florist shop, an all-night chemist, and so on. It was a good excuse to get dolled up and have a laugh.

I went in through the 'Here's Humphrey' set and sat down with the others to wait my turn. Max from Medindie Motors always went first. I guess somebody had one of his cars. The rest of us got there early just to watch Max stuff it up. All tarted up in his white suit and red and white spotted tie, he'd get his lines wrong fifty-four times until the crew were nearly wetting themselves.

Then I'd sit at a little table, lights everywhere, watch the camera move in, take a quick glance at myself in the monitor, hope like hell my make-up wouldn't go shiny under the heat of the lights, and feel a tickle of nervousness as the director counted down the seconds then pointed his finger at me to start.

Nervousness? What am I saying? I loved it. Show me a camera and I'm anyone's. I knew that being Patti meant I was advertising more than a hamburger or hot dog. I put on my best voice, stared straight down the barrel of the camera and it only cost me one hundred dollars a go.

One night I was ready, stirring up the crew, when the director frowned, pressed his ear-phone harder against his head to hear above the rabble, then hurried over and said, 'Patti. You're wanted on the phone. Your son's trying to kill himself.'

'Not again! Bloody hell. Let's get this over with, then.' I did my thirty seconds and took off.

When I got back, the Owl's Nest was chockablock. Cassie was trying to serve customers, but Pepe was out on Port Road, trying to get run over. My other daughter, Michelle, was as stoned as the entire cast of 'Hair'. She struggled to grip the tongs to lift up a sausage. She giggled, shrugged at the customer and had another go. Missed. Cassie wheeled Pepe back inside but, like a drunk telling his feet to go straight, he said, 'Now I'm going to break that window.' He swam towards it, dodged a policeman who came in, lost his way and went out to lean on the police car, which had just pulled in. He leant down and said to the policewoman, 'I'm on fucking drugs. I'm tripping. Don't you want to arrest me?' She just wound her window up, disgusted. It took a while to sort that lot out.

For all that, the return of my children gave me a new lease of life. They had so many problems and were such total pains in the arse that it was like the good old days. Once again I was needed. Now my daughters, married and divorced before they turned twenty, were women, and we had a common enemy and a common need to fill up the hours with something.

Algie, however, like an habitual criminal out on a good behaviour bond, didn't last long before he was back into his nasty ways. To an outsider he would have appeared so nice. He kept the Owl's Nest spotless, ran it like clockwork, just as though he was still in jail. Maybe he had never really left. Algie had the tattoos to prove he was a tough guy. I wore his bruises.

Algie was a Jekyll and Hyde. Every morning when I woke, I looked at him to see which one I was lying next to. One day he was a charming, attractive, brave person – Algie had a calm courage that day he was wired by the police and met an alleged Mafia drug runner. Another day he was unpredictably cruel and uncontrollably violent. Our life was a constant strain. We tested each other, took pot shots from our trenches, probed for the enemy's weakness.

# Skinny Minnie

*Algie ran away on R and R again. For a while we had peace and* prayed he would never come back. During these times, Cassie was at my side. She also helped in my escort agencies. She trained the new girls, and did lots of the rotten jobs, like checking new girls out for crabs.

My Skinny Minnie was a trouper. A television producer phoned me to ask if I had a girl suitable for a commercial. Straight away I thought of Cassie. This could be the break she needed.

I rushed her off to the Nilia's for a special hair-do. We spent ages choosing the dresses she'd take. She made up her face, collected her handbag, and sailed off into her dazzling future, Mum right beside her.

A few of the girls waited at home, dying to hear her news. If we returned. Hollywood here we come.

At about five o'clock, we dragged ourselves into the lounge-room, flopped into chairs and held out our hands for a drink. Cassie cracked open the stubbie, took a swig, wiped her mouth and gave us all a grin.

'Well?' Rachel asked.

'I was a secretary.' Poor old Skin. Her voice was all disappointment. 'So much for getting dolled up. They gave me a pair of specs, very prim and proper, to perch on my nose. I think it was an ad for a hotel manager's convention. So I sit behind this big desk and carry on answering the phone and what not. Suddenly this huge, toothless footballer bursts in the room and rushes at the table, laughing like a pack of drunken hyenas and makes a lunge for me. Phew. He's a very noisy person. I look up, fiddle with my specs and say some dribble like, "Goodness me." I swing around in my secretary's chair, my legs open, black stockings and suspenders, but no knickers. Then a bloke, I think it was one of the hotel bosses, gets the bright idea of chasing me through the suite. He wears just a raincoat and I'm supposed to carry on and squeal.'

There was silence in the lounge-room. Then a snort, a laugh burst out from somebody, and Cassie gave a tired grin.

'The lousy mongrels only paid me sixty dollars. End of film career.'

Cassie was my daughter all right. One night she came home wearing nothing but a blanket. She wasn't too pleased. 'The bloke was real thrilled,' she said. 'Very happy for his two hours' worth. I looked at my watch and told him it was time for me to have a shower and put on my lippy. "But I love you, I love you," he said and he was clinging on. I peeled him off and went to the shower. He opened the door and I jumped with fright. What's he up to? I thought. I told him it's against the rules for him to come in while I'm showering. He ripped back the shower curtain and flung all my clothes at my feet. "That'll keep you here," he said.

'That pissed me right off. I picked up my clothes, shoved them in a heap under my arm, put on my spiked heels and stormed out totally starkers, except for the shoes. Down the passage I walked to the lifts, down the lift to the ground floor. Ping! The lift door opens, and so does the mouth of a security guard waiting there to get in the lift. He just stands like a statue, his walkie-talkie held in mid air. I push past him and head across the lobby for the front doors.

'The driver must have seen me. As I opened the doors and stepped out, he ran with a blanket and wrapped it around me. The security guard hadn't moved.'

Another client who didn't please her all that much was a dirty old man. Skin came home furious, went straight into the office and yelled at Kasey. That was unlike her. Normally she'd laugh things off. Not that night. I went in to see what was wrong.

Skin was waving her fist at Kasey. 'I phoned and said, "I've left the iron on," and all you did was say, "We're going flat strap here and don't have a car."'

Cassie turned to me. 'So much for our security. That rotten old bugger had locked me in with him.' She glared at Kasey. 'It's your job to get me out of there. What if he'd been a psycho?'

Kasey just shrugged. 'What could I do? Anyway, you know how to look after yourself.'

Cassie stood in disbelief, then turned her back on Kasey and went into the lounge. I followed her.

'The old feller was disgusting. He climbed all over me. Oh, yuk! Then he locked the door and stood with his back to it. He wanted me to live with him for nine months and have his baby. He wanted an heir. That's when I phoned Kasey. He said it'd be no good getting me out because we'd have to refund the money.' Cassie clenched her fists. 'Sometimes that Kasey is as weak as piss.'

'You're telling me nothing,' I said. 'If I'm not here he lets the girls get away with murder. Anything to keep the peace.'

'Anyway,' Cassie said, 'I wasn't about to bash the old bloke. So I climbed back in bed, thinking I'd sneak out when he fell asleep. But he was as jumpy as a cat. Every time I moved, he was out of bed and standing with his back to the door, although I reckon he must have fallen asleep once, because he peed all over me. That was it. I marched for the door, and was out before he could stop me.'

Next day a guy phoned. 'Can you send Cassie out?'

'Sure,' said Kasey, and paged a car.

Cassie was about to get in the car when she asked the address. She couldn't believe her ears. She slammed the car door. Not the dirty old man again. Kasey sent another girl, but the old man wouldn't let her in. 'I want Cassie to give me an heir.'

Cassie was the one I depended on. She'd have a go at anything, and rarely complain. One day, in the club, the stripper didn't show up. So I went to Cassie and said, 'Bet you wouldn't strip.'

'Bet I would.'

'No you wouldn't.'

'Would.'

'Okay. Do it now.'

I gave her a quick lesson, and she went on stage. There were just a few businessmen sitting around tables for lunch. Cassie started her bumps and grinds. She jiggled to the music, took bits of clothes off, cocked a leg in the air, bent over and showed them a bit of this and a lot of that. She was going really well. That girl's a natural, a real hard worker.

But the four blokes at the front weren't even watching. Cassie did her best to get their attention. They ignored her and went on eating and talking. I saw her getting mad. Suddenly she jumped off the stage, grabbed the nearest bloke by the hair, spun him around, shoved his head right up between her legs, and gooshed it all about. She lifted his face and leant down to speak right into his eyes. 'If I've got the decency to get up there and take all my clothes off, you can at least have the decency to watch. So watch me, you bastard. This is my first time.'

Then Cassie climbed back on stage and finished her act. The businessman watched her every move, but I noticed he didn't eat any more of his lunch.

Another of my best girls was a schoolteacher, Charmaine. She was hot. She wore crotchless knickers or none at all. She would screw a client on the way up in the lift, or a total stranger if he was lucky enough to be catching the lift. That was Charmaine. She would have a man against the wall of the lift even if there were others there. She was married with kids. Charmaine was very much in demand because the clients didn't have to wait to get their clothes off, or hers. The drivers were shit scared of her. Butter wouldn't melt in her mouth, but my toughest drivers were jelly if they saw her number come up.

Some of the girls were as nutty as a fruitcake. There was Penelope. One day she went out with hair and came back bald. She had a gorgeous figure and she reckoned the bald head made her look totally sexy. I made her wear a wig, and we had a blue over that. So she wore a wig, but when she'd arrive at a client's door with the driver, the driver would say, 'Good evening Mr Smith, this is Penelope.' She'd lift the wig like a man raising his hat, and scare shit out of the client.

One night, I'd just fallen into bed and gone to sleep. The birds were singing in the trees. The sun was rising. There was somebody in the bed with me, can't remember who, just a body for the night. He must've been okay, because he was still there. Then I felt somebody touching my thigh, and a girl's voice whispered, 'Patti, Patti, are you awake?' I opened my eyes and two inches in front of my face is this pussy, staring at me. This hairy thing. Then I heard Penelope's voice. 'Patti, I think I've got crabs. Look.'

All the universe was a huge close-up image of this thing in Cinemascope wide lens stereophonic action. Oh my goodness, I wished I hadn't drunk the extra bottle of champagne. I shut my eyes.

The voice went on in a stage whisper. 'Patti, can I borrow your shaver?'

'No way. Take it home and shave there.'

I went back to sleep, and had nightmares about aliens from outer space. These great big nippers were eating through the wall, coming to get me. Somebody was patting my leg. I opened my eyes. Terror. There was this horrible creature with no hair staring at me. I'm sure it winked. I looked up at the bald head and screamed. The bloke next to me woke up and yelled, 'What is it?' Penelope. Great little worker, in shit all the time, and every time I heard her voice I trembled.

# The Owl's Nest

*Algie came back, was nicey-nice for one day, and then got stuck in.* 'Look how old I am. Over thirty. I want to do something for myself. Look at me. Beer gut, hair going thin, bloody great pouches under my eyes.' Then he got really shirty. 'It's all right for you. You've got everything you ever wanted. What have I got? Fuck all, that's what.'

He lit a cigarette and paced about our bedroom like a caged animal. Four steps one way, turn, four steps the other, turn. 'Why don't you let me take some real responsibility instead of just serving in the lingerie shop or as cook in the fucking Owl's Nest?' I knew where this was leading.

'Other women love me, treat me with respect. Why not you?' Algie kept on and on at me. 'You let Kasey do everything. It's too much for one bloke. I could help. I've got heaps of good ideas on what to do with the agencies. Why don't you listen to me? Why?'

'Because I'm Patti.'

I had Algie's brother Crowbar watched, until I had the proof that he was robbing the till in the Owl's Nest. He was robbing us blind. I told Algie, who exploded with rage.

'What are you, you bitch? Accusing my brother.' He smacked me across the face. Then he stormed into the bedroom and yelled for me. I saw Kasey peep out of the office, and then close the office door.

Inside the bedroom I saw Algie pointing to his suitcase. 'Come on, shithead, lift it down, or are you a totally useless slut?'

While my arms were in the air, lifting down the case, he punched me in the ribs. I dropped the case and fell to my knees, gasping for air. Algie threw the case on the bed, and snarled, 'Crawl over here to it, then lick my foot.' I crawled towards him, my eyes focused on his feet. Slowly one shoe lifted and moved back for the kick. I didn't believe he would do it. He was just trying to terrify me. The shoe hit me on the side of the head and I rolled over. He sneered down at me, 'That's for fucking crawling.'

That was it. I had to get away from this madman. To give myself some time to think how to make the final break from him, I booked two tickets on a Pacific cruise, and took one of my best girls, Sheena, with me. When I was a child at Pickering Street, there was no escape. Now I could buy it.

Of course, the cruise was no real escape. I was seasick before we left the wharf, and spent the cruise throwing up and worrying about the business. Had the cars been put in for their service? Were the girls soft-soaping Kasey to get more pay? What if the faulty tap on the cappuccino machine burst and the machine boiled dry? For sure, Algie's mate, that bastard, would be using the Owl's Nest for drug deals.

I phoned every evening from the ship. Algie gave me shit, accusing me of all sorts, and I decided that being a Madam was one long headache. I planned ways to eliminate Algie from my life. None, except perhaps murder, seemed likely to work. Anyway, what was the use of running away, if I had to come back!

One night, soon after my return from the cruise, I heard crashing in the Owl's Nest. Kasey ran to me. 'Algie's locked himself in the shop. He's got two bottles of scotch and he's smashing things with a baseball bat.'

I went to the shop door. Algie rushed towards me. Thank God he had locked it. He waved the bat at me and screamed, 'You fucking bitch.' Then he staggered over to a big vase of flowers on the counter, raised the bat and swung it. The vase exploded, water and flowers gushing across the counter. They were the flowers a gay friend had bought me as a welcome home gift.

Algie began to demolish the shop: chairs, coffee machine, cups and plates, everything. I stood and watched. Algie kept glancing out at me. 'You slag moll. I'm going to blow your brains out.'

Cassie was beside me. She shook with rage. We watched Algie destroy our shop, our months of work. Night after night Cassie had slaved away to build up the business. 'I'm going inside to find a gun,' she whispered. 'I'm going to kill the rotten bastard.' She ran to the house at the back of the shop.

I knew she meant it, and I hoped she would.

The police arrived and stood by me, watching Algie go berserk. He flung chairs, tipped over tables, laid into everything with the baseball bat. I wished they'd shoot him like a rabid dog. But it was only a domestic, and none of them was going to risk his neck by going in.

Algie pushed his face against a window and screamed at me. His face was twisted, mad, and I was very frightened. He was demented, snarling, as he yelled out that he would burn me with acid, hold a gun to my head and shoot out my brains all over the wall.

I turned to the police. 'You heard that?' They stared right through me. They'd heard it all a thousand times before.

Algie's mother and brother turned up. She was crying and said, 'Don't go near him. He'll kill you!'

Kasey had a key. He offered to go in and try to calm Algie. I ran back to the house and threw clothes in a case. All the bashings, all the years of work had come down to this.

My brain felt like a bomb about to explode. If I didn't leave him, it would come to blood one day for sure.

I lay on a hotel bed and racked my brains. I kept hearing Algie's voice. 'Look at you, you fucking moll. You're so ugly. Nobody wants you. Your kids all hate you. Nobody cares about you. Why don't you just go and lie out on the road in front of a semi? Do the world a favour. Make my day.' His words spoke for my father, my mother, my children.

There was an evil force in Algie that I couldn't deal with. One night he'd grabbed his rifle and chased me out of the house. I hid in the bushes among the dog shit while he hunted for me. Then he went inside. I crept to a window and looked in. He was snapping all the knobs off the stereo set. Then he ran into the bedroom, swept up a handful of my jewellery and began to pick at the diamonds with his pocket knife.

I lay on the hotel bed and went over and over the alternatives. How could I escape him? It was no good just running away. That only made him worse. He needed me, he craved the power I had, and the money. Without me, he was just a cheap crim. With me, he had expensive clothes, cars, a sense of importance. There was no way he would give that all up. But I would never give up my business.

The police could put a restraining order on him, but he had got wise to that, and shifted his tactics to mental cruelty. The torments left no bruises for a doctor to photograph. He would say, 'I'll be waiting for you. Maybe I'll be up a tree and shoot you. Maybe I'll be in the garage, behind the door, and when you drive home and get out of the car, you will seen what acid does to a face.'

It was a battle to the death, and I was really afraid for my life. Why should I give up all I had slaved for over the years? Why should he make me give up my life as Patti, and retreat into some pokey dump to live off the pension?

The battle against Algie had to be out in the open. It was also a battle for my money. 'What's yours is mine,' he said. 'I can take what I like, do what I like. One day I'll see you in the gutter, and I'll kick you like a mangy dog, and leave you to rot. All you'll have is a dollar and fifty cents of it will be mine.'

I had to find a way to get rid of him. It was no good trying to run or hide from him. I had to think of a way to stop him getting at me.

It was stupid getting him bumped off. I'd just end up in jail. Algie had already made a tape of someone I was supposed to have employed and who was threatening to have him shot. He'd given that tape to the police, just in case.

The simple solution of divorce would not work. He'd still persecute me. 'Revenge is everything,' he had told me. If I divorced him, I took away all his toys, all his posturing, his borrowed pride. He would still be out there somewhere, waiting. He was a vicious, violent little boy, who would smash anybody's toys if he couldn't have them. He would smash his own if he lost his temper. And

I was the best toy he had ever owned.

There was another compelling reason why I had stayed so long with Algie. All my adult life kept circling back to Pickering Street. If ever my life was to break that cycle it had to be now. I had to find the way out of a maze that kept leading back to the centre. Because Algie was the worst mistake I'd ever made, he gave me the best chance of discovering how to escape. He was the greatest threat. If I could overcome him, then I would be free of the hold my past had on me.

# *Legalisation*

*At this time another battle loomed over the horizon.*

During the eighties, Hindley Street began to die. Vagrants, race gangs and drug addicts moved in. The sense of family was going as organised crime moved in. Hindley Street lost its character of a main street in a small town. The people began to stay away. They went looking for a good time in the suburbs. The suburbs? Where was the glitter and beauty in suburban pubs or late-night shopping centres? Slowly the laughter and friendliness faded away.

A different family moved in. We all called them The Family, and they had some strange children. It was sleaze, drugs, corruption, videos of sex with little boys, the murders of children, stock market fiddles, official cover-ups called enquiries, and wild speculation by the rich. It was all connected. The corruption in the heart of Adelaide became visible.

The street girls looked like skeletons. I saw one kid as she shivered and shook, leaning against the window of Myers. She gave me a weak, frightened smile. 'G'day Patti.' She could only have been fifteen or sixteen, but she looked forty. Her face was haggard, her eyes were sunken, her skin yellow, her hands showed every bone.

I handed her a wad of money, and said, 'Get out of here.'

She grabbed at the money like a monkey and stuffed it in her handbag. Her lips stretched tightly over her teeth. 'No chance.' I saw her eyes look past me into the traffic. There was her pimp, cruising past, watching. She shuddered. 'He used to be my boyfriend. Told me that if I really loved him I could prove it by screwing a bloke.'

'Do you want to come home with me?'

Her eyes pleaded, but she shook her head. 'He'd kill me.'

'You'll be dead anyway in a few months. Do you know where you'll end up?' She looked at me like a kid in Grade Three who's been caught looking in the teacher's handbag. 'They'll find you one night, dead in an alley, because you're so wasted away you're no good for the game any more. There'll be no bruises on your body. Just a needle mark on your arm, a little hole which you didn't make, but who can know that? They'll call it an accidental overdose. That's how your boyfriend will fix you. An ambulance will come. The only words anybody will say over you are DOA.'

The kid just stood there, shaking and crying.

I put my face close to hers and said, 'Come with me now. If you're too scared to come to my place, I'll give you a ride to the bus station. But you've got to get out of here. Do you know anyone interstate?'

She laughed. 'My parents?' Then she fished a packet of cigarettes out of her handbag and lit a cigarette. 'Thanks, Patti. But no thanks. Now please go. He's getting mad.'

The next Sunday there was a spread in the *Sunday Mail* attacking street girls. Some Member of Parliament called Robin Millhouse gave the usual Festival of Light line about morality, corruption, crime, God's law. It wasn't fair to say those things about prostitutes. Why do the girls always get the blame? What about the men who use them? I got fired up and phoned a reporter. The media loved that and I kept feeding them stories.

The Millhouse attack on prostitutes gave me a cause. It helped to save my sanity during the last terrible times with Algie, who was away more and more, hacking around the countryside in one of the Mercedes Benz trucks I bought him.

Millhouse also helped the business no end. Every time there was a bit in the papers, or on the radio or tele the number of clients multiplied by four. He made me the Madam known all over the state.

In fact the poor man got such a going over in the press. He

wanted to get rid of us, to clean up the city, but ended up presenting the bill for decriminalisation. People called us Millhouse's prostitutes.

As it happened, although he was surrounded by a lot of self-righteous holier-than-thou fools in the Festival of Light, he had an open mind. He talked to me, he looked for the facts. Robin Millhouse tried to find the truth about prostitutes, and the more he found out, the more he understood us.

To me it was more than just a matter of morality. A woman's body is her own. Nobody, neither politician nor priest, has the right to tell her what to do with it, unless she is harming somebody else. In a strange sort of way we were fighting for women's rights. The prostitute issue was all tied in with the fights about abortion, homosexuality, and so on. I hated us being treated like lepers, and, knowing Adelaide, knowing my clients' names and occupations, I went troppo at the hypocrisy of some of the do-gooders.

Robin Millhouse was one of the rare men who had the courage of his convictions. Once he had got the facts, he still thought we were immoral, but he said it was necessary to face the reasons for prostitution and do something about them. There were facts like poverty, child abuse, hopeless government assistance for bashed wives and single supporting mothers, and a whole list of social problems, which helped to push some girls onto the streets just to feed their kids. The women's shelters were doing a great job – how I wish they were around in my earlier marriages – but how could they hope to look after the hundreds, maybe thousands, of abused women? In those days none of us really understood the extent of domestic violence.

Millhouse stuck by his guns. He didn't approve of us, but he turned his attack away from the working girls and onto society. He went on television and said our society lives a lie. 'I'm ashamed of the behaviour of some Christians,' he said, which got him in plenty of hot water.

He was a lawyer, but he admitted that the law was out of step with the real world. He saw that prostitutes were singled out for law enforcement when the really corrupt people were allowed to get away with murder. Bash the prostitutes and you've got a scapegoat to fool the public.

The public surveys showed that people approved of prostitution, provided it was kept out of sight. Just like the women who sat next to me in Nilia's hair salon. 'Oh no, Patti. We don't want you decriminalised. If it all becomes open we're scared of the names of men being discovered.' They needn't have worried. At that time, in law, the prostitute was named, but not the man. He was protected and the girl copped the criminal charges.

While all this was happening, one or two crooked cops in the Vice Squad increased their fear tactics. I got three or four visits a week. As always, the crime was not sex, but the money, and the rotten ones in the Vice Squad, the ones who ran their own girls and arrested mine, resented my wealth. Girls had their hands broken. Girls were blackmailed with threats to tip off their families with the fact that they were prostitutes. At the same time the do-gooders were attacking us, we were set up. My girls became afraid of the streets, and I had to increase my protection for them.

The day came for me to appear before a parliamentary enquiry into prostitution. So I went to Parliament House. I took one of my best girls, Camille, with me. Camille had the gift of the gab, presented herself with style, and had some brains. I was excited and curious as we walked up the steps and went in the narrow side door. Inside it was cool and dim, with long corridors going in all directions like a rabbit warren. The doorman led us along to a room, and showed us in. There was a big oval table with people there I had only seen in the newspapers or on television. Camille and I sat at one end of the table and faced them. A woman MP, just to my left, was giving us sweet smiles, but I could feel the bad vibes. This worried me, because I had romanticised these people. I imagined they were lion-hearts who would rescue my girls from the drug-pushers and crooked cops.

At first we were all a bit uneasy. I made a feeble joke. 'You must feel pretty good being called MP. I've got the same title, Madam Patti, and I'm laughing all the way to the bank.' They all tittered away, but I felt it was all fake. The men were awkward, couldn't come down to earth and be themselves.

The questions began and I was able to say my piece. 'Illegal, yes. But we are doing the state a service. There are a lot of sadistic men out there. If it wasn't for us, a lot more children would be abused, a lot more women raped.'

What these people didn't understand was that in fighting for decriminalisation I was threatening my own business. If the government ran brothels, if the working girls were made safe to operate without fear, the girls wouldn't need me. They could go independent and I stood to lose a fortune.

Perhaps I got a bit hot under the collar, but I began to give answers they didn't want to hear. 'If I'm illegal, why must I pay taxes? If I don't put in my tax returns and pay a whopping great fee, then I am sent to jail as a criminal. The government's living off prostitutes. You people here, part of your salary comes from prostitutes' earnings.'

I was naive. I hadn't woken up to the fact that when any government says 'enquiry' it really means 'cover-up,' and an excuse to make their lawyer mates rich.

As the debate heated up, it was a field day for the media. In April, 1981, 'Sixty Minutes' did a program on me and Millhouse, called 'The Unhappy Hooker'. To get more media attention I decided to hold a prostitutes' rally on the steps of Parliament House. I phoned the competitor agencies, but all I got was, 'You're fucking stupid, Patti. Let the girls look after themselves. I'm only in this for the money. Why would I want it to be legal?'

Two days before the demonstration the phone call came. 'If you go on those steps, you'll be shot.' Usually if they tell you, it's not serious. If it's real they just kill you without any warning. But I knew that man. He still lived in the old terror-tactics days of the seventies. I phoned the Vice Squad who said, 'Don't go. We can't guarantee you protection.'

So it was to be just my girls there. I had to fight them too. I told them, 'If we keep hiding, then we're hypocrites.'

'But Patti what if my boyfriend or mother or husband sees me on television? Whammo.'

That is one of the tricky bits of this business: trying to avoid the accident of a girl turning up on her own father's doorstep, or the disaster of a man opening the door to his own wife. It was another reason for me to have accurate files.

I had to pull out all stops to bully the girls to turn up. I got a pile of wigs, dark glasses, and made their faces up so their own mothers wouldn't have known them. I felt like a headmistress trying to get a mob of adolescent girls to go to church. But if they were game, even though they didn't believe in the cause, I had to look after them, cover for them as much as possible.

On the day, I was very proud of my girls. Our cars drove them to Parliament House, where they strutted their stuff and waved the banners. The media turned up in force. I stayed out of sight. That made me feel bad. The death threat was just another form of bashing. Do what I say or else.

I knew that voice on the phone. As the morning of the demonstration wore on I got a blinding migraine. But with what Algie was doing to me, and remembering Sid's bashings, I should have dragged myself onto those steps.

It was a measure of how bad those years were with Algie. He was taking away my strength. He was slowly but surely wearing me down. I was shocked at my own weakness, at how confused and pathetic I was beneath the surface. I thought that Patti the Madam had left the frightened little girl behind.

Later, when it came the day for the vote on the Millhouse Bill to decriminalise prostitution, I sat in the visitors' gallery with Andi Sebastian, the feminist, beside me. Down there was Millhouse. He had taken such a beating. He was up against the Adelaide wowsers. The churches had run the state for so long. They weren't fighting against prostitution, they were fighting to keep their power. Since the year dot those church schools had trained the kids of the rich how to inherit and keep power. This was not just about prostitution; it was about who was running the state. That's why it was so vicious.

Millhouse kept his word. He presented a Bill that effectively said, We may not like it, but it won't go away, so what shall we do?

I sat there in parliament and watched them all. I stared down at the men who were so afraid of losing votes. One by one I watched them cross the floor for 'conscience'. Gradually the house became full with tension. More and more were walking.

Andi Sebastian squeezed my hand as we leant forward, peering down, counting and re-counting. I could hardly believe it. Were we winning? Count again. Even-stevens. Shit. That left it to the casting vote of the Speaker, Bruce Eastick. I felt Andi slump forward. 'The Speaker always votes for the status quo.'

Afterwards, almost in tears, Andi took me to the Gateway Hotel and we got drunk.

# The
# detective's gun

*The phone rang. It was Bimbo.* 'Patti, there's a "D"'s gun on my cupboard.' Her voice was wild. 'What are we going to do?' Bimbo. That girl would be the death of me one day. How in heaven's name did she get hold of a copper's gun? Had she any idea of the penalties?

Bimbo was hysterical. 'Patti you've got to hide it. Where can we put it? No. No. I'll take it back. Patti, it's loaded.'

Then I got an idea. It was so wonderful I wanted to scream. 'Spare me the details. Just get yourself in a taxi and bring the gun around here quick smart before they come back to rip it off you.' I looked up and kissed my fingertips at the roof. Thank you God.

To calm myself I went into the kitchen and put the jug on for some coffee. I knew it would be stupid to lose this opportunity. I began to think it through. There were risks. By now the cops could think it was here. They would tear my house to pieces. If they couldn't find it, they would think I had sold it to a crim. That would mean arrests, charges, endless hassles. I already had a record of illegally possessing firearms. None of this mattered. Today was going to be one of the best of my life.

I called Cassie in from the backyard where she was sunbaking on a banana lounge. I told her my plan and a great grin spread across her face.

Bimbo arrived, white-faced, trembling, and carrying a solid-looking Country Road bag.

'Cassie, take that thing and hide it outside somewhere. On the roof.' Cassie put her hands on her hips and stared at me with that 'Aw-Mum' look.

I said, 'You don't expect me to do it? And it's no good asking Kasey to. He'd just flap around like a chook with its head cut off. Besides, we are the only ones to know about this.' Cassie gave a crooked grin, took the bag and went out the back.

'Now, Bimbo, from the top, tell me exactly what happened.' I needed the correct details. This gun was a top priority. It was vital that I knew if the cops were in the wrong.

She reached across the table and took one of my cigarettes. When she had taken two long drags, she said, 'A few of us went to the Black Rose after work, you know, to relax, let our hair down and wait for the sun to come up. Well, I was dancing away – you know, getting rid of the horrors. Maybe I had a bit too much to drink.' Two sniffs of a cork and Bimbo is anybody's. She went on, 'This "D" came in the door, looked around and gave us the big macho stare. We ignored him and just went on raging. He leant on the bar and watched me for a while. I was in my best black outfit, you know, the see-through that just shows a tit if I move the right way. I looked over at the "D". He was young. I didn't know his face. I reckon he was a rookie who'd just been given the plain clothes treatment.

'Anyway, after a while he came over, all Clint Eastwood tough guy bullshit, and grabbed my arm. Then, real heavy, he asked what my name was. I looked him straight in the eye and said, "Get fucked."

'His response was to put the hard word on me. So I took him home and screwed him all over the lounge-room. After a while we must've fallen asleep. I heard him pulling on his clothes and muttering, "Jesus. Six o'clock." Anyway, he rushes out and when I wake up there's his gun on the cupboard.'

Bimbo ran her fingernail round the edge of a rose printed on the tablecloth. I cupped my hands around my coffee mug and smiled. The cop was in it up to his eyeballs, and I knew just what to do. I pinched the cigarette from Bimbo and took a long, contented drag. I imagined myself taking the gun to the media, holding it up for the cameras. Heads would be rolling all over the Angas Street office floors. I could do it, and it would serve some of them right. But there was a better way to catch the fish I wanted.

While Bimbo went to the toilet I changed into my long black dress, carefully made up my face and fixed my hair. This was a showdown I intended to enjoy. I sent Cassie around to Bimbo's flat. She stuck a note on the front door. 'Bimbo. I'll meet you down at the Rose. Cassie.' She peeped in the window. They hadn't trashed the place yet. But they would, just to scare her shitless.

I looked at my watch. It was after the deadline when that cop had to sign in his gun at the end of his shift. Somebody was protecting him, and giving him time to find it.

When Cassie came back from leaving the note on the door, I said, 'Good girl. Now it's time to set up the big bust.' I took the girls to the Black Rose and we ordered a good meal and a bottle of champagne.

After a while two cops looked in the door. 'Is that him?' The cops looked young and frightened. Bimbo nodded. 'Relax,' I said. 'We're going to have some fun.' She glanced at me nervously. I said, 'Go over to the bar, and he'll approach you. Tell him if he wants it back to see me.'

Bimbo went to the bar and the rookie hurried to her, gripped her arm and whispered in her ear. He looked across at me, then around at the customers and, head down, came over to our table. He whispered, 'Where is it?' There was no need for him to worry about the sleaze bags at the bar. They couldn't have cared if we were all naked; well, the gay ones might have taken an interest in the 'D'.

I said, 'Do you mean your gun? The one you lost?' He pressed the palms of his hands together, and pleaded with me with his eyes. I snapped at him, 'Get your superior. I want to talk to him, not you.'

He jumped as though an electric shock went up his bum. Slowly, his eyes narrowed. But he went to do as he was told.

Sure enough, ten minutes later, a load of cops came in. Six of them went to the bar. Then who should stick his ugly face in the door but Big Shot. He motioned the young 'D' to stay over at the bar. Big Shot came to my table. 'What the fucking hell are you up to, Patti?'

'Sit down and let's talk about it.' I'll give him this, he didn't lose his cool. Big Shot sat, waved at the waiter and ordered his own bottle of champagne. Raising his eyes to mine he said, 'Come on, Patti. Don't play games. The top brass know all about it already.' Bullshit.

There was a long silence. Maybe I should have gone to the media. Just sitting at the same table as this bastard made my blood boil. I could feel my temperature rise. Big Shot tapped the rim of his glass. 'So you've taught the kid a lesson. I'm sure he'll remember you to the day he dies. But enough's enough. Why are you doing this?'

'Just for once the shoe's on the other foot. Now that young idiot and you know what it's like to be a working girl. Powerless. Shit scared of somebody in authority up at Angas Street. Knowing you can be taken to pieces whenever some bastard feels like it.'

Cassie handed me the gun. Big Shot slid out the magazine to count the bullets. No, we hadn't stolen one. He clicked his fingers at the young cop, gave me a murderous glare, and marched out.

That moment of triumph would last me a lifetime. I felt so good, I divorced Algie.

# *A gun to my head*

*One evening, two men broke into my flat and one put a rifle to* my head.

'Hand over the business and the girls, or you're dead.'

I wasn't with it, and said, 'No fucking way.'

My lack of fear surprised them. They mistook my bewilderment for courage. I vaguely remembered one of my girls, Jade, talking about some eastern states heavies she'd got mixed up with. 'Who are you?'

'Painters and Dockers. Smile.' He shifted the gun to my chest. That was supposed to mean, 'We're so mean we eat rocks and drink paint remover for breakfast.'

My rebelliousness started to simmer. I stared him down, and said, 'If you want to shoot me, do it. But there's no way I'm giving my business to you bastards.'

He blinked, looked over at his mate, and the gun barrel wavered.

I pushed my advantage. 'I've been threatened by the best. What the fuck are you?'

He stepped back and lowered the gun. His mate nodded, and said, 'You've got twenty-four hours to think about it. See you tomorrow night at the Berkley.'

I contacted Police Headquarters and told Assistant Commissioner Harvey all about it. Perhaps he'd like to meet these interstate hoods. I doubted they were really from the Painters and Dockers, who are genuine tough guys.

Next night I went to the Hotel Berkeley to show these pricks

I wasn't scared of them. Of course I was scared half to death, and took plenty of help with me: my son Pepe and his wife, one of my heavies, Jack, who I sometimes used as a bodyguard, and Algie. We had tea in the pub. While Jack was over at the bar, he took out his gun and showed off by twirling it around like Wyatt Earp. I hissed at him to put it away.

When it came time to meet the thugs, we went together towards the door. I saw through a window two detectives I knew. 'Quick. Hide the gun.' My son's wife stuffed it in her handbag. Things became rapidly confused. The coppers arrested Jack and Pepe's wife. I was in the back of a police car. There was no sign of the thugs. I saw a detective running past the hotel. It made no sense. They were arresting the wrong people.

We all went to the cop shop and I had to pay four hundred dollars to bail Jack out.

At this time, Algie was really after me. I had divorced him, and, just as I predicted, it did no good. He kept trying to wheedle or frighten his way back into my life. He had lost all the money and power he had with me. Sometimes he fawned to get it back. Other times he was schizo with anger. Just as a warning he had hidden behind my garage door, stepped out and held up a glass container. 'Acid. For your ugly face.' He tied me up, there in the garage, and sat in front of me. He held out a can of Coke and a handful of pills. In a soft, caressing voice he said, 'Go on, Pat, why don't you finish it? Here, just one little lot of pills and all the pain and fear are gone.'

He was also terrorising his girlfriend, whom he had been screwing from the first weeks of our marriage. She had his baby within nine months of our marriage.

She phoned me. She sobbed so much I could hardly make sense of what she said. 'Algie beating me . . . scared he's really psycho . . . will kill . . .'

The next time she phoned, Algie gloated aloud that he would love to run away with her. I snapped. I charged around to her place, Algie with me, and smashed her. As we left, Algie kicked her in the head.

That was one of the worst acts of my life. I was sick with guilt and deep fear that I was mad, as mad as Algie. There was no lower I could ever get. That poor woman had copped all my years of rage against Algie.

There was a knock at the door late one night. It was Algie again. He pushed his way in. Kasey was with me, and one of Jack's friends. Algie was glowering, but I was safe with the other two men there. He accused me of being on with Jack.

'So what? We're divorced. What business is it of yours?'

Algie jumped up in a red rage. He rushed into my bedroom and slammed the door. The men looked at me, at each other, at the shut door. What was going on? Then Algie flung open the door. He had my revolver in his hand. He held it up level with his eyes, and aimed it at each of us. He knew I always kept my gun on top of the wardrobe. Why hadn't I guessed? None of us moved. While we watched he slowly pulled back the hammer.

Algie said to me, 'I'll do eight years, but you'll be dead forever.' He stepped forward, put the gun to my right temple and I went into a kind of coma. Everything was in slow motion. I watched his finger tighten on the trigger. I saw the trigger move. There was no sound as he fired. He smacked me across the face with the gun, and was gone.

# *Prison*

---

*I went through the cheque book stubs. One thousand dollars, paid to* Algie as salary while he drove one of his trucks to Sydney. Six hundred dollars, paid to Algie as salary . . . Algie had drawn the dole while on my payroll. At this time he was taking me through the family court for half of what I had, but really had no right as he came with nothing and took everything. So my solicitor put him in for Social Security fraud. He was warned but he gave the solicitor the up sign. His girlfriend and I laid charges also against him for assault. I took her to the police and she showed her bruises. Now Algie was wanted by the State police for assault and by the Commonwealth police for fraud. Both lots went around together to arrest him. He was tried, found guilty, and put away in jail.

I had listened to enough crims to know what Algie's first night would be in prison. No television, no radio, no books, nobody to talk to, lights out at ten, and through the window the glow of the city lights – the streets. Shops, pubs, all out there.

Next morning the real boredom begins. Wake. Shave, shit, wait. Breakfast. Arrange a loan to get a TV, radio, some luxuries. Swap a John Lennon tape for an Elton John. Take ages to do this, so that it feels important, and fills up time. Talk about God to the padre, because born again means getting out sooner. Get another tattoo.

Revenge is everything.

I faithfully visited Algie. I waited outside the gates in the heat and flies with the other women and their kids. There was nowhere to sit. We women exchanged knowing glances. Why were we so dolled up? Our faces were painted, hair perfect, body doused in strong perfume. This was the best revenge. Pretend to care. He's locked up. Feel safe by seeing him locked up. We had the power to do anything we liked, see who we liked, go anywhere. He need never know. Suspicion is always worse than certainty. We didn't depend on them. But they counted down the hours to a visit. We queued up to press the button on the wall. 'What's your name? Who are you visiting?'

The door opened, I walked through the metal detector, handing over my keys and cigarettes. The screws were looking in all the wrong places. I had heard that a tennis ball, thrown over the fence, held a fortune in drugs. Trucks took drugs and weapons in. More than that got through, including one of my girls.

Then I went to the weatherboard room, Table 3. The prisoners were let in. Doctors, solicitors, land agents, child molesters, ex-cops, murderers, bank robbers, church elders; the man who chopped up his wife and kids – 'If you kill the ewe, then the lambs must die.'

Algie and I sat and faced each other. He reached out and rubbed his palms on my wrists to get the perfume for masturbation. He gave me his list. 'Please bring me my black jacky, brown cords, jocks and socks, blue truck bag, RAA card, and some photos of you and me together that I can stick in my photo album.'

He called me Trish. 'It's a bummer, but not the end of the world. I can't wait to come home. I've got stacks of making up to do. You're beautiful, Trish, honey. Hey and look at me! Big fucking deal. I'm thirty-five nearly, and I've got tits. He, he. Jesus, so old. I even got slaughtered at darts. Remember that joke about prostitutes – had more pricks than a dart board. Good one. Think I'll take a sickie tomorrow. Just can't be stuffed getting up for work. My ulcer is playing up anyway. As long as I remember the right name for the medicine, the doctor will believe me. Twelve months of this.'

I screwed his best mate while Algie was inside. Algie got to a phone. 'I love you, Trish. Can't wait to get out and show you how sorry I am.' He sent me long love letters, with SWALK

(Sealed With A Loving Kiss) on the bottom.

Then came the thunderbolt. The padre contacted me. Algie had made a full confession of his brutality to me. The padre was sure he was turning over a new leaf. All the right signs were there.

This went straight to my craziness about Algie. Now that I had punished him, I began to feel guilty. I had never lost faith that some day I could force him to reform. Knowing Algie was like bad sex with somebody I was supposed to love. If I refused, I felt guilty. If I did it, I resented it.

My weakness was not being able to handle his vulnerability. When he asked me, cowering, to bring him a thermos flask for his cell, or his old T-shirt, I began to feel a pang of pity for his helplessness.

When the padre spoke to me, he was pretty sure that Algie had at last woken up to his problems, and knew how to deal with them, if somebody out there would give him another chance.

Algie came out of prison early and I married him again. Three days later he tied me up in a chair. 'Six months you took away from my life. Six months.'

I had to buy him a Mercedes truck to keep him away from me. Then it became a trucking business.

# *The collapse*

*Thus I gave myself up to the final reign of terror. I was on permanent* overdose of tranquillisers because I couldn't face the reality of how mad I was to just give up all my hard-won freedom – just like that – because I was so off my brain to get the love I was denied as a little girl.

My abandonment of hope was in some ways as treacherous as my mother's abandonment of me.

Life became a mad slide into ruin. Algie was insane for revenge, and even police protection couldn't guarantee my safety. When Cassie got married, Algie terrorised the wedding from out there in the dark. We kept knives with us. He was out there in ambush, waiting. During the reception he slunk out of his lair to scratch and deface the cars before running off into the night. When I saw the thousands of dollars of gouges on my LTD, I went white with rage and leapt into the car to chase after him. 'Don't go out there,' the police warned. 'That's what he wants. He's waiting for you.'

In earlier times, as when Big Nick died, I'd had nervous collapses. Now, ruled by fear, the only way I had to go on was to exist in a daze of nerve tablets. I dared not think about the reality of what I had done in re-marrying Algie. My brain was so far away with the fairies, that I was incapable of running the agencies, the trucking company, the shops, anything. Kasey kept the agencies going, but the finances became more and more of a mess.

Tax time was drawing near and the account books were a dog's dinner. I had to move fast, or I'd be in jail for tax evasion on a huge scale. I tried sorting through the cartons of cheque books and receipts but it was hopeless. So I employed an accountant. Well, Shonky O'Shaughnessy had been an accountant, until he was struck off the register. I handed all the mess over to him and told him to sort it out.

He performed miracles and the tax department couldn't find one fault with my annual statements. With a huge sigh of relief, I told Shonky to stay on and run the accounts.

Run them he did. Right down to nothing. He was so smart I had no idea, when I made my regular inspections of the books, what he was up to. Shonky milked the accounts so systematically that by the time the warning bells rang we were past the point of no return.

It was a simple thing that gave him away. I couldn't make sense of some figures he gave me. There was too much money missing. Shonky gave a little cough, and almost whispered, 'I've tried to keep this from you Pat, but you need to watch out for Kasey. He's been having more than a little flutter, if you know what I mean. In fact, the amounts are monumental.'

My temperature went up. Kasey ripping me off for gambling debts? Sure, Kasey might be weak in some ways, but I had lived with him for almost twenty years. He was not a sneak thief, and he certainly wasn't a compulsive gambler. He had a thing against gambling, and had to be nagged to even go in an office sweep for Melbourne Cup Day.

I roared at Shonky to get all the books and bring them to me. I wanted every cent accounted for.

There was no money to check. Only astronomical debts. How could one man dispose of so much money so fast? Over the years, Algie had gone through thousands with trucks and cars and other expensive toys. The money I should have invested for my future, he had squandered. I hadn't minded because I couldn't imagine the escort business running into hard times. But Shonky had made debts many times the cost of three new Mercedes Benz trucks.

Shonky disappeared. So did a lot of the books. One carton of cheque books was found in Wingfield Dump. Algie again. It wasn't just Shonky. There were a lot of people salting away my fortune, leaving me with the bills.

My business collapsed like a card house. Just like that. All gone. I had to sell the trucks and shops, just to hang on to the agencies. Then I found that I was thousands in the red for rent Shonky had siphoned off. I just didn't have the cash to pay. The agencies began to fold. The girls went elsewhere for work. I was helpless to stop the crash. Almost overnight I was back to one grubby little office and a few girls. My house gone. Everything except my LTD that would be the last they took. Algie made sure he was there for the pickings. I had bought and given Cassie a red Jaguar. But he sneaked in, stole the car and drove it away to hiding.

All those years of battling. I couldn't handle how fast my life fell into absolute ruins. The world of finance is unreal. With human problems you can usually have time to sort things out. But where money is concerned you can have a fortune when you go to bed, and be a pauper when you wake up. It's like money is not real. It can literally go up in a puff of smoke.

When the last of my eighteen agencies was sold to meet another debt we'd discovered, I had nowhere to go. I retreated to the country. Here I lived in the same isolation, the same kind of living death Nan must have known. I lay in bed until noon. Then I sat in a chair and watched television until the set went white and hissed, sometime after midnight. I sat awake, too frightened to sleep, because as soon as I closed my eyes, all I saw were the ugly scenes of my past, replayed endlessly by my brain. Replayed to horrify me, and show in terror after terror that there were no answers to explain my life. It was a meaningless emptiness.

I knew I would not kill myself. I suffered a single blessed gift. It was not happiness. It was the torment of real feelings. I lived alone, listening to all the voices within.

I was not entirely alone. Mad Jack wandered around the district. I wasn't afraid of him. He was mad from grief. His wife was gone, and son was dead. 'He's off his head,' the police warned me. 'Better lock your doors at night. He ran naked through the main street once. Said his dead mother told him to.' I had nothing to fear from Mad Jack. He was a huge Russian man. He called himself Jack Strong. Mad Jack wrestled the invisible bear that wandered among the sheep in the paddocks. They were colossal battles. They hurled themselves into the fray, tooth and claw. The sheep scattered to the far fence. Neither Mad Jack nor the bear ever tried to kill each other. They wanted to be able to play again next day. Each evening, as the sun set, he passed by and lifted one hand to me in greeting. I left a light burning all night, and the door opened in case he wanted shelter from the freezing winter rains and frosts. Once he spoke. He paused in mid step, frozen for a moment, and then slowly turned his bearded face to me. With an enormous, joyous smile, he shouted, 'Love.' One afternoon he sat down in the paddock, poured petrol on himself and lit a match.

Before I was ready, I returned to the city.

# Perverting the
# course of justice

*For sanctuary, I went to live with my old friend Ralph. One day, I* was feeling down, sitting in an armchair, a *Women's Weekly* open on my lap. I read a page, went to turn it and realised I had no idea what I had just read. Pictures and stories swam in front of my eyes.

The atmosphere was heavy and I was on edge, suffocating in this stifling house. The air was loaded with the electricity of a storm that would not break. Voices came through the window. Ralph and strangers. Men. Somebody said, 'Patti?' Ralph said, 'Not here. No idea.' A car drove off.

The phone rang. Automatically I picked it up and heard Kasey's voice. 'Patti, they're after you. The NCA.'

The National Crime Authority? What could they want with me? I wandered the house, brooding on this new threat that hung over me. What was the NCA? Not like the ordinary cops, who knew me. Ordinary cops and working girls – people need us even if they don't approve of our ways. But what could the NCA have on me? I was out of the game, and was hardly a threat to the nation. All I had heard on the grapevine about the NCA was that they were a law unto themselves, could trash houses, invade anybody's privacy, and used bottom-of-the-barrel cops as their heavies.

Without warning, I felt stung. I was not going to run and hide. I got the number from 013 and phoned the NCA office. 'I hear you're looking for me?'

'Where are you Patti?'

'Doesn't matter. You listen to me. I know what you're all about. If you want to speak to me, give me the courtesy of agreeing to a time that won't embarrass my friend. He lives in a Trust Home area, and the neighbours mustn't see. If you bring a woman cop, which you must, get her to wear an ordinary overcoat, and not a cop's hat. I'll give you a time and address if you will wait until tomorrow when my friend is at work.'

When I said the address, the NCA cop gave a little laugh. A dizzy spell hit me and I went to my handbag for the tablets. My blood pressure was through the roof. I was putting on weight like I couldn't believe. My body was cashing in its chips. Without my tablets I'd almost certainly have a stroke. I dreaded the possibility of my brain suddenly going without warning, of being found on the floor days later, or of trying to live with half my body paralysed.

Next day I tidied Ralph's place and put out coffee and cups. It was like the old days when the cops came. It began to rain. That would keep the neighbours inside. I put a Valium in the palm of my hand and looked at it. This little tablet would zonk me, but I was terrified of a blood pressure attack while the NCA were here.

A car pulled up, and standing on the front verandah were two heavies escorted by a woman cop in police overcoat and hat. Across the road people stood watching on their verandahs. Ralph would go right off his brain.

I held the door open. 'Come on, come inside, quickly.' They shook the rain off their coats and stepped into the lounge.

I gestured to the coffee table set with cups and a plate of shortbread biscuits. The older man said, 'No thanks, Patti. You are to come with us.'

My face set hard to conceal my panic. 'Where?'

'We'll talk about it in the car.'

My brain shouted, No! I was struggling to put my responses onto automatic pilot. But the confident, aggressive Patti was gone. I asked, 'Can I take my car?'

'No. We'll bring you back.'

I thought, Yeah, sure. Somehow, I managed to make my voice sound stronger. 'Are you arresting me?'

'No.'

That was a relief. 'Well, what's the problem? Do I need a solicitor? What's it about?'

'We'll talk to you in the office.' So I locked the door behind us and got in the back of the car with the female cop.

The NCA went a crazy way to city, round and round Thebarton, Hindmarsh, over to Parkside, and then into the alleys of the West End. What were they up to? Little boys acting out their fantasies.

The woman asked, 'Do you mind if I have your handbag? I want to go through it.' She carefully examined everything made of paper – tissues, cigarettes, sweets wrappers, the lot. Watching her pick through my bag made me feel strange, so I closed my eyes and sank back into myself, trying to conserve my tiny reserve of energy.

We pulled up at the back of a building I didn't recognise. Thank God it wasn't Angas Street police headquarters. I hated the thought of prison cells. Stinking coffins. To be locked up would be to die, suffocated. We went through a back door and along a maze of passages. I felt like a prisoner being taken to execution. A door was left open and instinctively I looked in. Through the window I saw the Trattoria Restaurant. Ah, I knew where I was. But I was filled with foreboding. The real world seemed to be slipping away from me. To test the strength of my voice I forced out some words. 'Why all this bullshit? You can baffle me with science, but not bullshit.' They didn't answer.

We entered an office: a wide, open room, full of lights and people sitting at computers. The instant we walked in all the typing stopped; all heads turned to look. We were expected. In line, heavy, me, woman and heavy, we walked to a partitioned off room. Inside was a desk, and a chair out in the middle, for the SS interrogation. The woman cop carried a chair in from the office and sat behind me, the position supposed to unnerve the criminal mind. One guy sat behind the desk, and the other stood by my left shoulder.

'Coffee, Patti?' It was the boss, being courteous, while he shuffled papers on the desk. What was on those pages?

'Yes.'

'Cigarette?'

'Alpine. Menthol, you know, in the greeny-blue packet.' Shut up, Patti, you sound frightened.

There was a little comedy while they tried to find some Alpine, and eventually sent somebody out to buy some. We all sat in total silence while they stared at me. In my mind's eye I was out in King William Street, walking to the deli, pushing aside the coloured strips of plastic at the shop door, chatting to the owner.

When the footsteps returned the cop beside me went to the door and brought in two packets of cigarettes, which he handed to me. That worried me. Why two? How long was this going to take?

'We're going to take a statement.'

I was so shocked that all I could do was ask lamely, 'Why?'

'Harvey.'

I had known Assistant Commissioner Harvey for years. He was a good policeman, one of the old school. If he was in trouble, I would help. He had looked after me when the arse-hole in Vice Squad was harassing me and threw me off the Globe Derby Trotting Course. I had given him a name or two when kids were murdered.

The men held their left wrists up high, and pressed the timers on their watches. 'Synchronised at twelve twenty-five, exactly.'

Then they began; a hundred questions about Harvey and lots of other names, but Harvey was always their target. I tried to keep with them, I told what I must, all the time trying to work out their game. After almost an hour my head was spinning, and I unconsciously reached into my handbag for a tablet.

The boss nodded at his mate and said in a sudden, loud voice, 'You paid Harvey.'

I pushed my brain to keep up with them and not get trapped. 'No. Harvey and I knew each other, but never money.'

'Patti,' he said very quietly, 'Do you want a solicitor?'

'What! You ask me now, when I asked you at the house?'

The men laughed and went just outside the door, where they whispered to each other. The female cop kept asking me for names. Then she dragged her chair around so I could see her, and said, 'Did you know Chris and Geoff got married? I was one of

Chris's bridesmaids.'

I knew Chris and Geoff from the good old days of Hindley Street. I remembered Cassie and me out on the town, her eyes bright with excitement.

The men came in and asked about more cops. Then they asked me to name corrupt cops. I refused, even though I could have named plenty. The men went out for more discussions.

After two and a half hours of this my brain started to go haywire. I could feel it speed up, names racing through at a hundred miles an hour. This was not an arrest, but I couldn't leave. They kept on about Harvey, until I said, 'This is a load of crap. A waste of your time and mine. I don't know what the hell you are on about.' They didn't even hear me.

From behind me the woman's voice said, 'Are you going to do it now?'

'In about three minutes.'

What were they talking about? I was in a nightmare with ideas and faces flashing though my mind. None of it made sense.

The boss suddenly pushed a piece of paper right close in front of my face. 'Patti, we are placing you under arrest for perverting the course of justice.' My jaw dropped. I felt it. I heard it snap. My brain spun down and down like a whirlpool. 'Along with Assistant-Commissioner Harvey and Detective Eric Douglas.' I swayed on my seat.

I was numbed, like I'd been needled. I was alive but dead at the same time.

The woman said, 'They'll strip you of your jewellery over there. Let's get some off now to save the hassles.'

I tried to undo the clasp of the gold chain around my neck, but my fingers wouldn't work. They had turned to stone. She stood to help me. Her fingertips were soft, gentle, and I felt her breath on the nape of my neck. She tugged off the jade-stone ring from my beloved Nick. The man began to make a list on a piece of paper.

I held up my left wrist, but the woman couldn't get the bracelet off. She struggled with the clasp that I had fixed so the bracelet would never come off, not even in death. I saw the tiny images dangling and chinking together. At one end was the key, and far away at the other end, the heart it could never open. Next to the key was St Christopher, the protector, with the cross and baby Jesus on his shoulder. Then the gold letter 'P', in a wreath, to know it's me. A horseshoe for luck, the tips pointing up so the luck couldn't pour out. My witch on a broomstick: sweet, laughing witch, all in black, flying across the moon, away from the men who would tie her to a stake and burn her body. In the centre of my bracelet was the crucifix, on each side of which were hung an axe and a gun. These were for Algie. Then a dice, a present from Algie. He, who had stolen thousands, spent eighteen dollars on this tawdry piece. Then the Ankh, fertility symbol. Finally, the ballet shoe for the little girl of Pickering Street who dressed up in noisy crepe paper and danced on the road.

Next thing we were in the car and went around five corners to get to the car park at the back of Angas Street, just across the road from the NCA rooms. One man each side of me, we walked to the door. An arm reached in front of me to press a button. Eyes appeared in a slot in the wall. The heavies let go of me and walked away. The door opened and the policewoman held me lightly by the elbow to guide me in. I was being led around like a two-year-old. I had no control of my brain. It had clicked off.

She said, 'Now we go over to that desk.' She handed all my belongings over in a little bag. The cop tipped it up and spilt everything in a pile. He poked it about with the tip of his biro, and checked against the list. Then he looked at the bracelet on my wrist. I was sinking way down inside myself.

'I've given her permission to keep it on.'

'Why?'

'It won't come off.'

I thought of the lock-up places. They smelt filthy. I remembered the mad women clinging like cats to the wire fences at the mental hospital, screaming. The world was closing in, pressing me down under a pillow. My body was there but my soul was floating away.

We were somewhere else and the policewoman had my fingers in a hard grip. She pushed them down on a pad, rolling each

320

fingertip in the ink. She shoved my fingers in a bucket of white glob, like velvet soap all boiled up. I shuddered uncontrollably. I was as helpless as a baby, and she had to help me wipe my fingers.

Next would be the cell. My whole body was going rigid.

'We're going to let you out now,' the woman cop said in my ear. 'On your own bail.'

We stood there for twenty minutes while she filled out forms. I thought, They've got no right. What does 'perverting the course' mean? A pervert watches sex acts.

'They're out the front waiting for you now,' she said.

I panicked. Who's waiting? What are they going to do to me?

A big, burly sergeant took my arm. He thrust a plastic bag of my belongings in my hand. Then he and the woman led me to a door. We were out in a lane and it was raining. I saw men with television cameras rush across the end of the lane.

'What's going on?'

'Nothing.'

'Cover her. Cover her.' There was a raincoat over my head. Then I was pushed into the back seat of a car and we roared away.

'What in God's name has happened?'

The man in front turned around and said, 'You will appear in court at 9.30 tomorrow morning.' We pulled up outside Ralph's house. 'Now we are coming in to search.'

'No! It's not my house.'

'We will.'

'No. Have you a warrant?'

He nodded and took a piece of paper from his suit coat pocket.

'At least wait until he gets home.'

He smiled at me. 'You can't honestly say you're not guilty, Patti? I'll tell you something. You're looking at doing two years at least.'

'What for?' Immediately I visualised myself in a cell, locked away from my children, shut away from the night life, from the river and hills. A terrifying future life flashed past my eyes.

'Two years, without a doubt.'

They hoisted me out of the car and I tried to think of some way to stall them, so that Ralph could be there. 'What about my car? Why don't you check that out first?' I felt some control flowing back.

The woman and her boss gave each other the look. Oops, they had forgotten. The woman stood by me while the man ransacked the car. When he opened the glove box, he gave a shout, and began to throw things everywhere.

I laughed, and the woman looked at me as though I was mad.

'You're going to put the frigging lot back,' I said.

The woman cop found some coloured placards in the boot. 'All Parliamentarians Are Hypocrites'. She gave me a grin.

The male cop backed out of the car and held up a piece of folded alfoil. He held it out, triumphant, hysterical. He and the woman peered closely at it as he carefully unwrapped it. I saw their faces turn red. Cadbury's Caramello.

Then they began on the house. Ralph walked in and saw the mess. 'What's going on?' He looked just as he did before going off his tree.

'I'm sorry Ralph. I can't stop them.'

He looked at me, and I knew it was finished between us. Time to move out, be alone again. Automatically, I began to tidy the kitchen. I put some dishes on the sink and got out the detergent. Like a robot, I washed the dishes while the cops searched the house. I cried, thinking this was the last time I would stand at this sink.

As soon as the NCA had gone, Ralph got stuck into me, but the door bell rang.

It was Kasey. 'Got something to tell you.' He went to the kitchen and sat.

I waited. 'Well?' My head was still spinning from the arrest.

'I've got bad news. Eddy died this afternoon.' The man who was once my husband was dead.

Bits of me scattered everywhere, like a smashed vase. Michelle's father, gone.

'They're cremating him tomorrow at three. But you're not wanted there.'

Next morning I drove to Angas Street Courts. I wandered into the building, and hung about at a loss. The building was threatening and strange. My fate was to be decided in these walls.

Where did I go? What was I supposed to do?

I walked into a court room, and stood looking about. A man glanced up from his desk at the front, where he was sorting out a pile of papers. Then I saw the look of recognition in his face.

'You must be Patti. Where is your solicitor?'

'Solicitor?'

He put down his papers and said, 'Who's looking after you?'

'Nobody.' My blood ran cold. The committal was about to start. 'What am I supposed to do?'

The man stood up. 'I suppose I could get Bill for you.' He walked up to me and said, 'You come with me.'

He took me down a corridor to an office that had the label Legal Aid. I didn't know what was happening. I was in shock, and felt as though I'd been hit by a truck.

The man, I think he was a clerk, knocked on the door, waited, then opened it. The clerk introduced me to the lawyer Bill Braithwaite, who said, 'Hello Patti. Looks like we've got our work cut out for us. Please sit down.'

One morning, seven days after my arrest, I arrived at Bill Braithwaite's office. He looked at me with a worried expression. In a quiet voice he said, 'Your family's looking for you.'

'What family? I don't have a family.'

'I've got a message for you. Your Aunty Jean is in a bad way. She's in the Queen Elizabeth Hospital. I'm sorry, Patti, but she's not expected to last the day.'

I raced off to the hospital. Aunty Elsie, Veronica's mother, was there to meet me. It was she who insisted I be contacted. I held Jean's hand, and watched her breathing fade away. She was in a coma. I looked at the old, hard face, and remembered what a tough life she'd had. It seemed a thousand years since those days and nights when Nan and I went to Aunty Jean's for refuge from the drunken violence of my father. I thought of the Christmas Day when I handed out my pathetic brown paper parcels, and the adults disinterestedly put them aside. I thought of the day my father returned from war and scratched my face on his rising sun badge when he threw me in the air. Aunty Jean had taken me into the toilet and smacked me for ruining everything. While Aunty Jean quietly died, I sat in silence and wondered what she had thought of her life when she got near the end. Now she was just a body, the spirit already gone. It was exactly a week since Eddy died.

On the first day of the committal hearing, when I went into the court it was so jammed with people that there was no place for the accused – Harvey, Douglas, and me – to sit. I was made to sit away from Harvey and Douglas, and told not to look or speak to them. Even a glance could be misinterpreted. All around me was the crowd of police, media, and lawyers. The room was stifling and the air was filled with excitement.

I thought back over the weeks of preparation for the trial. The phone bugging. The NCA men working three shifts to have me watched every hour of my life. I would see them sitting in their car near my flat, the temperature about 40 degrees in the shade. 'Die you bastards.'

Algie was in court as a witness for the prosecution. Oh, no, I thought. That's the lid on my coffin.

The first morning of the trial was a farce. The room was so like a sauna that it was almost impossible to breathe. The young magistrate had to adjourn the trial to the next day in a court in Wright Street.

The trial began in earnest and the NCA called witness after witness to show I had a conspiracy with Harvey and Douglas. I was supposed to be paying them off to drop charges against Jack.

But Harvey's solicitors were really good, and began to tear the evidence to pieces. Witnesses for the NCA parroted their prepared lines. The NCA even had Jack using a name nobody used for my son's wife, who hid the gun in her handbag, the night of the arrest at the Berkeley Hotel.

When Algie walked up to be questioned my heart sank into my boots. To my utter amazement he told the truth, and dismissed the ideas that I was connected to drugs and police corruption.

The trial lasted two weeks. Each morning my daughter, Michelle, dragged me out of bed, poured me into my pantihose, and filled me with coffee. Every third morning Michelle got me to Nilia's for my hair. I refused to go to court like a bag of shit.

On the day the verdict was given, I stood in a trance of fear that the magistrate would send me away for two years. I didn't hear a word he spoke. I was repeating the Lord's Prayer over and over. I was there and not there, real and not real. Then all around was shouting and cheers. Michelle touched my shoulder and I jumped. Coppers were shaking my hands, media blokes waved and grinned at me. I saw Mr Harvey with tears in his eyes. I heard a voice say, 'It's all over. You're free.'

Free?

I walked toward the door. Strange faces pressed around, people yelled. A plain-clothes cop standing with an NCA officer grabbed me by the shoulder. 'Patti Walkuski. We have a warrant for your arrest.'

I stood stock still. 'Arrest?'

'There is an unpaid fine of $60 for a parking offence involving one of your trucks in Sydney.'

My god. Sydney? Trucks? That must have been three years ago.

'Unless you pay the fine, you will be arrested.'

I opened my handbag and began, with trembling hands, to try and open my purse. How much cash had I on me?

An Adelaide CIB detective leant forward and asked me, 'What's the matter?'

'The NCA is going to arrest me for an unpaid parking fine.'

'What! How much is the fine?' The CIB man reached for his wallet. 'If you can't pay up, I'll give you a loan, Patti.'

Outside the court cameras flashed. A hand gripped my elbow and propelled me through the mob. In a panic I did now know what to do, or where to go. My mind slipped into a wild free-wheeling confusion.

I drove home somehow. I made a cup of tea, and tried to get myself together. It all hit me the next day, and I went to bed. I pulled the blanket over my eyes and shut out the world.

# *Medusa*

*Even though we were innocent, Harvey, Douglas, and I paid heavy* penalties. Harvey was demoted, and developed a cancer that killed him. Douglas was re-instated, but his career was under a cloud. I was ill with pneumonia, and in the delirium of my fever kept waiting for a letter or some token of apology from the NCA.

As I slowly regained my health, I drifted for the first time, into a new, different kind of life that I couldn't understand. I think it was called 'normal', although the NCA still dropped in to visit. I married Bernie Crompton, a kind, caring man. It was so weird, so difficult to be with a man of manners and thoughtfulness. At last I had a good husband, and didn't know what the hell to do with him. My life had been all fights, but old habits die hard. I gave poor Bernie hell. After five weddings I had found the best husband, and knew I'd have to divorce him if we were to remain good friends.

We went about our lives as voluntary helpers with street kids. To our disgust we soon sensed that there was corruption in the administration. Those kids were being ripped off. Bernie, who had a college education and understood accounts books, challenged the administration. But those books were well and truly cooked, or went missing, stolen goods suddenly disappeared, and so Bernie and I got out in disgust.

We'd had some good times and tragedies with those kids. So many were from good homes of respectable parents. Funny how many kids came from strict religious families. Like so many of us, they were not good enough for their despotic parents. A fifteen-year-old, Colin, had a father who was a church elder. Colin was on the streets until he lived with Bernie and me. He tried to commit suicide every time there was a north wind. He'd run out into the traffic and try to get skittled. But the bus drivers and taxi blokes knew about him and always had their eyes peeled going past our place. Then one day Colin went back to his home, sneaked in and stole his father's credit card. He used it to try and buy a car. When the salesman got suspicious, Colin ran out onto the road and, not looking, went straight under a bus. I cried for that boy and the waste of his life. Another child sacrificed on the altar of righteousness.

It was not always sad. Those kids taught me a trick or two. If you wanted a good feed on Sunday, you'd go to a church. To sit at the back, pretend to pray a bit, and look all mournful was good for a Hungry Jacks lunch with a family. For the full Sunday Dinner with lamb roast and mint sauce in the luxury of somebody's home, you had to give a few Halleluias, go to the front and beg to be saved. Being taken home also gave you a good chance to see what was worth stealing for when you sent your mates back to knock the goodies off.

One morning in late 1989, at six, somebody bashed at our door. Outside was the gabble and hiss of two-way radios. I opened the door to six big storm troopers. It was the NCA back in town. They ransacked the place. Took every bit of paper they could lay their hands on. Photos, the dictionary – you name it, they thought it held state secrets. My videos, licences, passport, private letters. The lot. Anything not nailed down. One gorilla even climbed up in the ceiling to snuffle and scratch around.

I sat on the lounge and watched. 'Why? What are you looking for?'

'Can't tell you,' mumbled Hero Number One.

'What! You come in here, wreck a home, and I'm not told why? What right have you?'

'Don't blame us. We're only following orders. And we don't apologise.'

I glared at him and said, knowing it was useless. 'What you pull to pieces you'll fucking well put back.' I remembered how they'd trashed Ralph's place.

There were NCA cops in every room and one outside in the car. 'Well at least have the decency to turn your radios down. You're waking half the neighbourhood.'

Then the penny dropped. The NCA style is to raid everybody they imagine is guilty. I picked up the phone. But I was too late. By the time I got through to Kasey, my former manager, they were already there. 'They're just coming through the front gate.'

By the time I got there with the cameras and crew of 'A Current Affair', they had demolished the place. Kasey's mother was sitting at the kitchen table, shaking with fear. They had ripped her bedroom to pieces, torn the mattress open to look for drugs. She was in her eighties, in the last stages of cancer, with only a few weeks to live. Did they really believe she was a heroin pusher?

I asked the NCA cop, 'What are you looking for?'

He wouldn't answer.

I watched the tele and saw the wreckage of Kasey's home. Then I learnt what it was all about. The South Australian Attorney-General had written to the NCA, asking for an investigation. I was supposed to have said that Attorney-General Chris Sumner went to my brothel.

The reporter kept talking about my 'brothel'. Many years ago, I'd owned a massage parlour for about three months, and left it to the girls to operate. Otherwise, in the years that I'd been a Madam, I'd run up to eighteen escort agencies. My girls went out to the clients in hotels and motels all round the city of churches.

I was stung by the double accusation that I was 'common' and a 'criminal'.

Then a TV reporter said that in conversations with me about Sumner, bla bla bla . . . I was stunned. What the hell was going on? Where had she got her information? I had never met her.

I phoned a reporter at the Adelaide *Advertiser*, who had followed the details of my story since the Harvey-Douglas case, and had got to know me. He agreed to run a story.

Later it all began to make some kind of crazy sense. There

were people in Adelaide using my name to smear Sumner. The beat-up about Sumner supposedly using my girls was a way of putting the boot into him while he was down. If it was done right, Patti's name would destroy Sumner and, perhaps, bring down the South Australian government.

Whatever their reason, the media were no better than the NCA. They could say what they liked, knowing it was their word against mine. It was child's play to use me as a pawn and then, after the damage was done, make me look unreliable. What credibility would a judge give to the word of an ex-Madam?

And so began another bewildering time of NCA interrogations. Locks, security, cameras, the whole Hollywood charade, as though they were heroes in an FBI movie. Because I had no money, I was assisted by the Legal Services Commission. Back I went to Bill Braithwaite's office, and he kept tapes of our voices . . . Then the Commission appointed two new lawyers, who were supposed to help me. Soon after the investigation, one of them was himself appointed to the NCA.

The NCA harassed me about Sumner. Time after time they quizzed me about exact dates, places, names and events that were supposed to have happened way back in the seventies, when Sumner was alleged to have been seen outside one of my non-existent brothels. Times, and dates and conversations. Pressure, pressure.

Besides Sumner they kept making hints about other matters. Day after day they said, 'Now Patti. We've got new allegations against you.'

I lashed back. 'Why are you doing this? Why are you going on and on?'

'Don't blame us. If we get allegations we must act on them. You're not the only one in the industry we're visiting.' But it was me they were visiting most.

I had to act against them. They brought out the Irish in me. Every morning I picked up the phone and made my regular wake-up call to the NCA listening in. Patti, the threat to the nation started the day with 'Good morning arseholes.'

On my fiftieth birthday, 5 December 1990, I was called in by an usher to an NCA court. Take the Bible and swear to tell the truth. Two and a half hours. I had to stand and fight my battle.

I had nothing to gain by telling lies, and there were lots more truths I could have said if I'd ever wanted to set up other respectable citizens.

As it happened I wasn't the only bunny. During the Sumner business, the prosecutor for the NCA was changed. There was a big shemozzle going on about the NCA. It was under attack itself for inefficiency. And this whole mess went back to 1989 when the government had called in the NCA after a TV beat-up about allegations of corruption among police and public officials in South Australia, especially in the heart of the State – good old Suppression City, Adelaide.

My first surprise, under questioning, was that they already knew what Sumner was supposed to have done with the girls. They let it slip by their questions.

They kept hammering away at the question, 'Was Chris Sumner a customer? The name Sumner is on one of your books.'

They left off the Sumner business and started on about some other, heavier stuff. Drugs. Secret bank accounts. Ridiculous questions, like, 'Have you got videos of Members of Parliament with working girls? Audio-tapes.'

If they could make any of their fantastic notions about blackmail stick, then they would finish me off. I was looking down the barrel at far worse than the two-year sentence they'd threatened me with during the Harvey-Douglas case.

Operation Hydra, they called it, as though there was a widespread network of crime I was involved in. I was told I'd been given the code-name Medusa. What a laugh. At least I had a hair-do before I appeared in public. I suppose, like most people, there were a few people I'd love to turn into stone and drop in the Port River. But, Patti the big-time crim? The evil woman threatening blackmail on the lives of innocent politicians? Drug Queen? Who were they kidding. At this time of my life I was so gaga with stress I couldn't have organised a piss-up in a pub.

It wasn't just Sumner who wanted their name cleared. I wanted the truth about me to be known. I watched Sumner on television. He carried on about being a victim, about waste of public money. I felt the same.

In the end, the enquiry completely cleared Sumner. There had been one man who had been using his name when seeing prostitutes, and another man who was a dead ringer for him. It was a bit of bad luck.

It took me a long time to work out who'd set up the other allegations about me.

Somebody, anonymous of course, had made the initial phone calls that were quoted by the media. At first I thought it must be Algie. It had his cowardly style. The NCA reckoned it was a prostitute. I got word that it was my own son's father-in-law.

How do you explain all the hatreds? Medusa. Her face and her hair of twisted snakes turned people into stone. She was supposed to have died when a bloke held up his shield like a mirror and she turned to stone by seeing herself. Not me. I've got plans for Patti.

# *Postscript*

---

*Patti lives alone now in a unit with a sign 'House of Hope' above the*
front door. Bernie is still a friend. 'Bernie is a good bloke, a
kind, a gentle man. I didn't know how to handle him, so I had
to divorce him. That doesn't stop him calling in nearly every
day to make sure I've taken my blood pressure pills.'

In her front garden is a concrete elf, a reminder of the days
of her childhood beliefs. The elf is a jaunty little chap. He has
pulled his pants down and gives all visitors the brown-eye.

Behind the front door is the most frightening hand weapon
imaginable; just in case of an unwelcome guest.

Eager to make something of her middle years, Patti took
courses and passed certificates. She ran a shop in Semaphore,
with Cassie, to sell off her wardrobes of clothes. She has organised a marching club for women, and runs a select social club.
After all these years, Patti has a pair of tap shoes, and the girl
who dreamed of becoming a ballerina now attends tap-dancing
lessons. What the hell. There's a dance in the old dame yet.

Patti becomes quite unmanageable when one of her grandchildren visits.

Patti has a pastor, Ray Thyer, once an underworld figure. He
puts his heavy hand, diamond ring and tattoos, firmly on the
writer's shoulder in a friendly grip. In his gruff, kindly voice
he says, 'Now you do Patti proud in her book. We may be a
bit over the hill, Patti and me, but we're still not beyond doing
some very nasty things.'

For a while Patti became a born-again Christian. She is a bit of a prodigal, and Ray needs to have the occasional chat. Patti is not quite convinced that God is good.

She dreams of reconciliation with her mum and those of her children who have cut themselves off from her. Regarding the various men who brutalised her, Patti doesn't show any inclination to forgive them. 'There are some things that should never be forgiven. To do so is a total denial of justice. Why should I?'

Patti refuses to retire from life. 'Maybe this book will open doors. I want to do something worthwhile, exciting. There is so much of me not yet fulfilled.'